D1590985

HOME ECONOMICS

HOME ECONOMICS

Domestic Fraud in Victorian England

REBECCA STERN

The Ohio State University Press / Columbus

Library of Congress Cataloging-in-Publication Data
Stern, Rebecca.
  Home economics : domestic fraud in Victorian England / Rebecca Stern.
      p. cm.
  Includes bibliographical references and index.
  ISBN 978-0-8142-1090-1 (cloth : alk. paper)
    1. Fraud in literature. 2. English literature—19th century—History and criticism. 3.
Popular literature—Great Britain—History and criticism. 4. Home economics in literature
5. Swindlers and swindling in literature. 6. Capitalism in literature. 7. Fraud in popular cul-
ture. 8. Fraud—Great Britain—History—19th century. I. Title.
  PR468.F72S74 2008
  820.9'355—dc22
                                    2007035891

This book is available in the following editions:
Cloth (ISBN 978-0-8142-1090-1)
CD (ISBN 978-0-8142-9170-2)

Cover by Janna Thompson Chordas
Text design and typesetting by Jennifer Shoffey Forsythe
Type set in Adobe Garamond
Printed by Thomson-Shore, Inc.

∞ The paper used in this publication meets the minimum requirements of the American
National Standard for Information Sciences—Permanence of Paper for Printed
Library Materials. ANSI Z39.48-1992.

9 8 7 6 5 4 3 2 1

For my parents, Annette and Mel, who make all the world a home

Contents

———⌒ᴠᴠᴏ———

Illustrations

Illustrations

Acknowledgments

———— ∽ ————

A S GOOD FORTUNE would have it, completing a book about fraud means that I have a great many upstanding and outstanding people to thank. In abandoning my dissertation to begin work on *Home Economics*, I kept with me the indispensable wisdom of Helena Michie, Bob Patten, and Marty Wiener, who trained me to be both an ambitious reader and a respectful historian. At Rice University and since, I have benefited immensely from the intellectual rigor, good humor, and camaraderie of Caroline Levander, Chuck Jackson, Andrew Yerkes, Louise Penner, Jill Carroll, Myanna Lahsen, Mitra Emad, and Padmaja Challakeree. To Eileen Cleere, I owe a special debt of gratitude for being so smart and inspiring, for reading drafts of chapters, and for being so much fun.

An NEH Summer Stipend, and Andrew Mellon Fellowships at the Harry Ransom Humanities Research Center and the Huntington Library were instrumental to conducting the research for this book. The University of South Carolina provided crucial travel support and the release time that allowed me to complete this project; before that, Ball State University provided much-appreciated summer funding for research and writing. Among the many librarians who have helped me over the years, I am particularly grateful to Julie Anne Lambert at the Bodleian Library's John Johnson Collection of Printed Ephemera. Without her wide-reaching knowledge and deep generosity of resources, I might never have "met" the Tichborne Claimant, nor have encountered the rich wealth of ephemera and ballads that fill out

———— ∽ ————

these pages. Pat Fox at the Ransom Center in Austin was unerringly cheerful as I submitted a barrage of pink, yellow, and blue slips. My time in Austin was joyful and productive, and I am grateful to the staff at the HRC for their part in that joy. In getting this manuscript "between boards," I have taken real pleasure in working with the The Ohio State University Press; particular thanks to Eugene O'Connor for helping me navigate the perilous waters of copyedits, and to Sandy Crooms, my acquisitions editor, who gave this book a home.

I could not have written *Home Economics* without the smart insights, sustained encouragement, and capacity for laughter of many friends and colleagues. I began my work at Ball State University, where Lauren Onkey, Bob Nowatzski, Kecia McBride, and Pat Collier offered this book its first feedback. Chris Thompson, Beth Campbell, Eric Lassiter, Frank Trechsel, Carolyn Mackay and Larry Nesper fed me well, both literally and intellectually, and kept me laughing. To Tom Koontz, Patti White, Joe Trimmer, and Paul Ranieri, I offer sincere thanks for being so wonderful and so understanding.

The gang at the Dickens Universe heard and responded to early portions of the introduction, and provided encouraging words at key moments. Sincere thanks to John Jordan, John Bowen, Jim Buzzard, Joe Childers, Amanda Claybaugh, Carolyn Dever, Natalka Freeland, Eileen Gilloly, Gerhard Joseph, Priti Joshi, Sally Ledger, Carol MacKay, Teresa Mangum, Andrew Miller, Catherine Robson, Hillary Schor, Carolyn Williams, Alex Woloch, Robyn Warhol, and Susan Zieger. The insights, scholarship, and evolving work of fellow Victorianists Emily Allen, Nancy Henry, Tim Alborn, George Robb, Jen Hill, Leila May, John Plotz, Marlene Tromp, and Tammy Whitlock have helped me to develop my own ideas, and inspired me to attempt intellectual feats that, if not readily attainable, have nonetheless led me to climb. I have deeply enjoyed sharing with Ellen Rosenman attachments to both the Yelvertons and *Mary Price*. Maria LaMonaca was my writing buddy for the crucial years of completing the manuscript; for her camaraderie, generous readings, and good humor, I am thankful. Celeste Pottier was a wonderful research assistant and friend as I prepared, at long last, to let the manuscript out of my hands.

I will tell anyone who asks how much I adore my colleagues at the University of South Carolina. The book owes a great deal to the rigor and acumen of Greg Forter, Susan Courtney, Nina Levine, Mindy Fenske, John Muckelbauer, Carol Harrison, Tony Jarrells, Gretchen Woertendyke, Holly Crocker, Dan Smith, and Ed Gieskes, many of whom participated in the colloquium that helped me to sort through my most recalcitrant chapter. As I worked towards completing the manuscript, they were steady sources of support and

Acknowledgments

inspiration. And Steve Lynn was the best Chair ever, in the whole history of the world.

To my dear, dear family and friends who are family, I offer deep gratitude. Laura Helper deserves special mention as my writing comrade of over a decade now—in the darkest nights of revision, she was shiny and bright, a warm and wonderful star. I couldn't have done it without her. Rachel, Laurie, Leah, Stephanie, Sara, Jeanne, Max, Thelma, Suki, and Becky: you women rock my world and I love you for it. Annette and Mel; Liz, Michel, Alexander, and Aidan; Jon, Elisa, and baby Leo; Kenny and Beth; Evan; Benjy and Toni—I love you all so much. Thank you.

An early version of chapter 3 appeared in *Nineteenth-Century Literature* 57 (2003): 477–511. My thanks to the journal and its publisher, the University of California Press, for permission to reprint here.

Introduction

Fraud at Home

The Private Life of Capitalism

Thus fraud is the order and hum of the day,
While honesty's kick'd like a strumpet away,
Pimps, sharps and pickpockets join hands with defaulters
Some waiting for places—and others for halters
Sing Tantarara Rogues all!
—"Frauds and Pickpockets, or Rogues All!"

JOHN SADLEIR WAS a household name even before his body turned up on the Heath. A major player in a number of banks, Chairman of the Royal Swedish Railway Company, and a former Junior Lord of the Treasury, Sadleir held a choice position in Britain's economic pantheon. He was no angel, to be sure—he resigned his ministry post after revenging himself against a man who had failed to support him—but the public had nonetheless learned to respect him as a financial genius. That public paid attention, therefore, when the London *Times* reported on February 18, 1856, that Sadleir's body had been found at dawn on Hampstead Heath, next to a bottle and a silver cream jug that bore his crest. The slippery traces of essential oil of bitter almonds on both the bottle and the jug added intrigue to the story: despite its fragrant potential to invoke homey memories of marzipan and pear cakes, essential oil of bitter almonds contains prussic acid, better known today as hydrogen cyanide. The bottle was labeled with the word "poison" in at least four different places, thereby eliminating any doubt, and allowing the *Times* to pronounce Sadleir a suicide, even before the inquest.

That the story would be a sensation seemed a foregone conclusion, but the terms of that sensation shifted the following day as the nation began to discover why so successful a financier had sought so gruesome and solitary an end. Initially, the *Times* recorded "an impression that the deceased had disordered his mind by over-speculation" ("Suicide of Mr. John Sadleir" 1856). Within a week, it became clear that the extent of that "over-" was staggering, and that the financial and mental "disorder" the deceased had left in his wake was enormous. Revelation piled on revelation: Sadleir's securities for loans and businesses proved to be fraudulent, and the Tipperary Joint-Stock Bank, of which he was the primary creditor and to which he had appointed his brother James as chairman, failed. Sadleir had transferred money from rightful accounts to his own. He had manufactured counterfeit deeds, prying wax seals from legitimate documents and pasting them onto forgeries (*The Times*, 26 February 1856).[1] In a shockingly blatant memorandum, he had instructed James how to doctor the books so as to feign the solvency of a bankrupt bank. In the end, it became clear that Sadleir's suicide dovetailed with the imminent discovery that he had "swindled the public to an amount little short of half a million" (ibid.). The *Times* noted wryly that "as a forger he seems to have been remarkably successful. . . . At the close of last week it was added that many forgeries on private individuals had been already made out, and that the discovery of many more was anticipated. On the whole, this seems the greatest crash made by any individual in recent times" ("Adjourned Inquest"). As the ensuing weeks brought to light balance sheets that were outright lies, falsified books, and a barrage of phony titles and securities, a national panic ensued. One of the great frauds of the century, Sadleir brought down with him businesses, banks, and innumerable private citizens.

The individual investor garnered what may seem a surprising proportion of the press coverage. For example, the *Times* printed the full account of the inquest and various articles on the large-scale implications for the banking industry and the stock market, but it also granted substantial space to Sadleir's ruin of private shareholders, some of whom were so fortunate as to recoup two shillings to the pound, but most of whom lost everything. On February 28, the correspondent from Ireland concentrated almost entirely on personal stories, including an extract from the Kilkenny *Moderator* that detailed Sadleir's ruin of "a struggling farmer, residing near Annamult," and of "a humble publican in Thomastown [who] was a depositor to the amount of about 500*l*., the savings of his whole life. Many similar cases," the journalist noted ruefully, "might be recounted." According to an extract from the *Waterford Mail*, those "similar cases" involved even more tragic subjects: "We regret to find so many of the shareholders described as widows and spinsters. These ladies have, we fear, invested all their property in such shares, and they will not be able to book up to meet the claims of depositors" ("Suicide" 1856). On March 10, another journalist remarked that Sadleir "was a national calamity," in part because "the social position of the majority of the sufferers has been more clearly ascertained. We hear of small farmers, traders, clerks, assistants, police-officers, &c., who have lost their little accumulations from the thrift of many years. The provision for families is gone—the fund which had been provided for the support of declining life in many instances is gone too" (*The Times*, 10 March 1856). In conveying the personal details of the financial disaster, the journalism took on an emotional, novelistic tone that had far more to say about the social ramifications of Sadleir's fraud than about its strictly financial elements.

A wide array of weekly and daily papers published excerpts from Sadleir's final letters, the melodramatic tenor of which reinforced how literally his swindling hit home. "I have committed diabolical crimes unknown to any human being," he wrote in one published letter. "They will now appear, bringing my family and others to distress—causing to all shame and grief that they should have ever known me." Another selection portrays him wishing, "Oh, that I had never quitted Ireland—Oh that I had resisted the first attempts to launch me into speculation! If I had had less talents of a worthless kind and more firmness I might have remained as I once was honest and truthful [*sic*]—and I would have lived to see my dear Father and Mother in their old age—I weep and weep now but what can that avail" ("Suicide" 1856). Coupled with the sad tales of widows and spinsters, of humble publicans and struggling farmers, the swindler's laments for the familial happiness he had forfeited, for the "distress . . . shame and grief" he would bring to his "family and others," rendered his corporate deceit a drama of private, emotional suffering. Throughout the journalistic coverage, the technicalities of his swindles remained amorphous and nondescript, but their effects on private lives appeared in vivid detail.

This tendency to concentrate on fraud's personal consequences conformed to a more general trend that emphasized the perils of commercial enterprise for the home, its contents, and its inhabitants. The press was only one form of popular culture that, in cautioning against the dangerous effects of speculation, turned to the emotive power of ruined widows, children, and hardworking fathers to render its pathos complete.[2] *Fraud and its Victims*, for example, performed at the Royal Surrey Theatre in 1857, closes with a remonstrance to remember that many of the "poor wretches in the streets" are "honest fathers of families, trembling widows, and helpless orphans, who have been robbed of their all [by] . . . smooth frauds of men—who dare to stand erect amongst their fellow men—while their victims perish in the streets or die unthought of in their miserable garrets" (Coyne 1857, 49). Representations of the middle classes worked within similar parameters: William Powell Frith's *The Race for Wealth* (1877–80), a Hogarthian series of five narrative paintings that depict "the career of a fraudulent financier, or promoter of bubble companies," includes as its centerpiece a dramatic portrait of a family gathered in their well-appointed breakfast room at the moment they learn of their impending smash (Frith 1888, 2:141). While the series includes a diversity of settings, including the Old Bailey and Newgate prison, Tom Taylor's 1880 exhibition pamphlet advises viewers that "These five pictures are to be looked at as the five acts of a *domestic* drama dealing with the real life of the day" (Taylor 1880, 2; emphasis added). Together, these texts exemplify a general rule wherein both fictional and nonfictional representations of fraud stressed its power to reverse the proper relationship between private and public space, to expose the vulnerable members of the home to threats that lay beyond its doors.

Or, I should say, that *ideally* lay beyond its doors: the threshold of the home hardly kept the marketplace at bay. Although Victorian England is famous for revering the domestic realm as a sphere separate from the market and its concerns, this book follows the past two decades of scholarship in feminist and cultural studies in taking the Victorian ideology of separate spheres as precisely that—an ideology, one that operated alongside, and crucially depended for its popularity on, a reality that offered no such clear separation.[3] That is not to say that "public" and "private" did not operate as recognizable categories of knowledge or fields of action; it is, however, to assert the fact that daily life frequently involved the public and the private impinging on, operating within, and conflicting with one another.[4] "Domestic fraud," the focus of this book, depends for its surprise and its cachet on a formal tenuousness of categorization in which the separation of public from private inevitably, predictably, and consistently fails. While that failure may have helped nominally to bolster the appeal of political projects that promised to erect better fences between difficult neighbors, it also paradoxically cultivated a marked appetite for narratives of invasion, seepage, and contamination that asserted the impossibility of maintaining firm boundaries. The most frequently cited of sources, Ruskin's famous paean to the home in "Of Queen's Gardens," contends that "so far as the anxieties of the outer life penetrate into it, and the inconsistently-minded, unknown, unloved, or hostile society of the outer world is allowed by either husband or wife to cross the threshold, it ceases to be home; it is then only a part of that outer world which you have roofed over, and lighted fire in" (Ruskin 1891, 115–16).[5] Here, Ruskin's "inconsistently-minded, unknown, unloved, or hostile society" references the increasingly complicated milieu that was "the outer world," in which fraud was one of the more popular quandaries. As one early-nineteenth-century tour book of sorts, *The Frauds of London*, observed, "Petty forgeries and frauds . . . seem to multiply and advance with the opulence and luxury of the country; and to branch out into innumerable shades, varying as the fashions of the year" (1826–27, 3). Fraud was one of the leading "anxieties of the outer life" that both sustained the fantasy of hermetically separate worlds, and proved its utter impracticability.

Far from being an isolated haven of fiscal safety and ignorance, even the most modest home was a site of purchase, exchange, and employment. Within its walls, men and women hired or worked as servants, contracted marriages, managed children, and obtained furniture, clothing, food, and labor. While popular representations of market fraud reinforced the fact that domestic life was vulnerable to the stings of the marketplace, Victorian culture at large identified the home itself as a place of business. The household was subject, therefore, not only to the effects of fraud in the "outer world," but also to swindlers who worked within its perimeters, taking advantage of its vulnerabilities just as market swindlers manipulated traders in banking, commerce, and other ostensibly "public" fields of exchange. Herbert Spencer remarked in "The Morals of Trade" (1859) on the

> gigantic system of dishonesty, branching out into every conceivable form of fraud, [that] has roots which run underneath our whole social fabric, and, sending fibres into every house, suck up strength from our daily sayings and doings. In every dining-room a rootlet finds food, when the conversation turns on So-and-so's successful speculations, his purchase of an estate, his probable worth—on this man's recent large legacy, and the other's advantageous match; for being thus talked about is one form of that tacit respect which men struggle for. Every drawing-room furnishes nourishment in the admiration awarded to costliness—to silks that are "rich," that is, expensive; to dresses that contain an enormous quantity of material, that is, are expensive; to laces that are handmade, that is, expensive; to diamonds that are rare, that is, expensive; to china that is old, that is, expensive. And from scores of small remarks and minutiæ of behaviour, which, in all circles, hourly imply how completely the idea of respectability involves that of costly externals, there is drawn fresh pabulum. (Spencer 1892, 146)

Spencer notes the widespread "roots" of fraud that found nourishment and bore fruit in every Victorian house. The expensive material goods that raised the costs of admiration rendered the home a commercial site, a fact that even a cursory glance at a Victorian housekeeping book made clear.[6]

Domestic fraud was both a fact of daily life and a primary ingredient of Victorian popular culture: nineteenth-century texts are crowded with impostors who come to the door assuming the shapes of tradesmen, reputable doctors, or long-lost relatives; with servants who misrepresent their credentials, make off with personal property, and otherwise compromise the economic integrity of the household; with food that is not nearly so wholesome as it appears; with false suitors who threaten the stability of normative domestic relationships; and with two-faced acquaintances who undermine the social and fiscal credit of friendship, romance, and the family. In the face of such figures, which provide the subject matter of the pages that follow, this book argues that domestic fraud was a fundamental component of the Victorian imagination.

Because my chapters provide a history of cases and categories of fraud that operated within locations that have traditionally been construed as domestic, my definition of "domestic fraud" is partially spatial. More significantly, it is conceptual. Alongside the multiplication of joint-stock corporations and the rise of a credit-based economy, which dramatically increased swindling in the Victorian money market, the threat of fraud took shape both in actual household commerce and in popular ideas about ostensibly private, more emotive forms of exchange. For example, while the Sadleir case in and of itself does little to illuminate swindles that happened within the home and among domestic relationships, it does establish how powerfully fraud operated as a cognitive, affective trope. As I've already noted, the journalistic coverage departed repeatedly from the world of legislation, agencies, and banks to focus on sentimental and domestic components of both Sadleir's and his victims' lives. Furthermore, it insistently rendered Sadleir's fraud a social problem, by attending assiduously to his debasement of the public's personal—as well as financial—investments in him. According to the Victorian economic journalist David Morier Evans, Sadleir "had the power of impressing upon others a high opinion of his own value" (1859, 227). His election to Parliament and his appointment as Junior Lord of the Treasury derived almost entirely from his capacity to promote himself as a financial Midas—to prompt outlays not only of money, but of trust. One *Times* writer observed that Sadleir's fraud was unparalleled, because "The present period, for the majority of Englishmen, is one of economy, not speculation. In the midst of all our caution, however, of all our thrift, of all our circumspection, a knave slips unawares into the camp and swindles his fellow-subjects out of the enormous sum of 1,000,000*l*. sterling" (*The Times*, 10 March 1856). Sadleir's swindling, then, had the potential to affect even those subjects who had not entrusted him with their money; the writer speaks for "the majority of Englishmen," who, despite "all our caution, . . . all our thrift, . . . all our circumspection," had allowed the "knave" to enter "the camp" and had believed his fiction of respectability, even if they hadn't bought into his ventures. Some months later, when rumors began to circulate that the financier had been seen walking the streets of New Orleans and Paris in an Elvis-esque afterlife, many people suspected that he had even counterfeited death by "simply . . . playing the trick, so well known both in history and romance, of a pretended death and a supposititious corpse" ("Curious Speculation" 1856). Although subsequent articles argued convincingly that Sadleir was decidedly dead, the gist of these stories suggests the ways in which Sadlier had compromised personal as well as fiduciary trust.[7]

In other words, although Sadleir's operations had financial aims and effects, the costs of his swindles were not simply economic. The media consistently emphasized that Sadleir had culled and therefore compromised more intimate forms of capital, suggesting, as the parodist Douglas Jerrold wrote in 1839, that "swindling . . . has indeed a far more comprehensive meaning than that superficially awarded to it" (7). Within the British legal system, it is in fact startlingly difficult to exaggerate the breadth of that meaning. To this day, "No precise legal definition of fraud exists. In the public service, the term is used to describe such acts as deception, bribery, forgery, extortion, corruption, theft, conspiracy, embezzlement, misappropriation, false representation, concealment of material facts and collusion" (Great Britain 2007, 123).

In a practical sense, the fluidity of Victorian law reflected ongoing Parliamentary debates about governmental interference in a market that boasted both unprecedented success and increasingly endemic dishonesty. As George Robb has noted, "Even safeguards against fraud were regarded as undue restrictions of freedom. Fraud, or no fraud, the disciples of Adam Smith resented all state interference in the economy. The government could not, so the argument ran, make people honest by act of Parliament" (1992, 25). Ideologically, the cultural evidence of the period, from art to literature to street ballads, from journalism to political economy to parliamentary debates, testifies to a correspondingly flexible sense of what it might mean in the popular imagination broadly construed to be a fraud, or to be defrauded.

In this context, then, a comprehensive understanding of the scope of fraud requires conceiving of investment in the nonfinancial, as well as financial, senses in which it operates in capitalist culture. Victorian popular texts emphasize the desires, risks, fears, and hopes involved in investment, rendering it a practice far more complex than the simple outlay of cash. To invest is to extend credit, or faith, with the implicit understanding that the sum of one's capital, energy, and trust may be lost. That is not to say that nineteenth-century Britons conceived of financial and social speculation as the same thing; it is, however, to insist that less material forms of exchange work like, on, and alongside the exchange of financial capital.[8] As Pierre Bourdieu argues, "It is in fact impossible to account for the structure and functioning of the social world unless one reintroduces capital in all its forms and not solely in the one form recognized by economic theory" (1986, 243).

The other forms of capital to which Bourdieu refers are powerful components of both "the structure and functioning of the social world" and of Victorian popular culture. For example, in Julia Pardoe's *Speculation* (1834), the
well-to-do Nichols advises his friend Frank that "matrimony . . . is the best
speculation extant; ay, it beats the joint stock companies hollow; for you may
embark in it with no other capital than good eyes, ready wit, and unabashable impudence" (1: 6–7).[9] Novels, plays, and poetry, as well as journalism,
parliamentary reports, and legal parlance, emphasize the cultural property of
education, artistic savvy, and worldliness; such social valuables as connections,
a family name, and general *savoir faire*; and (a category beyond the scope of
Bourdieu's own work), affective assets, implicit in such expressions as "I give
my love," "you stole my heart," and the less desirable property of "emotional
baggage."[10] Each category of capital carries its own potential for investment;
each involves its own series of risks, losses, and rewards. Furthermore, and
perhaps most importantly, each category intersects complexly with the others.
The nineteenth-century credit system, for example, relied so heavily on the
properties of education, social connections, and self-presentation that it was
nearly incomprehensible when divorced from them.[11] As Anthony Trollope's
Robinson in *The Struggles of Brown, Jones, and Robinson* (1861–62) playfully
notes, the social and economic fields shared various significant features, not
least of which was a susceptibility to fraud:

> Credit I take to be the belief of other people in a thing that doesn't really exist.
> When you go to Smith's house and find Mrs S. all smiles, you give her credit
> for the sweetest of tempers. Your friend S. knows better; but then you see she's
> had wit enough to obtain credit. When I draw a bill at three months, and get
> it done, I do the same thing. That's credit. (9)

As Trollope's speaker draws a bill, grants Mrs S. credit for a good character,
and then winks at the reader about the false promise behind both, he suggests how less material, more portable, forms of capital not only circulated
more easily than land or gold, but were also considerably more vulnerable to
counterfeiting.

The acquisition of cultural capital ostensibly requires the investment of
time, energy, or other forms of libido (Bourdieu's central examples of cultural capital are education and "self-improvement"), but the proliferation of
quack doctors, false gentlemen, and characters who feigned educational and
professional acquisitions that they never actually possessed suggests the ease
with which a savvy swindler might counterfeit, rather than actually obtain,

various cultural, social, and affective assets. The situations in which domestic assets changed hands might also be duplicitous—as in the cases of servants who purposefully soiled clothes so as to claim them as perquisites, which I discuss in chapter 2, or of men who seduced young women by staging fake wedding ceremonies, which I discuss in chapter 4. Because Victorian England employed such a broad vocabulary for the category of personal property (including such "goods" as "good eyes, ready wit, and unabashable impudence"), the situations in which one might be swindled were both diverse and widespread. Most significant to my argument here is that the stakes of domestic exchange, and hence of domestic fraud, might involve money or material goods, but were by no means restricted to them. Not all interpersonal scams fell within the province of the home, of course, but the majority of Victorian popular representations locate fraud within the confines of domestic relationships.

The articles, ballads, novels, poems, melodramas, illustrations, and paintings that provide the cultural evidence for this book illustrate how the social aspects of a potentially abstract economic system permeated the plots and thematic concerns of a wide array of nineteenth-century British print culture. As these archival materials make clear, narratives of domestic fraud appeared in many disparate sorts of texts. Because Victorian communities tended to read widely *across genres*, consuming literature alongside other popular forms that negotiated economic debates, tensions, and fantasies, my methodological commitments in this book follow the generic distribution of the evidence, situating literary works more familiar to modern readers among texts that are now less recognizable, because they are noncanonical or nonliterary. More cultural history than literary criticism, *Home Economics* engages a diversity of primary material both to demonstrate the breadth of Victorian interest in the risks attending fiscal and personal investing, and to offer a significant context for the tensions, commitments, and tropes that readers of Victorian literature encounter regularly. Where I generally forego extended analysis of canonical texts, I hope that readers will not find it difficult to extrapolate useful connections to them.

To be sure, the tendency to represent economic trouble in social terms was not an exclusively Victorian phenomenon. Puns on words like "counterfeit" in early modern culture confirm that the perils of the marketplace have both been operative within British popular consciousness and figured within social contexts since the advent of capitalism (see Robb 1992). In *Henry IV, Part One*, for example, Falstaff puzzles the link between counterfeiting and life itself, as he rises like Lazarus after his battle with Hotspur:

'Sblood, 'twas time to counterfeit or that hot termagant Scot had paid me scot and lot too. Counterfeit? I lie; I am no counterfeit. To die is to be a counterfeit, for he is but the counterfeit of a man who hath not the life of a man; but to counterfeit dying when a man thereby liveth is to be no counterfeit but the true and perfect image of life indeed. (5.4.120–26)

The endearing convolutions of Falstaff's logic signal some of the basic fascinations that arise in a society with developing forms of capitalist endeavor and expanding domains of mass culture. Throughout the seventeenth and eighteenth centuries, the hazards of private banking, of the emerging credit economy, and of the stock market reinforced a set of perceptual paradigms based in risk that increasingly governed popular representations of ostensibly private, more emotive, forms of exchange. In *Pamela*, for example, Richardson's heroine famously deems her "virtue" more valuable than jewels, land, or money, and the drama of the novel's first half depends almost entirely on Mr. B's increasingly spectacular attempts to swindle Pamela of that prized property. *Moll Flanders* similarly derives much of its piquancy from Moll's sly, *social* depredations and from the various erotic and romantic deceptions practiced on her. Yet Falstaff, Mr. B, and Moll circulate within a wide array of storylines to which swindling contributed but was not yet so ubiquitous a plot element as it became in the nineteenth century. By the mid-Victorian period, that is, the figure of the fraud was a stock character of the novel; of both high art narrative paintings and cheap illustrations; of the various newspapers, which had multiplied in both number and readership since the early modern period; and of the parlance of the law courts. One feature unique to the Victorian fraud plot, therefore, is its prevalence. It is difficult, in fact, to identify a single Victorian novel that does not engage in some way with the potential for social or emotional swindling.

More significantly, Victorian texts take a distinct approach to the problems of counterfeiting and duplicity with which Falstaff engages so playfully. Nineteenth-century popular discourse nearly universally characterizes fraud as an inexorable component not only of some abstract, far-off market, but of daily life. In 1858, the minister at Lambeth Chapel preached to his congregation,

Walk through our streets in this great city: you have lies on either side of you, compelling attention in every window. Scarcely an announcement will bear the test of simple truth. Things are declared to be what the author of the declaration knows them not to be. You know not whom to trust, or what to trust. You submit to fraud as an unavoidable necessity, and accept falsehood as a part of the established order of things. Truth you know of in the abstract, but truth practical you despair of. It is an attribute of God, a heavenly virtue,—impracticable in this ungodly world. This is the miserable inference you are tempted to draw. (Shepherd 1858, 9)

Victorian representations reflect various attitudes toward the persistence of fraud. Some are sardonic about honesty in general, and so take an entirely ludic perspective on swindling; others regard fraud as a deplorable inevitability but rely on the fake to establish the "true gold" of some exception to a disheartening rule. Regardless of attitude, regardless of form, the preponderance of Victorian cultural texts not only characterize fraud as a social menace far more prevalent than any purely economic problem but also maintain that fraud is integral to the field of social exchange—that it is not only inescapable but, potentially and paradoxically, a necessary evil.[12]

To illustrate, consider one resurrection of John Sadleir in popular literature. In Charles Dickens's *Little Dorrit* (1857), Sadleir appears as the isolated, guilt-wracked Mr. Merdle, a swindling financier who ruins entire communities and eventually takes his own life. The early numbers of *Little Dorrit* were already in print when Sadleir committed suicide, and the plans for the novel reveal that Dickens had already determined that his hero, Arthur Clennam, would suffer a financial smash. However, when he began writing the novel's sixth number, just two days after Sadleir's death, Dickens drew on the incident to add currency and depth to his novel's fraud. His letter to John Forster about the number confirms direct influence: "I had the general idea of the Society business before the Sadleir affair," Dickens writes, "but I shaped Mr. Merdle himself out of that precious rascality" (Forster 1874, 3:159). As Norman Russell observes, "Dickens's depiction of Mr Merdle was coloured in some part by recollections of George Hudson, the 'Railway King'"; and the fall of Strahan, Paul & Bates in 1855 "could certainly have suggested an effective means of effecting [Clennam's] ruin"; but Sadleir provided a more specific and sensational anchor for the novel's plot of market fraud (1986, 134).[13]

However, although *Little Dorrit* certainly attends to the disastrous effects of financial speculation, domestic fraud in both its spatial and ideological contexts dominates the novel's concerns. As in the press coverage of the Sadleir case, the particulars of Mr. Merdle's business remain obscure and inaccessible. "Nobody knew with the least precision what Mr. Merdle's business was, except that it was to coin money," Dickens writes. His Sadleir takes shape in "a jungle of overgrown sentences" in which he is "Gigantic Enterprise, The Wealth of England, Elasticity, Credit, Capital, Prosperity, and all manner of blessings" (*Dorrit*, 331, 578). "The City" appears briefly, but then only to emphasize that Merdle's business is precariously mobile. When Mrs. Merdle complains that her husband carries his "business cares and projects about, instead of leaving them in the City, or wherever else they belong to," she emphasizes his propensity to carry fraud directly into domestic space and the field of private life (333).

Correspondingly, Dickens bestows the finest precision on his portraits of individual homes. The novel is full of exact and exhaustive descriptions not only of the Merdles' overstuffed house, in which "there was so much Powder in waiting, that it flavored the dinner" (209), but also of William Dorrit's cozy jail cell in the Marshalsea prison; of Arthur Clennam's funereal manse; and of the Plornishes' parlor, including its delightful faux pastoral mural. By the novel's close, each of these sites has served as a backdrop for interpersonal swindles, many of which intersect with, but are not reducible to, the crash of Mr. Merdle's enterprise. *Little Dorrit*, in short, might be summed up as a horror story about the ubiquity of fraud.

The *Times*'s remark that Sadleir "had disordered his mind by over-speculation" recurs in *Little Dorrit* in the trope of speculation as disease. This analogy was already a well-established component of a larger anti-capitalist rhetoric, in that it underscored the porousness of supposedly "separate" spheres: the metaphor of illness suggests the potential for a "sick" marketplace to infect the home and its inhabitants. An early humorous pamphlet entitled *A Cure for Deceit*, for example, describes the symptoms that signal the onset of depredation: "An intense itching in the skin to do as much mischief as possible to everyone about you, a total absence of all good feeling for others, and a great desire to 'SWIM' yourself at the expense of 'SINKING' your friends—A love of FLATTERING every one and an entire absence of one good requisite for an honest character."[14] Elsewhere, John Lalor's *Money and Morals*, published in 1852, worries in similar terms about the "highly contagious passions of the human mind which prompt men to seek sudden accessions of wealth" (84). In keeping with the representational strategies I have been discussing here, the rhetoric of economic ailment stressed the potential for misguided speculation and greed to contaminate investors' relationships not only to the marketplace, but also to their friends and families.

In *Little Dorrit*, Mr. Merdle's "Complaint" is apparently a mysterious medical condition; after his suicide, however, it becomes clear that "the late Mr. Merdle's complaint had been, simply, Forgery and Robbery" (*Dorrit*, 593).[15] Much earlier in the novel, Dickens sets up the metaphor of contagion that eventually structures the mania for misguided investing, associating it with the danger of allowing disease to cross boundaries with impunity.[16] In a chapter entitled "The Progress of an Epidemic," he postulates,

That it is at least as difficult to stay a moral infection as a physical one; that such a disease will spread with the malignity and rapidity of the Plague; that the contagion, when it has once made head, will spare no pursuit or condition, but will lay hold on people in the soundest health, and become developed in the most unlikely constitutions; is a fact as firmly established by experience as that we human creatures breathe an atmosphere. (476)

The ailment in question in this passage quite explicitly has nothing to do with the Plague proper; this is the fever for speculation. "Bred at first, as many diseases are, in the wickedness of men, and then disseminated in their ignorance," Dickens writes, "these epidemics, after a period, get communicated to many sufferers who are neither ignorant nor wicked" (487–88).

Significantly, this same chapter suggests the means of communication, as Dickens brings his reader into a scene of domestic warmth, namely the Plornishes' shop-parlor. It contains a *trompe l'oeil* ("a little fiction," Dickens calls it) painted to resemble the exterior of a Happy Cottage replete with sunflower and hollyhock, a faithful dog, and a pigeon house.

No Poetry and no Art ever charmed the imagination more than the union of the two in this counterfeit cottage charmed Mrs. Plornish. It was nothing to her that Plornish had a habit of leaning against it as he smoked his pipe after work. . . . To Mrs. Plornish, it was still a most beautiful cottage, a most wonderful deception; and it made no difference that Mr. Plornish's eye was some inches above the level of the gable bedroom in the thatch. (478–79)

The Plornishes' "little fiction" seems safe enough—delightful, even—but proleptically, the implications of this passage are decidedly more ominous. The Plornishes prove to be key actors in promoting the name of Merdle among the working-class denizens of Bleeding Heart Yard.[17] "Mrs Plornish," Dickens writes,

habitually held forth about him over the counter, in conversation with her customers. Mr. Plornish, who had a small share in a small builder's business in the neighbourhood, said, trowel in hand, on the tops of scaffolds and on the tiles of houses, that people did tell him as Mr. Merdle was the one, mind you, to put us all to rights in respects of that which all on us looked to, and to bring us all safe home as much we needed, mind you, fur toe be brought. (476)

As Mrs. Plornish chats up the name of Merdle in her shop room, Mr. Plornish endorses him from the very rooftops of the homes he builds in Bleeding Heart

Yard, exemplifying the novel's deep connections between domestic exchange and corporate fraud, and reinforcing its anxiety about the propensity of fraud to compromise the "safe home." More subtly, however, the Plornishes reinforce *Little Dorrit*'s general concern with forms of fraud that have nothing whatever to do with investment proper. Indeed, Merdle and the financier who inspired him are completely extraneous to the novel's central plot, which involves the romance between Amy Dorrit and Arthur Clennam, a man raised in a house so riddled with familial fictions—a sham marriage, a sham mother, a stolen legacy—that it literally implodes in the novel's climax.

The plotting becomes quite convoluted, and here I map only the ways that *Little Dorrit*, despite its status as Dickens's longest and most overt study of the Victorian money market, renders swindling a domestic (in this case, familial), as well as a financial, problem. At the novel's moral center is Amy Dorrit, a veritable homemaking wonder who can turn even a prison cell into a site of domestic comfort.[18] In fact, Amy paints pretty murals of domestic felicity from the novel's start. She supports her father's tranquility, first by maintaining his fantasy that neither she nor her sister works; and later, when he falls into dementia, by taking to an "imaginary pawnbroker" his "pompous gold watch," his sleeve-buttons, his finger-rings, and his clothes. As Janice Carlisle notes, "She is the one who maintains the 'pious fraud' that her brother Tip is a visitor, not an inmate, in the debtor's prison" (1975, 200). More significantly, Amy begins her life with Clennam "with the inception of a new fiction, a new instance of secrecy" (ibid., 203).

Within the novel's overt logic, Amy offers a promising alternative to its unhappier homemakers: in particular, she seems well equipped to create an honest abode for Arthur, her employer's son, who eventually becomes her husband. The reader learns, however, that Amy's capacity to keep things tidy has its darker side. Amy's relationship to the Clennam family involves a codicil that is meant to leave her a substantial inheritance. The codicil derives from her uncle's patronage of Clennam's real mother, a beautiful young singer with whom Arthur's father had the misfortune to fall in love. Despite the fact that Clennam senior is devoted to and secretly has a child (namely, Arthur) with the unnamed singer, he is coerced into marriage with a severe, cold woman whose father is in business with his family. Within a year of her marriage, the severe, cold, woman (now Mrs. Clennam) learns that the man she has married is not the man she had bargained for: she had been promised a husband of strict religious upbringing, whose "uncle's roof had been a sanctuary to him from the contagion of the irreligious and dissolute" (*Dorrit*, 644); she gets instead a man who has fathered a child and is in love with another woman. When she learns that the contract into which she has entered is based on a series of lies, Mrs. Clennam is outraged and deems herself "the instrument of . . . punishment" for her husband and his lover (648). She demands of them compensation that, she feels, will distribute the sense of loss more evenly among "investors."[19] That payment takes the material form of young Arthur Clennam's body. Confronting the singer, Mrs. Clennam demands,

> You have a child; I have none. You love that child. Give him to me. He shall believe himself to be my son, and he shall be believed by everyone to be my son. To save you from exposure, his father shall swear never to see or communicate with you more; equally to save him from being stripped by his uncle, and to save your child from being a beggar, you shall swear never to see or communicate with either of them more. (648)

In other words, her solution to the fraud that has been practiced on her is to compound deceit, to add the fraud of maternity to the fraud of her marriage. And she never reveals the codicil, which Arthur's uncle had intended to atone for the singer's suffering, until the blackmailer, Blandois, threatens to expose her.

Ironically, therefore, the novel's conclusion depends not on the resolution of domestic fraud, but on its perpetuation. Well after Merdle's suicide and the fall of his "Wonderful Bank," Mrs. Clennam brings both codicil and confession of Arthur's true parentage to Amy Dorrit. "I will restore to you what I have withheld from you," Mrs. Clennam declares. "Forgive me. Can you forgive me?" (658). As the reader has been taught to expect, Amy has nothing but compassion for the woman who has robbed her of her legacy and the man she loves of his true mother. But in coming into possession of her own property (which at that point is only knowledge, the fortune having gone the way of Merdle), Amy accrues Arthur's as well—and she keeps it, just as Mrs. Clennam had kept it before her. Because the series of lies that defrauded Arthur of his true birthright remains in Amy's possession, the happy close of the marriage plot reiterates the terms of the family swindle that structures the novel's central story. While Little Dorrit would readily give over her available economic capital to her husband when she marries, she keeps to herself the social and emotional property of his parentage (681).

Amy's behavior may not fit the convenient American definition of fraud as the intentional deception of a person for the purpose of depriving that person of property or causing that person injury in other ways—and certainly, one may choose to distinguish between the pious and the less pious strains of swindling. Nonetheless, Arthur and Amy's "modest life of usefulness and happiness" is predicated on the *very same duplicity* that characterizes Mrs. Clennam as a swindler. [20] Thus this novel, which transmogrifies John Sadleir into Mr. Merdle and treats speculation as a species of Plague, represents the home as infected space even after both Merdle and Mrs. Clennam have fallen. The happy home, in fact, is presumed to be happier for the fraud Amy Dorrit maintains.

At the novel's close, a minor character, Ferdinand Barnacle, argues, "We must have humbug, we all like humbug, we couldn't get on without humbug" (616). Although Dickens guides his readers to reject such explicit cynicism, one cannot help but wonder whether, living in the age of Sadleir, he found it difficult to imagine even a domestic contract free from humbug in some shape or form.[21] And, to be sure, Ferdinand Barnacle has a point with regard to Victorian culture: "we all like humbug" concretizes a crucial component of the popular appetite.

The following chapters trace "humbug" through the rooms of the Victorian home, to examine literal occurrences of swindling that plagued family legacies; master–servant relationships; the trade in food and drink; and the business of marriage. Chapter 1 examines the case of the Tichborne Claimant, a butcher from Australia who claimed to be the long-lost heir of the Tichborne estates in Hampshire. His legal trials in the 1870s—at that time the longest in British legal history—generated an abundance of printed materials, including ballads, cartoons, melodramas, alphabets, and parodies. These texts establish the enormous popularity of the case, but they also underscore the importance of narrative to both economic and social processes of investing. I argue that mid-Victorian popular culture offered a significant opportunity to engage with risk within a virtual, if not an actual, context. The Tichborne case in particular negotiated contemporary debates about speculation, particularly about the discrimination between who had the right to access the risks and thrills of the market, and who did not. Clearly situating economic dishonesty within a family setting, the Tichborne Claimant emphasized the subjective profits that an audience might accrue in engaging with domestic fraud. Thus the case operates more broadly to illustrate the concomitant social forces that worked both to discipline actual frauds and to distribute and promote stories about them.

My second chapter examines the context in which anxieties about domestic fraud became most visible, namely middle-class Victorian attitudes toward servants. Domestic administration was a particularly volatile activity in that it foregrounded the home as a site of employment, as its own marketplace perhaps different but in no way divorced from the world of commerce. Themselves forms of capital, servants had capacities for mobility and circulation that replicated the operations of capital beyond the home. A plethora of ballads and chapbooks relate the escapades of footmen who make off with the good silver, and various other domestics (such as "The He-She Ladies' Maid") who prove not to be what they seem. This chapter concentrates on the complicated distribution and management of property within the home, demonstrating through "character" plots, "eye-service," and the perquisite system the integration of business and domestic perspectives about the rights of access I discuss in the first chapter.

Chapter 3 turns to the problem of food adulteration and the crisis it raised in the 1850s as increasing numbers of merchants were found to be cutting flour with alum, for example, or enhancing the appearance of potted vegetables with copper or lead. In this case, the market entered the home both literally, in the shape of adulterated foodstuffs, and more metaphorically, as individuals carried the principles of microscopy (instrumental in detecting food fraud) into social interactions, minutely evaluating one another for authenticity. The scandal of food adulteration was thus manifold in its effects: at the same time as it generated parliamentary inquiry and public education, it was also part of a larger social transformation by which the domestic population was taught domestic suspicion. I include here a close reading of Christina Rossetti's "Goblin Market" and a broader discussion of Mrs. J. H. Riddell's 1866 novel *The Race for Wealth,* which features a food adulterator as one of its two male protagonists. Although this character initially enters the adulteration business to the honorable end of reclaiming his family's estates, Riddell suggests that fraud is perilously contagious. Lawrence becomes increasingly involved with dishonest practices, slipping easily from adulteration to adultery in a double tragedy of market and marital deception.

The Race for Wealth provides the transition into the fourth chapter, which argues that the rise of popular interest in failed marriage plots in the mid-Victorian period owes as much to the prevalence of domestic fraud as it does to the oft-cited Matrimonial Causes Act of 1857. The former raised issues of fiscal and personal responsibility, while the latter stimulated and reflected a growing skepticism about the value of marriage as an institution. Narratives of false marriage, bigamy, impersonation, and gold-digging grew increasingly popular. I argue that this fascination testifies to a crisis within the family: no longer certain what constituted "real" or "true" connubiality, the public sated both curiosity and anxiety with narratives of swindlers whose schemes for economic, social, or physical profit worked by manipulating the tenuous values of the marriage plot. Drawing evidence from historical and cultural materials including literature, legal cases, newspaper accounts, illustrations, and ballads, I focus in particular on the wildly popular Yelverton marriage case. The public fascination with the trials of Major William Charles Yelverton, who staged not one but two dubious marriage ceremonies to Marie Theresa Longworth, is emblematic of a larger appetite for narratives of marital deception and depreciation.

My conclusion turns to futures both economic and temporal. In closing this book, I engage the rise of economic lingo in nineteenth-century mothering manuals alongside legal debates about the Victorian futures market, both of which took on a peculiar urgency in the 1860s. At the same time as domestic pundits were emphasizing the need for rigorous childhood training in order to prevent a future riddled with economic dishonesty, Parliament was voting to make the market even more free by legitimizing futures trading, which had long been illegal because of its susceptibility to fraud. From that discussion, I turn briefly to more recent history, to Martha Stewart and Enron, to *Hustle* and *The Riches*, to consider the enduring appeal of domestic fraud in current popular media.

The appetite for quick riches, alongside the tales of impersonation and duplicity more central to this study, combined to furnish British culture with innumerable fraudulent narratives and narratives of fraud. Tracing these stories, this book examines how economic dishonesty permeated widely held conceptions of public and private life, personal value, work and familial roles, and the character of intimate relationships. Throughout, I aim to elucidate not only the salient details of particular plots, but also the wider concerns about capital, value, and social exchange that structured their relationship to Victorian popular consciousness.

1

Genre Trouble

The Tichborne Claimant, Popular Narrative, and the Dangerous Pleasures of Domestic Fraud

———— ✀ ————

I N 1874, THE COURT of Queen's Bench sentenced Arthur Orton to four-teen years penal servitude. The charge was officially perjury, but less for-mally the Court punished the defendant for his audacity in daring to imper-sonate the missing heir of one of England's prominent families. Orton's most successful claim was ultimately to the title of nineteenth-century England's greatest impostor, better known as the Tichborne Claimant. This chapter uses his status as a Victorian sensation to theorize the relationship between the perils of actual fraud and the consumption of popular narratives about it. In brief, I argue that a common set of interests inspired the widespread fascination with accounts of both interpersonal and financial deception, but that there was a significant difference between attitudes toward narrative and approaches to actual cases of economic dishonesty. Stories that allowed con-sumers to participate vicariously in affective and domestic forms of investment provided an opportunity to engage with the risks of speculation within a virtual environment. That capacity to play with risk was particularly attrac-tive in a culture that was confronting the reality of fraud within the home, and that increasingly depicted the money market as a mystifying and perilous field, unsuited to all but educated specialists. The growing popularity of plots about outrageous interpersonal cons, in which duplicitous characters emo-tionally (and often financially) bilked credulous "investors," corresponds with increasingly vocal debates about access to the market, its risks, and its profits,

———— ✀ ————

and about that market's relationship to the home. Those debates in general, and the Tichborne case in particular, reveal an emergent social readiness to allow, and even to encourage, engaging the risks of fraud within the field of popular entertainment, and a simultaneous widely held urgency to cordon off and to punish the more material consequences of domestic malfeasance. In the Tichborne case, the law intervened to impede the capacity of invented narrative to impinge on real property, but there was little trouble with the Claimant's fictions, so long as they kept to the generic category of imaginative entertainment.

Throughout this chapter, I draw on multiple meanings of investment, referring both to monetary speculation and to cathexis, the investment of libidinal desire in an idea, a person, or a thing. I am, therefore, playing somewhat fast and loose with the Victorian distinction between speculation and investing: technically, the former signified rash and often unprincipled outlays of money or credit, while the latter, characterized by lower rates of return and hence lower risk, referred to a more prudent and respectable designation of resources.[1] My conflation of terms is not meant to elide the fact that many Victorians sought to establish a difference between the two, but rather to recognize both the difficulties of distinguishing the one from the other and, more centrally, the continuum between financial and libidinal encounters with risk. I emphasize that continuum to establish the intimate grounds on which Victorian speculation operated, and to demonstrate the power of narrative to motivate interest in both economic and social ventures.[2]

Investing in Narrative

Because this is a chapter about stories, it seems only right to begin with a good one. The "good story" rarely lacks for ethical pitfalls; generally, in fact, it corresponds with the pattern that Thackeray comically observes "both in life and in novels which (and the latter especially) abound in villains of the most sombre sort" (*Vanity Fair*, 6). Arthur Orton, the "villain" of the tale of the Tichborne Claimant, was hardly somber—rather, he was colorful, daring, and quite literally enormous, weighing in at over three hundred pounds by the time the guilty verdict was handed down. The *Standard* decried him as "The most daring swindler of our times, the most audacious rascal that ever devised a scheme to delude a nation, the most consummate perjurer, and hypocrite, if not worse, that our age has known" (8 March 1872). In contradistinction to Sadleir, whose notoriety he ultimately trumped, Orton's "scheme to delude a nation" began with a smaller scheme to delude a family: his national swindle

FIGURE 1.1
Sir Roger Charles Doughty Tichborne, 1853 (Photograph).

thus flatly depended on a series of stories about a household. His fame came only after he initiated the legal proceedings that ultimately led to his incarceration. And it is not surprising that he received so much popular attention. In the course of his trials, Orton called into question the integrity of one of the oldest families in England: he claimed to have seduced Katherine Doughty, one of the daughters of that respected family, and left her pregnant; and he successfully passed himself off as the family's missing heir to the heir's mother, the Dowager Lady Tichborne.

The "goodness" of this story thus has little to do with its moral sensibilities (although one might assign it any number of morals). Rather, it is "good" in its richness of detail and event, in its careful balance of the credible and the fantastic, and in its capacity to capture the attention of its consumers. In that the tale of the Claimant thereby corresponds to the larger shape of stories about fraud, it serves here not only to entertain but also to illustrate, first, the tendency of popular narratives to feature scenes of swindling that are domestic and intimate; and second, the ideological stakes that such stories solicited among the public that made them popular. Furthermore, to the extent that it models significant forms of affective engagement with Victorian narrative, the

Claimant's story merits greater attention from scholars of both literature and culture than it has yet received, at least among American academics. Given his notoriety in England, the Claimant has accrued surprisingly little stateside notice.

∽

The trials themselves were complicated, but the basic story behind them is both eminently narratable and relatively straightforward. [3] In 1854, Sir Roger Tichborne set sail from Rio de Janeiro, Brazil, to Kingston, Jamaica, on a ship that was lost at sea. Like everyone else on board, slender young Sir Roger was assumed to have drowned, but his mother refused to believe him dead (see figure 1.1). Persisting even ten years later in her belief that her son was still living, Lady Tichborne placed advertisements for her missing boy in newspapers as far away as Australia. In 1866, her faith was rewarded in the shape of a hefty man from Wagga Wagga who claimed to be Sir Roger (see figure 1.2).

Subsequently alleged to be Arthur Orton, a poor butcher originally from Wapping who had taken up the alias of Tomas Castro in Cuba, the Claimant dismayed most all of Sir Roger's close relatives. First of all, they had finished mourning Roger, who was no great prize—one commentator observed that he "was not particularly intelligent, nor did his general cultivation do much to supply his native deficiencies or to enable him to do credit to his rank and social position" (Morse 1874, 11). The family was also quite happy with the current heir, who was just a baby. More seriously, the Claimant hardly resembled the man he said he was, and he was strikingly bereft of familial and scholarly knowledge. But Lady Tichborne in her dotage cared not a fig for such petty details. Rejoicing over her rediscovered son, the Dowager was able to shelter Orton from the family's objections and to grant him an allowance of £1000 per year. When she died in 1868, however, the long and checkered legal story of the Tichborne Claimant took precedence over the story of happy return. The Tichborne relatives declared the Claimant, now eager to inherit, an impostor, and the Claimant, strapped for funds, responded with a civil suit to eject the tenant of Tichborne Hall.

In attempting to discern whether the beefy man who presented himself as the Tichborne heir was the same slim man who had disappeared some ten years earlier, the courts pursued a wide range of evidence. As Rohan McWilliam records, "The Claimant was rigorously cross-examined and found wholly ignorant of Sir Roger's past; in particular, he could not speak French (which Roger had been brought up speaking), or read Latin (which he was taught

∽

FIGURE 1.2
The Tichborne Claimant, 1872 (Photograph).

at Stonyhurst)" (1991, 46). Beyond these questions of intellectual erudition, the court interrogated the Claimant's knowledge of family history, the sanity of the Dowager Lady Tichborne, and material evidence of text and body, including handwriting and, finally, a tattoo that Sir Roger allegedly had that the Claimant decidedly lacked. The tattoo testimony effectively ended the civil suit and precipitated the criminal trial for perjury, of which the Claimant was convicted in 1874. Although he was sentenced to fourteen years in prison and has come to be known as Arthur Orton, excepting one confession, which he issued upon his release from prison and later retracted, the Claimant maintained to the last that he was a Tichborne done wrong.[4]

To term the Tichborne story "popular" is to understate the case considerably. The Claimant took center stage in the public imagination between 1867, when he swore before the Lord Chancellor that he was Roger Tichborne and sought to claim the splendid family estates in and beyond Hampshire, and his conviction in 1874. His legal trials, which began in 1871, were the longest the British public had ever seen; they garnered years of public attention.[5] As the *Observer* remarked in 1874, "For the greater part of the seven years since the Claimant appeared on English soil it may be said that no subject whatever occupied so large a space of the human mind" (quoted in Woodruff 1957, xiii).[6] George Cruikshank imagined a "final Tichborne juror" still sitting in the year 1930, his companions all dead from "the disease known as 'TICHBORNE ON THE BRAIN,' a malady which we regret to say has carried off an immense number of people."[7] That the drama took a prominent place in the British popular imagination is evident in the public demonstrations and national controversy it inspired in its day, and in the dizzying number of documents, illustrations, and other ephemera that survive into the present. These include comics, ballads, alphabets, illustrations, horse races, newsletters, tea towels, and at least one attractive Staffordshire figurine.

In beginning both this chapter and the last with dramatic stories, I conform to a typical scholarly formula in which a compelling narrative serves to whet an audience's appetite, to engage their interest, to solicit an investment in the argument to follow. As I noted at the outset, however, this story also broadly performs the dynamics I mean to analyze, namely the power of narrative to prompt its consumers to buy into a particular set of ideas, or (less felicitously) to propel them into the game of opposing them. The Tichborne Claimant was a regular Lothario of narrative seduction: in seeking recognition of his claim, he utilized a series of powerfully evocative tales that rallied both the national support he obtained primarily from the working classes and the predominantly upper-class countermovement that eventually sent him to prison.

To date, most scholarly work on the Claimant has focused on the social tensions between these two groups, rather than on the specific domestic context of the stories that motivated, for example, the backing Orton garnered from the working classes and the derision he received from their wealthier compatriots. For example, Rohan McWilliam's astute analysis highlights the question of fair play, noting that the Claimant had over eighty witnesses, alongside a paltry seventeen for the prosecution, and that the final damning tattoo evidence came out quite late in the game. By the time of the criminal trial, McWilliam notes, the Claimant "was bankrupt and could not pay for his own defence. In contrast, the crown engaged six of the finest lawyers of the day to prosecute him. To the popular mind, it was clear that he could not get a fair trial and that the government and the legal profession were closing ranks to crush him. The Claimant became both a popular martyr and hero" (1991, 47). In a related vein, David Wayne Thomas remarks on the general liberalist bent of the debates surrounding the trials, and the Claimant's utility for mapping the rise and fall of progressive sentiment in England. The ostensible Sir Roger's decision to abandon the trappings of rank and privilege for a simpler life overseas also invigorated his generally working-class supporters, as Janet Myers observes. "The defense argued that the family members who disavowed Roger did so not because he was an imposter [*sic*], but because he had humiliated the family by choosing to lead a humble lifestyle in Australia" (1999, 113).[8] Enthusiasm for the Claimant was thus a multifaceted liberal challenge to upper-class elitism.

The trials undeniably engaged with national tensions about power, privilege, and property rights, but here I want to emphasize how powerfully their tremendous popular appeal depended on the household backdrop against which the debates took place. The Claimant's stories located political conflicts among deeply personal contexts. In attempting to access not only the financial resources of the Tichborne property, but also the family name and the social relationships that went with them, Orton targeted various of the domestic, nonfiscal forms of capital—including trust, reputation, prestige, and affection—that circulated in Victorian England. Thus, in the Tichborne case, fraud was explicitly a concern that not only impacted but actually occurred within the home. It involved stakes most anyone might hold, and investments that most anyone might make. This drama was, in short, a paradigmatic story of domestic fraud.

Thus, although both McWilliam and Thomas have expertly elucidated the liberal concerns of the trials, and their analyses inform my own, I want to suggest, beyond the specific uneven situation in which the Claimant placed himself, that the literally familiar nature of the stories surrounding the case was responsible for much of its appeal. As many critics have noted, the trials called attention to the intimate dynamics of gatekeeping that kept many citizens from sharing in the opportunities that were open to the "respectable" classes. Key among those opportunities was the capacity to invest, and key among the vehicles that mobilized interest in this case were the forms of affective capital that its domestic context mobilized. Like the domestic fraud plot in general, the Tichborne case achieved much of its popularity by offering the opportunity to amuse oneself with peril, to play with the emotional elements of investment within an explicit context of risk.

Chapter 1

Investing in Risk

I'm arguing here that part of the appeal of investing was the thrill of chance. In so doing, I'm working to complicate the work of both Elaine Freedgood and Mary Poovey, who have suggested that early financial journalism employed a rhetoric of individual exception to promote a more general rule of security about the money market and its growing perils and opportunities. "Even when a specific article exposed financial misdeeds," Poovey writes, "by doing so it implicitly dramatized the financial system's ability to police itself and thus helped normalize the operations of a financial world still subject to catastrophic irregularities and still largely unfamiliar to British readers" (2002, 23). Freedgood makes similar claims in her remarks about the earlier financial journalism of Harriet Martineau and J. R. McCullough, contending, "What classical political economy attempted to do, particularly in its popularizations, was to cleanse the economic realm of contingency and uncertainty, to make it predictable" (2000, 16). Within the realm of popular culture, various tales also promoted the market as a sure and wonderfully swift route to class transcendence. As D. Morier Evans noted in 1859, "It is with the railway mania of 1845 that the modern form of speculation may be said to begin, and the world has not yet recovered from the excitement caused by the spectacle of sudden fortunes made without trouble, and obscure individuals converted, as if by magic, into *millionaires*" (1859, 2). While Evans aims to see the world "recover" from this spectacle, which led innumerable men and women into financial ruin, the "magic" he references suggests the enduring appeal of the market.

However, Evans's *Facts, Frauds, and Failures* includes over seven hundred pages of disastrous market stories about fraud and smash. As such, it is far more characteristic of Victorian investment narratives than the writings in political economy that Freedgood and Poovey identify. In contrast to the stories of McCullough and Martineau, most popular Victorian texts tended to *emphasize* the vulnerability of the average person to con artists and swindlers, both within and beyond the stock market.[9] For example, John Lalor's 1852 *Money and Morals* offers what might serve as plot summary of many mid-Victorian works:

> The quiet maiden annuitant, the hard-worked country surgeon, the plodding clerk who has cut pens over the same desk for a quarter of a century, nay, the parson himself, . . . feels his blood begin to mount, and the fever to set in, when the El Dorados of Capel Court and its neighbourhood are opened to his imagination. The temptation is strong, but the result, if he yields, is generally deplorable. The chances are a hundred to one that he is bit. (84)[10]

Lalor's blunt assessment of speculation paints a far less sanguine picture than that which one finds in the works of early financial journalists. Even if, as Poovey writes, the latter "sought to depict the financial sector, which they represented as a culture unto itself, as a law-governed, natural, and—pre-eminently—safe sector of modern society," popular materials representing the circumstances and consequences of economic dishonesty—including conduct information, dictionaries of flash and cant, ballads and cartoons, pamphlets and broadsides, novels and melodramas, and even much of the financial journalism itself—were far more interested in representing investments that ended in ruin (2002, 22–23).

That tendency is rather surprising, given that so many lower- and working-class citizens fought bitterly to gain and maintain the capacity to play the market. Throughout the nineteenth century, financial investment was a relatively cloistered practice, available most readily to those who had already received the stamp of legitimacy. Not only did it require either capital or credit, which many people lacked or had only in limited supply, but the Stock Market was also a comparatively closed space.[11] Early in the nineteenth century, stock jobbers (or traders) cultivated an atmosphere "calculated to raise the hopes of novices, to puzzle the wits of out-door speculators, and sure to have the effect of diminishing the property of those who are not members of their fraternity" (Practical Jobber 1816, 12). Furthermore, prior to the Joint-Stock Companies Acts of 1856 and 1857, and the Joint-Stock Banking Companies Act of 1857, if a company or bank failed, its shareholders were liable "to their last shilling and acre," which produced a level of risk prohibitive to many potential investors. The new legislation rendered shareholders liable only to the extent of their investments, which initially seemed to promise both better access to the market for all investors and a more equal distribution of capital amongst the laborers that produced it. However, as Donna Loftus observes, although "limited liability was seen by many reformers as a mechanism for democratization by incorporating working-class men into the free market," the specter of a truly open market proved more an impediment than a spur to the nascent legislation (2002, 93). After much debate, the Acts that finally emerged in 1856 and 1857 were carefully constructed so as to preserve, as best as possible, the exclusion of the working classes. Loftus notes that the ideals of reform promised to "democratize the market by allowing anyone of 'recognized integrity and capacity for business' to obtain capital" (102), but the amount of red tape Parliament incorporated into the Acts ensured that "the management of capital emerged as complex and technical and requiring expert knowledge" (105).

The debates about limited liability brought to the fore longstanding prejudices against overly emotive and insufficiently "trained" speculators, namely women, the clergy, and the poor.[12] Many pundits argued that the emotional susceptibility of these groups made them frighteningly vulnerable to the scammers who were increasingly visible in the market. At the same time, however, the government took a predominantly *laissez-faire* approach to swindling: regulations meant to police fraud were quickly overturned, or coexisted with other regulations that nullified their effects. As a writer for *The Saturday Review* observed, "By common law, no mere fraud is criminal at all; and even now, it is only in exceptional cases that delinquencies of this nature are made amenable to punishment" ("Treatment of Fraud" 1856, 340).[13] In the ideological competition between safety and peril, the dominant group opted to maintain the pleasures and profits of living dangerously, even as they worked to prevent more vulnerable investors from engaging the same risks their legislation elected to preserve.

The Tichborne Claimant became a flashpoint for the lower classes' outrage about the double standard. As Thomas has observed, the Claimant provided a forum for the working classes to respond to the condescension inherent in many liberal programs for the poor, which regarded their ostensible beneficiaries as so many ill-educated children who might be made more comfortable but ought neither to be trained in autonomous intellectual pursuits nor to join the rank of their benefactors. The generally wealthy anti-Claimant party attributed their opponents' beliefs to a simply pathetic level of straight-on credulity, noting the alarming readiness with which the masses were willing to believe the stories of a man who was so clearly a fraud. Significantly, many of the popular debates about the trial concerned the incapacity of the Claimant's supporters to properly estimate the narrative powers of the man they backed. As Thomas notes, even the eminent economist Walter Bagehot weighed in on what he saw as the scope of public gullibility, characterizing the willingness to credit the Claimant's story "incredible . . . to all persons of trained intellectual powers" (quoted in Thomas 2004, 99). That question of intellectual training, Thomas argues, reiterated the patrician attitude that the poor would do well to leave the work of right judgment to their betters. Popular credulity, furthermore, confirmed the rationale for "protecting" poor investors from the market.

To the dismay of the upper classes, the Claimant constructed alternative forms of access to the dynamics of investing. On the one hand, he did so quite literally by offering *shares in himself* in 1870, as part of an effort to raise money for his legal expenses. The Tichborne Bonds "consisted of a promise, signed by the Claimant, to pay the holder £100 within a month of his getting possession of his estates, on condition the holder did not sue him unless and until he had secured the estates" (Woodruff 1957, 165). The bonds were to sell for £65 apiece and, at least initially, were intended only for his close supporters. However, they quickly appeared in "public houses, market places, and amongst crowds at sporting events," for sale at greatly discounted rates of £20 to £30 (Annear 2002, 269).[14] The Bonds encouraged the people who bought them to wager on monetary gain, but they only partially explain the Claimant's enormous popularity. The latter had more to do with the Claimant's ability to inspire investments that were more abstract than actual and hence were accessible to both supporters and detractors—even to those who did not have £20. In brief, the Claimant offered the public the opportunity to engage with his cause affectively.

The Claimant's story mobilized powerful personal and political investments among the Victorian public, and it notably emphasized a *lack* of both emotive and economic security. Whereas Freedgood contends that the strategy of exceptionality in popularizations of political economy was about managing risk, and that "Work on risk is always aimed—symbolically or materially—at increasing safety and reducing danger," the actual glee about fraud in some of the more humorous Tichborne ephemera, for example, indicates a set of concerns and interests that differ substantially from the pursuit of safety or consolation (2000, 11). In popular culture more generally, stories of swindling certainly produced an element of Schadenfreude that appealed across classes: readers could celebrate their own relative security in comparison with others' misfortunes. However, the popularity of stories about impostors, frauds, cads, and swindlers cannot be chalked up to a desire to feel safe, especially when one considers how these tales functioned in relation to forms of capital that were not quantifiable in pounds and pence.

Virtual Investing

Current work in behavioral finance tends to coincide with the trajectories Freedgood and Poovey map for early financial journalists: it is primarily concerned with tracking the relationship between risk and investment, shoring up investor confidence, investigating how investors generate feelings of security, and explaining "irrational" investment behavior. In contrast, other risk researchers attend to the unique thrills and pleasures that accompany experiences of danger. For example, Jonathan Simon writes that, in "extreme sports," such as "climbing, big-wave surfing, white-water rafting, helicopter skiing, transocean solo yachting, and sports car racing . . . risk taking is not simply an irreducible by product of pleasurable actions, but in some respects the very source of pleasure" (2002, 180). Simon argues that this direct access to pleasure exists *even for those who engage with the extreme only virtually,* through such secondary media as magazines, books, and television. In keeping with Simon's claim, I want to suggest that Victorian tales of fraud and deception appealed to their consumers' desires to engage actively with dicier forms of speculation and to participate in the thrill of risk. There were clear profits to be made in doing so. As Simon argues, hazardous activities, whether enacted really or intellectually, "function as resources for self-fashioning. . . . [in that] they provide practical experiences, ideas, and narratives around which new kinds of subjectivity are being created and popularized. . . . They provide, as it were, access to and a view of certain kinds of mentalities, skills, relationships, and objectives" (180–81). Risk generates creative pleasures that are available to secondary (or virtual) consumers, who participate in new forms of identity by experiencing and coping with peril imaginatively.

Of course, the recreational pursuit of risk differs significantly from its status as fact in modern life, and willing entry into a virtual environment of danger is not equivalent to involuntary encounters with threat that characterize daily experience in commercial society. Simon emphasizes that summiteering (the form of climbing that fetishizes getting to the top), for example, which dominates the popular literature on mountain climbing, tends to stress the suspension of laws and social relationships that characterize ordinary activity.[15] "This," he argues,

> allows survivors of abusive marriages and cancers to find in climbing a counterpoint to their experiences. The experience of radical threat in the domestic and health contexts is combined with the complexity of relationships, the vulnerabilities of being embodied, and dependence on various kinds of expertise. Climbing, in contrast, allows radical threat to be completely externalized. (191)

Simon's argument coincides with Freedgood's remarks on Victorian representations of mountain climbing, in which she argues that the appeal of risk depends on its contextual distance from daily life:

> Embracing danger in the Alps reinforced the idea that England, or that part of it inhabited by the middle class, had become so safe and secure that it had lost all possibility of providing challenge and difficulty. The idea that one needed to engage danger in the outside world because it was no longer readily available in England provided a kind of psychic security. (2000, 121)

—cɦɔ—

Unlike their mountain-climbing counterparts, the social climbers who dominated literary works found no need to leave England in search of peril. Many, in fact, found little need even to leave the house. As I note above, the majority of Victorian texts emphasize the risks not only of the market but also of the home, and in both sites, one of the preeminent risks was fraud. Providing narrative tension by dealing with clear and present dangers, these stories offer "psychic security" only through their status as texts. That status was certainly not insignificant: nineteenth-century literature and art and journalism and caricature, and drama, about the risks of fraud offered an important opportunity to *choose* to engage with risk. Choice itself helps to explain some of the pleasures of these texts: assuming a sense of control or power suggests access to a realm of volition that is unavailable under ordinary circumstances. In contradistinction, then, to representations of extreme sport, in which risk becomes desirable through its capacity to suspend the conditions of daily reality, narratives of fraud not only served to indoctrinate their consumers into an emerging economic system; they also provided an opportunity to negotiate temporally and physically proximate dangers from a vantage of empowerment.[16]

The pleasures these texts offered intersected with implicit fantasies about investments and profits within explicit storylines. In *Facts, Frauds, and Failures,* Evans notes that "the ruling passion is the grand desire to make money expeditiously, for the purpose of gratifying luxurious propensities, or of indulging in an imposing ostentation" (1859, 5). As this passage suggests, the standard fantasy of investment had less to do with having more money or more things than with having access to the world of money and things and to the power that that elevated subject position would provide. As Herbert Spencer remarked of commerce more generally, "the chief stimulus is not the desire for the wealth itself, but for the applause and position which the wealth brings" (1859, 145). The dream of speculation almost inevitably involved the potential to gain entry to a closed world and thus emphasized the inequities in a capitalist social system that granted privilege to an elite group and kept the majority of the populace on the outside looking in. Access depended on various paraphernalia: sumptuous furnishings, beautiful clothing, fine horses, and the requisite cellar of gorgeous wine. Together, these became the vehicles by which an initially poor man might hurtle past those who might snub him. At the same time, while his proceeds would include money and the material trappings of wealth, these were simply appurtenances to the condescension that an individual might obtain. The complex fantasy of class transcendence, then, reveals the forms of psychological, as well as physical, property that were instrumental components of any investment, that prompted investment in speculation itself, and that produced the pleasures of virtual speculation.[17] Within the Tichborne case, the potential for the working classes to acquire these sorts of affective proceeds helps to answer Rohan McWilliam's ironic question: Why should an "anti-aristocratic plebian movement be so keen to assist a man in joining the aristocracy?" (2007, 194).

Affectionate Investments

Affective speculation, with or without its monetary trappings, is both unavoidable and risky. It is a constant activity of "real life" and a dominant component of popular media. One might or might not buy stock or use banks, but it was not easy to suspend more emotional forms of investment. Stories of domestic fraud, then, both engaged with risk in the real world and presented a suspended forum in which to meet its challenges. For example, consider another good story about another wicked man, this one certainly familiar to most readers of British fiction, Mr. Wickham of Jane Austen's *Pride and Prejudice*. Technically a pre-Victorian work, Austen's novel sets the stage for much of the century's literature in offering what might be best understood as an opportunity to rehearse the practice of speculation. Before she obtains her reward of economic and matrimonial satisfaction at Pemberly, spunky Lizzy Bennet must come to terms not only with "the mortifying conviction that handsome young men must have something to live on as well as the plain" (*Pride*, 134), but also with the fact that some of those young men lie like snakes. Charming, impoverished Mr. Wickham's "appearance was greatly in his favour; he had all the best part of beauty, a fine countenance, a good figure, and a very pleasing address" (64). His lively speech and agreeable carriage win him admission to the neighborhood around Meryton, while his manufactured tale of woe at Mr. Darcy's hands helps him initially to obtain Lizzy's loyalty and affection.[18] "A military life is not what I was intended for," Wickham tells Elizabeth. "The church *ought* to have been my profession . . . and I should at this time have been in possession of a most valuable living, had it pleased [Mr. Darcy]" (70). When Wickhams's true character comes to public light, however, the reader learns not only that Darcy has already compensated him for the living, but also that Darcy disowned Wickham for his efforts to persuade his sister, the young heiress Georgiana, to elope. Upon Wickhams's subsequent decampment with Lydia Bennet, the reader learns that he "was declared to be in debt to every tradesman in the place, and his intrigues, all honoured with the title of seduction, had been extended into every tradesman's family" (260).

Because narratives solicit social and emotional, as well as monetary, forms of capital, Wickham's facility with fiction—specifically, his capacity to give falsehood the guise of truth—has prompted the novel's characters to invest in him on a number of registers, granting him various forms of credit: the tradesmen allow him to purchase luxuries and necessities without restraint; the tradesmen's daughters give him access to their bedrooms; the community allows him admission to balls and parties, where he attempts to forge romantic liaisons with young women like the newly wealthy Miss King, and sympathy for the sufferings he claims Mr. Darcy has inflicted on him. Most importantly, Lizzy, our heroine, initially buys his story sufficiently to accept it as truth and to accept him as a potential suitor. Wickham's compelling stories, in other words, encourage those around him to extend both financial credit and the privileges—including intimacy—of a middle-class lifestyle that most of Austen's readers either aspired to, already enjoyed, or exceeded.

Readers also invest in Wickham, but they do so virtually, with the distance and provisional engagement that fiction allows: they risk neither real debt, nor real ruin, nor (precluding the unusually empathetic reader) real heartbreak. The novel nonetheless takes its readers in, so to speak, and offers them a number of potential responses. One might participate in Lizzy's initial trust in Wickham, and hence in her disappointment and dismay at his moral bankruptcy. One might respond to Wickham with outrage and a sense that the boundaries of respectable society require stronger protections from spendthrifts and scammers. One might take pleasure in Wickham's capacity to con the class that would like to exclude him—for indeed, he receives no punishment but that he is to stay married to Lydia and to join a regiment in the North. And one might take masochistic pleasure in pain that offers the luxury of voluntary encounter, and rather enjoy the fact that one has been made to suffer.[19] Regardless of the lens through which readers interact with this particular plot, its very availability for engagement summons them into the complicated, otherwise cloistered practice of investment, in which they gamble on or against Wickham, with relatively little actual risk.

There are clear implications here for the larger category of Victorian fiction. As Joseph Litvak notes, there is "a powerful fantasy of legibility at the heart of Austen's fiction as a whole: the fantasy that, at least in reading one's acquaintances, one *does not* have 'to take the false with the true' since one can learn to distinguish reliably between those with genuine class and those who are merely vulgar poseurs" (1997, 50). That capacity to practice discernment without risking either face or fortune becomes all the more important when one recognizes that most all of fiction's bad boys participate in some permutation of imposture. In this book, I am most interested in those whose plots explicitly threaten economic or symbolic forms of capital, but there are myriad other cases that invite readers to rehearse their skills of detection. The scammers and seducers fall to the end of a continuum on which, staying within Austen's oeuvre alone, one might note various lesser examples: in *Sense and Sensibility*, Willoughby professes love for poor Marianne Dashwood but marries the heiress, Miss Grey. In *Mansfield Park*, Henry Crawford devotes himself to Fanny Price, only to run off with Maria Rushworth. In *Persuasion*, Mr. Elliot's eagerness to reconcile with the Kellynch family derives entirely from his desire to ensure that Miss Clay not spoil his chances of becoming Sir William.[20] All of these men compromise the faith of their social trustees, and all solicit the reader into a relationship based simultaneously in pleasure and suspicion. For Litvak, that relationship opens the way into the wider sense of distinction that is fundamental to both his argument and my own: the power of fiction, he argues, "consists in large part in its implicit flattery of the reader, whom it congratulates for *having* the distinction to *make* distinctions, for setting herself apart from the upstarts by whose pretentious impostures she might have been taken in" (1997, 50; emphasis in original). In returning now to the Tichborne case, I want to emphasize that the fantasy of being able to set oneself apart from "pretentious impostures" is one of fiction's significant pleasures.

The Claimant seems to have taken a page out of a Victorian novel: he was, one of his lawyers said in the first trial, a man who "had gone away from home for a dozen years, and had been immensely surprised and pained to find on his return that his identity was disputed, and that difficulties were thrown in the way of his resuming his old position" (Atlay 1899, 269). Like Austen's charming man, Orton played upon both financial and domestic fields, using the power of narrative to solicit backers for his legal fees, his decidedly upper-class appetites, and his filial claims; in his wake, he left unpaid creditors and spoiled reputations. Popular interest in his stories reveals how the appeal of virtual risk applies to the field of libidinal investment in interpersonal relationships, and how narrative instrumentally produces those investments in both real and virtual environments. Within the field of narrative, Orton's escapades generated the pleasures of fiction, but unlike his fictional counterparts, whose popularity he shared, the Claimant targeted actual property: for him and the family he attacked, the stakes were real. Two of the most powerful narratives of the trial—the tales of a lost son restored to a devoted mother, and of the Claimant's avowed seduction of his cousin Katherine—provided much of the incentive for the public to invest in the affective components of this troubled family story and in the larger political agendas they endorsed. Like popular stories about fraud in general, these narratives offered up the opportunity to engage with risk through potentiated emotional investments in characters, plot lines, and outcomes. However, because the events took place in real time, on English soil, among English citizens, and with regard to English property, the stories surrounding the trials had the potential to be deeply dangerous.

In her essay "Affective Economies," Sara Ahmed argues that the linguistic constructions by which we express emotion construe feelings as personal belongings (as in the phrase, "I *have* a feeling"). However, she contends, no matter how language may promote a mental landscape wherein "emotions become property; something that belongs to a subject or object, which can take the form of a characteristic or quality, . . . emotions work as a form of capital: affect does not reside positively in the sign or commodity, but is pro-duced only as an effect of its circulation" (2004, 119–20). In other words, affect is an effect of exchange, valuable insofar as its agents esteem it. Just as emotions are mutable and vulnerable to the fluctuations of the social market-place, the emotional capital one might invest in an individual, a story, or even in the value of emotions themselves does not reside in the particular form of affect, but rather in its fungibility.

Victorian culture placed significant value on the affectionate economy of the nuclear family. While the realities of domestic exchange often failed to measure up to their idealized standards, that failure rendered those standards no less powerful, no less evocative. The vast majority of popular texts figured the cheerful family as the benchmark of worth, wherein the dynamics of alliance and reproduction took shape as stratified forms of capital in which emotions significantly outweighed cash. In treating the economy of domestic life, conduct books, novels, and melodramas consistently argued that famil-ial happiness counterbalanced any measure of hardship, while riches could not even begin to compensate for the emotional deprivations of corrupt relations. In Dickens's *Nicholas Nickleby*, for example, rich, deceitful uncle Ralph's London home brims over with "the softest and most elegant carpets, the most exquisite pictures, the costliest mirrors; articles of richest ornament, quite dazzling from their beauty, and perplexing from the prodigality with which they were scattered around" (*Nickleby*, 229). Yet Ralph leaves his poor relations to live in comparative want, in a simple cottage on the other side of town. The impoverished Nicklebys nonetheless render their home homey with their domestic camaraderie and their zest for "every frugal pleasure." They take an almost disturbing joy in discovering the details of their new abode: "One day it was a grape-vine, and another day it was a boiler, and another day it was the key of the front parlour closet at the bottom of the water-butt. . . . In short," Dickens writes, "The poor Nicklebys were social and happy; while the rich Nickleby was alone and miserable" (436–37). The beautiful contents of Ralph Nickleby's beautiful home provide him the social advantage that allows him to condescend not only to his brother's family, but also to lords and their lesser satellites. However, within the larger rubric of the novel, Ralph's psychological perspective has little value: here, the affective outlook of choice is familial devotion.

Despite this panegyric to the domestic hearth and its affections, *Nickleby* and the culture that consumed it placed a high premium on financial success. The novel may be remarkable for the baldness with which it links sentimental attachment to fiscal profit, but it simply makes plain a general truth that the Victorian family was a site of monetary, as well as emotional, trade. As John Bowen notes, "the family is not, cannot be, free of economic determinants, or the violence and conflict of the wider society" (1996, 109).[21]

The Tichborne case, too, vividly revealed the imbrication of tender attachments with elegant carpets, of familial devotion with a family's extraordinary wealth. In particular, Lady Tichborne's loyalty to the Claimant was inseparable from the economic components of maternal alliance—specifically, the forms of credit a mother might extend, and the material and social legacy she might leave to an heir. Lady Tichborne had used her position to provide not only credibility but also financial credit to the man who was ultimately convicted of imposture and perjury. On the strength of her support, he had been borrowing money steadily, even prior to his departure from Australia; she had granted him half her settlement as an allowance; and, were it up to her, he would take possession of the Tichborne estates.

Bram Stoker's chapter on Orton in *Famous Imposters*, which he wrote over a decade after the Claimant's death, notes the other side of this particular coin. In remarking the various "costs" of the trials to the Doughty-Tichborne family, Stoker's sympathy exposes his own investments in the forms of capital that Orton jeopardized. Beyond "having to spend vast sums of money [Stoker puts the figure near £100,000], as well as time and labour, in order to protect themselves from the would-be depredations of an unscrupulous adventurer," the family took a serious hit in social value, due to the unwanted public attention that the trials brought to their family's private affairs. Stoker's stakes in the case are hardly subtle; they inform even the grammar of his analysis. He writes, "To free themselves from a persecution, as cruel as it was vicious, [they] had to be pilloried before a ruthless and unsympathising mob, to have the privacy of their home invaded, and to hear their women's names bandied from one coarse mouth to another" (1910, 202). Recording the Claimant's multiple sites of incursion—the home, the family, and the names of "their women"—as violations of private assets, Stoker's grammar of ownership ("the privacy of *their* home," "*their* women's names") figures privacy, land, and reputation as equivalently valuable forms of property in which he and his intended readers held considerable stock. Bourdieu's discussion of honor in *The Logic of Practice* helps to explain the rationale behind the individual family's considerable outlay of cash, but it also suggests the series of social investments that motivated both the Crown and the public to buy in as well. Bourdieu writes, "The interest at stake in the conducts of honor is one for which economism has no name and which has to be called symbolic, although it is such as to inspire actions that are very directly material. . . . A family has a vital interest in keeping its capital of honor, its credit of honorability, safe from suspicion. . . . The defence of 'symbolic' capital can thus lead to 'economically' ruinous conduct" (1990, 120–21). Orton's claim to have illicitly accessed the valuable "property" of an upper-class woman's body thus not only lost him the sympathy that might have won him the estate, it also ensured that a good portion of his audience would back their beliefs with funds. For example, John Morse's *Famous Trials* records the sentencing in the second trial, in which "Mr. Justice Mellow . . . addressed the defendant in terms of great severity. Wicked and nefarious as was his attempt to present himself as Roger Tichborne, and so to obtain the vast property which of right belonged to the infant heir, this crime seemed almost to sink into insignificance beside the more infamous perjury concerning Lady Radcliffe" (1874, 233–34).

The seduction story was indisputably disastrous for Orton. It cost him the support of a large segment of the population that regarded propriety as *the* stabilizing force in the social economy. Complicated as were its effects, the basic facts are relatively simple. During the 1867 Chancery hearings, the Claimant provided a written statement that proved perhaps his greatest mistake beyond appearing on English shores. It referred to a sealed packet that, before departing for foreign lands, the young Sir Roger had deposited with Vincent Gosford, the family steward. According to Gosford (whom, incidentally, the family had since dismissed for financial mismanagement), the packet pertained to Katherine Doughty, with whom Sir Roger had fallen in love. Her parents opposed their marriage, largely because of Sir Roger's intemperate habits, and Gosford testified that the packet contained Roger's written series of promises to reform himself, including a pledge not to indulge his predilection for drink, and another to build a chapel to the Virgin if and when he was able to marry his cousin. Initially, the Claimant denied any memory of the packet, but he was miraculously able to reconstruct its contents after the Chancery hearings, when he learned that Gosford had destroyed the original. At that point, the Claimant produced a rendition of the packet that was scandalously different from that which Gosford described. In the written document he provided to his lawyers, Orton claimed that the packet had contained instructions to

Gosford to "show great kindness to my cousin Kate and let her have anything she required. My cousin give [*sic*] me to understand she was enceinte [pregnant] and pressed me very hard to marry her before I left" (quoted in Woodruff 1957, 95). In the trials, he testified that he had seduced Kate Doughty, who had by then become Lady Radcliffe.[22]

In some senses, the Claimant fanned his already roaring popularity by providing a source of derisive humor for the working classes—for example, a broadsheet, "The Tichbourne A.B.C.," gives "R" to "RADCLIFFE his cousin, who says, she never will / Confess she danced the *Can-can*, with Roger in the mill." But he also brought down on himself all the furies of outraged propriety, especially after Lady Radcliffe produced a duplicate of the original packet, which coincided with Gosford's version. Impugning a woman's reputation was not gentlemanly behavior, and various members of the public joined the battle against the Claimant in consequence.

Lady Tichborne's story worked upon an entirely different set of social investments. In fact, given the general national estimation for maternal affection, it is surprising that her assertion that the Claimant was her son was not simply decisive. Initially, common sense seemed to dictate that her word serve as law. As William Ellis wrote, "Imagine, I say, any low vulgar fellow here so circumstanced, over 20 stone in weight, crossing the channel to palm himself off upon a lady of title as her son, as the long-lost relative of uncles, aunts, and cousins still living, and moving in the highest sphere of society—an IMPOSTOR!!! Forsooth; why none but a MADMAN would attempt such a thing. . . . It is repugnant alike, to either sense or reason" (1873, 11). However, the many holes in Orton's story required more than Ellis's sort of logic could fill. Into the gap came the powerful tale of reunion, the Victorian stock in devotion, and the popular conception of maternal love as a precious and inalienable commodity. The ballad "We'll Not Forget Poor Roger Now" was only one of many to play to public sentimentality: "If there's any mothers standing round me, / I ask you truely [*sic*], every one, / If you think that you could ever— / Once forget a long lost son, / And so his mother recognised him / Which filled the family with dismay, / But suddenly she died, poor lady, / Or a different tale they would tell today." Flatly asking its audience to invest in the figure of the mother and, through her, in the son, "We'll Not Forget" summons the appeal of maternal attachment to bolster the Claimant's claim.

While the tale of maternal devotion reinforced the idea that the government was unfairly and illogically protecting the financial interests of the Doughty-Tichborne family, it also consolidated how the Tichborne affair conflated questions of economic and familial legitimacy. The "different tale" mentioned at the close clearly implies one in which the Claimant, sanctioned by his mother's authority, would have successfully assumed possession of both the family name and the family estates. Many of the post-trial ballads utilize the poignant rhetoric of attachment to imagine the alternate narratives the dowager might have made possible. "The Conviction of the Claimant," for example, avers, "If his mother had lived, / It would have caus'd a deal of bother / For she would have proved without a doubt, / He was her son Sir Roger." Much of the print culture produced to support the Claimant also emphasized his exclusion from familial affection, which it framed as an unassailable form of property: even in the more politically overt conversations about justice and "basic rights," the basic right to a mother's love had powerful appeal.

However, the reunion scene that initially seemed prime fodder for the Claimant's supporters proved so dubious as to be comic. In his initial letters, the Claimant "asked for money on no evidence of being entitled to any; and … inquired 'How's Grandma?' when Roger Tichborne must have known that he had no grandmother" (*Great Tichborne Case*, 16). Hawkins also reminded the jury, "He had talked about his grandfather, *whom Roger had never seen.* He said he was a private, whereas Roger was an officer; that he was educated at Winchester instead of Stonyhurst; that he had had St. Vitus's dance, which Roger never had" (Harris 1884, 209–10; emphasis in original). When mother and supposed son encountered each other for the first time in Paris, the Claimant lay in a darkened room with his face to the wall and refused to turn toward Lady Tichborne. "Must have been rather a strong maternal instinct," Hawkins remarked, "to recognize her son through the bedclothes!" (ibid., 210). As the Crown amassed more and more evidence linking the Claimant to Orton, the peculiarities of the Claimant's memory and the plain weirdness of his meeting with the dowager became increasingly suspicious.

Lady Tichborne passed away before either of the official trials was yet underway. The Claimant had testified before Chancery, the family had objected, and the court had requested additional information, which sent the *soi-disant* Sir Roger off to Cuba to gather evidence that he was the man he claimed to be, and to defend himself against the charge that he was Arthur Orton. The dowager died in his absence. Public stock in both the Claimant's and her own perspective suffered considerably with her decease. Whereas her living support had presented a difficult challenge for the Doughty-Tichborne family, her death allowed them to pursue more openly the defamatory logic that would undo the "bonds" of affection in which so many of the public had invested.

Chapter 1

Sensational Family Stories

In analyzing how the tales of mother and cousin played in the courtroom and in popular culture, I want to emphasize the significance of genre to what we now call "spin" in motivating very different kinds of investments in the same series of events. To begin, there were multiple versions of both stories. In the case of Lady Tichborne, the value of these renditions instrumentally informed the value of the same basic series of facts; in the case of Lady Radcliffe, Orton's lies did little to help him in court, but they titillated the national audience. However, whatever power he may have gained by providing the bawdier members of the population with salacious fantasies of a gentlewoman's body, he lost quickly when the exposure of his lies dovetailed with the equally titillating exposure of his own body. Stories about the Claimant's retractable penis became part of the legal record, thereby satisfying the appetites to which the seduction story appealed, while issuing a public warning about the consequences of making false claims. I'll have more to say about the Claimant's physical anomaly shortly.

First to the dowager: in working against the Lady Tichborne's testimony, the Crown mounted a masterful public relations campaign of sorts, one that acknowledged the sentimental power of maternal attachment at the same time as it discredited the attachment of one particular mother. The lawyers and the purveyors of ballads, in particular, together presented the dowager as an object lesson in the dangers of sentimentality, juxtaposing the material profits that hung in the balance for both Lady Tichborne and the Claimant against the emotional capital that had previously held ascendancy. In the hearings that began in 1871, the Crown made the dowager appear so full of motherly love as to be willing to accept as her son even a man who was in no way like him. As Hawkins argued, "All the world . . . believed that Roger Tichborne was dead. One poor, crazy, misguided soul alone refused to listen to the voice of reason—refused to believe that her first-born son was dead" (Harris 1884, 191). Even the Claimant's counsel was unable to discredit this line of argument. Interrogating Roger's old tutor in Paris, the Abbé Salis, Thomas Keneally asked, "'Was not she a truthful, honorable person?'. . . '*Elle avait la tête malade*,' responded the abbé, which is translated in the columns of the *Times* . . . by the unpleasant phrase, 'She had a diseased brain'" (Morse 1874, 48).

Given such felicitous primary material, it seems scarcely surprising that humor was the weapon of choice for divesting the mother's claims of both validity and sentimental appeal. "The Latest Tichborne Alphabet" dedicates D to the "Dowager Lady Tichborne," noting wryly, "'Tis sad she was insane— /

She really thought her shipwrecked son had come safe home again." "The Claimant's Woes, or Roger the Dodger" mounts a more boldfaced attack, suggesting that Lady Tichborne relied on a logic of likeness: "He makes small I's, and spells / Affection with one f, / And so he must be Roger, / He cannot be a dodger, / He could not spell, you know full well, / Which proves he must be Roger." It was true that Sir Roger spelled very badly, but so, the Crown proved, did Arthur Orton. While Lady Tichborne's reason (or want thereof) offered cause for laughter outside the courtroom, the analysis of the handwriting expert Charles Chabot within it traced the Claimant's spelling and scrawl, both, to the erstwhile butcher from Wapping.[23]

Even without the Orton connection, the mother–son drama ultimately crumbled under the force of the Crown's interrogation and "the evidence of numerous witnesses—some of them her [the dowager's] own brothers and sister, and one of them her own attorney—that . . . she had made up her mind to acknowledge the man who pretended to be her son, no matter whether she recognized him or not, and no matter how wild and false were his statements" (*Illustrated London News*, 31 January 1874). In effect, the team of lawyers managed to transform a sentimental story of reunion into both a cautionary tale about the perils of blind attachment and a sensational familial conspiracy that involved, at best, a mad and bereft mother and a scheming impostor. Initially, the dowager's account solicited both financial and emotional investments on the Claimant's behalf; ultimately, it offered its consumers only the opportunity to indulge in ill-advised emotional transports, thus conforming to the general perspective that sentimentality was rather too outré to serve for either moral example or effective political galvanization.[24]

Furthermore, Hawkins's opening arguments in the criminal trial reminded the jury that Lady Tichborne had potential financial, as well as emotive, profits to glean by defeating her husband's family. As Richard Harris observes in his *Illustrations in Advocacy*, Hawkins's remarks demonstrated a rare degree of forensic mastery:

> "Poor Lady Tichborne," says the learned counsel, "alone of all the world, clung to the belief that her son was not really dead." No tidings had been heard of the Bella, no news of the vessel or the crew, but still she clung to that belief. She was, moreover, not on good terms with the Tichborne family, and was not satisfied with the settlements. She had been left out in the cold, with no provision beyond her marriage settlement. Her income was limited. "Now," says the learned counsel, "such a person would be a ready tool to an imposter, supposing her own reason to be blinded by her feelings and her delusions." (1884, 196)

Hawkins's mention of the dowager's settlements suggests, first, that she "would be a ready tool to an imposter" potentially because of her own financial discontent, and second, that her role as "tool" may have been collaborative: she might have known full well what she was about when she took up the Claimant as her son.

Much of the available material about Lady Tichborne confirms that she was a complicated woman. Willful and difficult by Victorian terms, she had fought famously with her husband, from whom she lived separately for a significant portion of Roger's youth. She was also French and Catholic, and neither attribute served to bolster her credibility among the educated British public.[25] At least one journalist noted that young Roger had "passed his early childhood in a home most likely to embitter his feelings and drive him on his own resources. His father and mother led a miserable life. To use his own expression, 'his home was a very hell upon earth'" (*The Queen*, 23 July 1871). The *Illustrated London News* (31 January 1874) remarked on "that part of the case which related to the mother's recognition of him, . . . showing, from the letters of Roger himself and his father, that she was animated with the most insane hatred of his family." The Crown thus painted her simultaneously as a dedicated but mad mother, and as a vindictive and conscious opportunist who had a score to settle with her late husband's family. These perspectives revised the happy melodrama of reunion into a pair of tawdry sensational tales. In the one, she was a mother swindled by a gifted impostor; in the other, she was herself a fraud, eager to collaborate with the Claimant in order to reap her own profits.

As a rule, sensational plots *are* plots of domestic fraud: their thrills depend on incursions into private space and personal relationships. Their villains and protagonists engage in various acts of deceit, including forgery and impersonation, in order to gain access to social and economic property to which they are not legitimately entitled. In Mary Elizabeth Braddon's *Lady Audley's Secret*, for example, the eponymous heroine proves not to be Lucy Audley at all; rather, she is a bigamist named Helen Talboys, who pushes her first husband down a well when he threatens the privilege she has acquired with her new identity and her new marriage. In Mrs. Henry Wood's *East Lynne*, the supposedly dead adulteress Isabel Carlyle returns disfigured and disguised to her husband's home, to serve as governess to the children she had abandoned and, indirectly, to compromise the integrity of her husband's second marriage. In the closing chapters of Wilkie Collins's *The Woman in White*, the reader learns that Sir Percival Glyde has forged his own parents' marriage into the church register and hence forged his own right to his name and his fortune. His accomplice, Count Fosco, is a former spy who has crafted himself a new identity in England. Together, the men successfully scheme to take away Laura Fairlie's name and fortune by arranging her marriage to Glyde and then switching the body of her ailing identical half-sister, who is incarcerated in a madhouse, with her own. As these examples from the sensational "big three" suggest, most sensation fiction features characters who use false pretenses to access the profits of domestic relationships. They derive their narrative tension from the breach of proper boundaries and property rights.

By shifting the genre of the maternal story, the Crown set the stage for its rebuttal to the seduction claims, which essentially posed an inverse challenge to that which they had faced with Lady Tichborne. Lady Radcliffe was already "dancing the can-can" on the stage of sensation and needed to be restored to respectability. The Claimant's story of capering with his pretty cousin Kate in the hayloft was quite popular, exposing a gentlewoman to the scrutiny and derision of the public, giving "common mouths" access to Lady Radcliffe's name and providing the masses imaginative access to her flesh. The narrative retained its suggestive power even after it became clear that it was a lie, so that Orton's fictional incursions kept hold of their force and their appeal. Those incursions depended on a notion of private property that construed a gentlewoman's body as a commodity exclusively reserved for gentlemen, whose advantage would be mocked, if not desecrated, were a man who had elected to become a butcher in Wagga Wagga (or anywhere else for that matter) to access it. Thus, beyond the fraud that aimed at the Tichborne estates, Orton had committed a fraud upon Katherine Radcliffe and, through her, upon the privileged men of her class.

Within the courtroom and beyond it, Orton's opponents depended on sober codes of chivalry to mandate the defense of an innocent woman threatened by a "scoundrel": the Crown initiated the work of gatekeeping under the banner of defending a lady's honor. Harris's analysis of the case notes the complicated rationale behind the criminal trial. Technically, of course, it was designed to prove that the Claimant was Arthur Orton and hence guilty of perjury. However, it derived its legitimacy and much of its social power from its second objective of restoring to Lady Radcliffe the property of her reputation. As Harris remarks, the point of the trial "was not merely whether the defendant was Tichborne, but whether a lady, hitherto regarded as a virtuous woman, would be degraded, and perjured, in the eyes of the jury, her husband, her children and the world" (1884, 220).

The family's hired detectives had amassed an impressive array of witnesses and physical documents linking the Claimant to Orton. In addition, the lawyers recurred to written evidence from the first trial to prove that Sir Roger was nowhere near Tichborne at the time of the alleged seduction. Ironically, though, the Claimant's own counsel did much of the work of genre-shifting himself, by putting on the stand various witnesses who offered testimony about the Claimant's rare genital deformity.[26] Keneally initially intended this testimony to link his client to Sir Roger, who allegedly had the same "malformation," and to distance him from Orton, whose sister, Mary Ann, testified for the defense that her brother "had no malformation of the genital organs whatever" (*The Tichborne Malformation* 1878, 7). In response, the Crown brought to the stand Mary Ann Loder, Arthur Orton's lover in his youth, who averred that her former sweetie's equipment was indeed unusual. While the exposure of the Claimant's genital anomaly did nothing to confirm or disprove his identity with Orton, its discussion in the courtroom explicitly articulated the terms of access to various bodies. Keneally could not have anticipated how compatible this story would be to that his client had told about Lady Radcliffe, nor how its sensational cachet would help to appease the public's appetite for gossip as the tide turned against the Claimant. Orton's unusual penis shifted the public gaze from "cousin Kate's" body to his own and exposed the latter to scrutiny and derisive laughter.[27]

The Claimant's body was already a source of sensational thrill—the decisive tattoo, birthmarks in unspeakable locales, and the size of his earlobes were hotly contested points of evidence; his fat, too, made the supposed gentleman's body an occasion for popular discourse. The first trial had generated some speculation that the Claimant was "tattooed upon / His hoop de dodden do" ("Jolly Old Sir Roger" 1872), but the genital deformity proved both physically and legally emasculating to the Claimant, rendering him a public laughingstock. Sir Roger's childhood nickname of "small cock" emerged, as did *The Tichborne Malformation*, a pro-Claimant pamphlet that included Dr. Wilson's testimony that the Claimant's organ was quite small indeed:

> The penis retracts in a most unusual degree, so that on one occasion when he passed water, which had been retained for some hours at my express wish, the penis was absolutely out of view, and nothing whatever of it could be seen but the orifice from whence the stream issued. Yesterday I found the member more turgid, but I endeavoured to put it back towards the neck of the bladder with which it is continuous, and I found it perfectly easy to push the whole member out of sight. (3)

By making Orton's privates available to the public, the Crown both reasserted hierarchies of access and worked upon public investments in privacy. The scandalous exposure of the Claimant's retracting penis distracted from the salacious pleasures of the seduction story. Those pleasures "retracted," too, alongside increasingly persuasive evidence that the Claimant was a fraud. As the physical unveiling grossly echoed the revelation of his imposture, the grounds of narrative investment shifted. To say the least, the multiple forms of humiliating exposure certainly didn't help to encourage speculation on Orton's behalf. His emotive claims to disenfranchisement and discrimination stood no chance against the thrill and sensation of his exposure as a fraud, and his more comic public exhibition. As a source of bawdy bodily humor, the most he could hope for was pity. The criminal trial thus accomplished both the legal and bodily humiliation that many Britons associated with justice.

The Powers of Genre: Fact vs. Fiction

In the civil trial, the prosecution offered overpowering evidence that the would-be Sir Roger was indeed a fraud. In addition to the devastating effects of the lawyers' cross-examination, which made the Claimant and his witnesses failures on the stand, the Crown provided a slew of testimony establishing that the man who presented himself as Roger Tichborne was in fact Arthur Orton. The subsequent criminal trial, then, was responsible for translating proof into punishment.

But the scope of disciplinary action that the Crown set out to accomplish exceeded the simple function of law. When Arthur Orton was convicted of perjury and sentenced to fourteen years of hard labor on 28 February 1874, his career as poster boy for the working classes effectively ended.[28] However, even as the man himself lost his utility for specific political movements, his story kept its narrative power—and has maintained its popularity even to the present day. In the past decade alone, alongside the new scholarship I've been drawing on here, a major motion picture, a new popular biography, and a touring exhibit have joined the ranks of Tichborne ephemera.[29]

In other words, at the same time as the Crown used the generic evocations of popular fiction to dismantle the Claimant's public claims to truth, it took no action to detract from his popularity as a "true story." Rather, in much the same way as it had mobilized the properties of sensation to realign the allegiances elicited by the conflicting family stories, it utilized the distinctions between truth and fiction to expel Orton's claims on popular consciousness from the category of the real. Sentencing him physically to jail was only part of their success; they also sentenced him imaginatively to the category of popular entertainment. There, his story continues to function beautifully, without menacing the real lives, or real estate, of his consumers. By separating the "real" from the fictional, the Crown managed to quarantine the narrative

FIGURE 1.3

"Present State of the Tichnborne 'Bonds,' Dedicated to the Stock Exchange."

powers of fiction. The law, in this sense, operated as the Law in a Foucauldian capacity, cordoning off the genre of fiction from its powers to threaten actual property, exchange, and relationships.

I noted much earlier in this chapter that the experience of domestic fraud in daily life was significantly different from the experience of domestic fraud in popular culture, and I argued that the latter offered an opportunity to engage with risk within a virtual environment in which investing, in its various forms, was relatively safe. With an eye to the enduring power of the domestic fraud plot, I want to return to the monetary investments Orton solicited in the form of the Bonds, to make some final remarks about the Tichborne case and a larger point about Victorian popular narrative.

According to Woodruff, the Tichborne Bonds were the spur that initially prompted the government's intervention (see figure 1.3). They created a sense of urgency to

> prevent penniless adventurers from coming forward with frivolous claims. If such people could finance themselves by appealing to the sporting instinct of members of the general public, inviting them to have a gamble, stake £20 or £30 for a good chance of raking in a hundred, there was hardly a family in the country with great possessions who could view the prospect without disquiet. It meant that all the skeletons in family cupboards which might be clothed with legal significance . . . could become a new kind of commercial enterprise. This first great example needed to be dealt with very firmly. (1957, 165–66)

It is surely significant that the "sporting instinct of members of the general public" was less a problem than the vulnerability of "all the skeletons in family cupboards," and the threat those "skeletons" posed to the actual property of wealthy families. While family skeletons had long been standard fare in fiction, and the public's sporting instincts were already driving various forms of legitimate trade, the incursion of "penniless adventurers" on the property of actual families required governmental intervention.

The problem, in other words, was one of genre. Virtual investing in the form of libido was not only acceptable, but key to the operations of finance as well as fiction. In corporate enterprise, numbers, photographs, backers' signatures, and so on typically worked alongside a prospectus, as the components of a more or less overt story that ultimately had to do more than promise a finale of material gain: it also had to appeal to potential investors' interests in social, political, and cultural profits—to libidinal forms of "interest"—that would prompt them to buy into risky ventures.[30] These "stories" encouraged their marks to enter the world of fantasy, to dream of a better life, to cathect. As I've already noted, "better" usually meant increased access not only to power and justice, but also to other privileges of class that involved domestic comfort and were often explicitly familial.[31]

An effective fraud depends on an effective fiction. Like a successful novel, a successful swindle requires a narrative compelling enough to persuade victims to invest in (or extend credit for) products, ventures, ideas, or relationships that have no basis in fact. When a venture's sole purpose is to deceive its consumers, it requires a story of promise sufficiently gripping to prompt a willing encounter with a bad gamble.[32] Given that Victorian swindlers' narratives were frequently as delicate in detail as the increasingly elaborate banknotes that engravers designed to circumvent counterfeiting, it seems hardly a coincidence that the proper term for passing counterfeit notes was "uttering," nor that both fraudulent tales and tales about fraud made such excellent fodder for popular culture. [33]

Almost all Victorian plots depend for various of their pleasures on greater and lesser forms of domestic fraud. Charlotte Brontë's Rochester tries to stage an illegal marriage to Jane Eyre, and her aunt Reed tells Jane's uncle that Jane is dead; in Dickens's *Great Expectations,* Pip is led to believe Miss Havisham his benefactress, and we learn late in the novel that Compeyson had tricked Miss Havisham herself into a betrothal he never intended to fulfill; in Eliot's *Middlemarch,* Bulstrode keeps his discovery of Sarah Ladislaw secret from her mother and thereby obtains the whole of a fortune he would have had to share with her and her young son, Will. Significantly, most Victorian plots encourage readers to invest against the dictates of common sense, to bet on the long shot. We speculate against the odds that Jane Eyre will finally find some sort of familial happiness; that Will Ladislaw will come into his fortune; that Pip's expectations will prove, in the end, to be great indeed, and perhaps even that Miss Havisham will put on a fresh dress and throw out that nasty cake. There are no guarantees—and often, as in *Great Expectations*, there aren't any clear payoffs—but these tales nonetheless offer the pleasure of playing the game, even when the reader "loses." The capital one invests in these plots is virtual rather than material, and the violations of moral trade become sources of enjoyment rather than pain.

Fiction itself, of course, depends on a reader's investment of time and energy—hence the old Italian proverb that there is no thief like a bad book. However, when the field of narrative threatens real property, rather than time or other intangible assets, the game becomes serious business. When the Crown responded to the threat of the Tichborne bonds, it sought to divorce the virtual from the actual, to protect the family from becoming a site for market-based investment that would potentially allow strangers access to household property (in the case of Tichborne, that property included the house). At the same time, the legal arguments worked to maintain the virtual capacity of domestic investing by recurring constantly to the suffering of the Tichborne family. The government's exigency to draw a clear line between real incursions on the family and virtual domestic fraud (the stuff of novels, melodramas, and penny dreadfuls) sought to cordon off what had become a thriving trade in swindling, from what had become a rich source of recreational pleasure.

The Crown thus had little problem when Orton emerged from prison in 1884 and once again made himself a public commodity. No longer in the running for the Tichborne property, the Claimant earned his keep as a sideshow attraction, touring England and America as a B-grade celebrity. For his "act," he told the well-worn story of his life as Sir Roger. "Sometimes, for a change," Annear reports, "he featured in an illusionist's routine, being made to vanish from a chair swinging in mid-air" (2002, 401). The confession he issued in 1895 generated a bit of stir, and a bit more when he retracted it, but because he no longer posed a threat to valuable capital, there was no further legal action. The casket that contains his body bears the name Roger Doughty Tichborne.

✧

I have been arguing in this chapter that narratives work to open up their readers, allowing them to try on potential perspectives that may or may not fit. In Victorian England, popular stories produced a space to shop for virtual paradigms that might suit their consumers' real lives, but they also provided space to play in ideological perspectives they would never wear in public. Different genres of Victorian popular culture offered very different sets of imaginative possibilities: as a group, they offered a reader a range of opportunities to conceive of the realities among which he or she circulated, and the various ideological investments into which he or she might buy.

In the Tichborne case, the government attempted to protect the property of rich families. Despite the Crown's desire to keep frauds and their schemes away from the material goods in wealthy homes, Victorian households were already hosting an array of people who displayed misleading markers of legitimacy. And not only wealthy families were at risk: fraud was a very real problem in middle- and working-class homes as well. The following chapter carries forward the claim I have been making at the close of this one, namely, that the recreational attitude toward domestic fraud maintained an inverse relationship to its proximity to real life: the more material and valuable the form of capital, the more serious and disciplinary the popular response tended to be. The textual residues of those responses in popular discourse suggest, too, that generic contexts often varied according to the value of the property in question and the stakes a consumer risked in seeing that property compromised. Venturing on narrative offered a lot of room for experimentation. Venturing on the state of one's actual household was rather more serious business.

2

Brinks Jobs

Servants, Thresholds, and Portable Property

———— ⌒⌐ ————

I N 1859, CHARLES DEARLOVE brought charges against his family servant, Jane Robinson, who had removed to her own home various bits of property belonging to his. The legal proceedings enabled the Dearloves both to reclaim their possessions and to exact serious punishment for Jane, who was sentenced to one year in prison. Jane's appetite for her employers' property was so vast as to demand redress, but the inventory of her plunder is remarkable not only for its expanse but for its triviality: the items in question were small, ordinary bits of domestic material. Mrs. Dearlove testified that

> the prisoner Jane was our servant for about three months prior to 31st October, when I discharged her—after she was gone I missed a black cloth mantle, a silver pencil case, 4 towels, 2 plates, some egg cups, and a variety of articles—I accompanied the policeman to John Robinson's house . . . I saw a linen pocket handkerchief lying on the table—I said "That is mine," and gave it to the inspector—I saw a pair of drawers lying on the shelf, and said "Those are mine," and gave them to the inspector—Jane's box was searched in my presence, and contained a black silk mantle, a photographic portrait, 2 China crape shawls, a wool bag, a silk pocket handkerchief, a piece of glazed lining, a pink sash, a muslin collar, 7 books, 6 pieces of lace, a pincushion, and a lot of other things which were all mine—I had not given them to her. (Central Criminal Court 1859–60, 33–4)

———— ⌒⌐ ————

In addition, when the police inspector searched Jane's mother's box, he discovered

four towels marked with Mrs. Dearlove's initials, one pillow-case, five pairs of childrens' drawers marked, two pinafores, a night-cap marked, a night-shirt marked, a white frock, an embroidered collar, two pieces of embroidery, a piece of new chintz, three brown Holland jackets, a calico chemise marked, six china plates, a china cup and saucer, a dessert-plate, two table-covers, two pairs of socks marked, a boy's shirt, and a coloured frock. . . . a counterpane, a pair of gloves, two pieces of crape, a shawl, a pair of Angola socks, and also a number of articles which there was a doubt about at the time—they were shown to Mrs. Dearlove, and she said they were hers. (Central Criminal Court 1859–60, 34)

The sheer volume of Jane Robinson's spoils is impressive, yet towels, bits of china, scraps of cloth, and random pieces of clothing hardly seem the stuff of panic. Nonetheless, the markings on the clothing represent a larger sense of proprietorship that Mrs. Dearlove seems singularly concerned with maintaining: "That is mine," she repeats; "those are mine." The physical objects themselves, in other words, signified more broadly, and Jane's violation exceeded the simple realm of theft. She had made off with a series of objects that embodied their owners' personal investments in a particular type of domestic identity, and she had defrauded an investment of trust.

While servant fraud was not nearly so spectacular or sensational as the grand imposture Arthur Orton attempted, it was far more familiar, far more local, and therefore had rather less capacity to be entertaining. Standing at the threshold between theoretically public and private spaces, servants bore the brunt of the angst about the increasingly imperiled household. They were both in circulation themselves and mediums of fiscal exchange between divergent economies. Popular middle-class texts of fact and fiction expressed a marked anxiety about the subversive exchange of capital that servants might facilitate between individuals, between spheres, and between classes. In this chapter, I focus on the significance of literal possessions and of more amorphous forms of property (reputation, labor, security) in the changing legal, geographical, and social configurations of the household. Whereas they had originally served to mark the class status of the families that employed them, servants were gaining mobility and professional power. Mid-Victorian authors and illustrators made the most of both sorts of mobility, emphasizing the types of threat and property that servants might shuttle into and out of the home.

For the most part, servants take center stage only in texts that are now relegated to archives—in penny dreadfuls, like G. W. M. Reynolds's *Mary Price* (1852); in comic novels, like the Mayhew brothers' *The Greatest Plague of Life* (1847); and in the manuals, sermons, and pamphlets generated for a growing and newly professional class of workers. There are exceptions of course, but generally domestic servants appear only on the margins of canonical texts, as part of the scenery against which the central characters act.[1] Thus it is all too easy to move quickly past the "help" in *David Copperfield*, for example, who enjoy the Copperfield property a bit too much when David and Dora set up housekeeping. Yet, the anxiety those servants produce is significant. David remarks that their first housemaid, Mary Anne, "preyed upon our minds dreadfully. . . . We should have been at her mercy, if she had had any; but she was a remorseless woman, and had none" (*Copperfield*, 586). She enters their home with "a written character, as large as a proclamation; and according to this document, could do everything of a domestic nature that ever I heard of" (585). But good Mary Anne proves positively criminal: when David finally summons the nerve to fire her, he is surprised at her mild departure until he discovers that the teaspoons are "deficient" and that Mary Anne has borrowed "little sums . . . in [his] name of the tradespeople without authority" (590).

The context of the written but false document, the missing spoons, the perilous economy of trust, and the fundamental balance of domestic economy were vital components not only of Dickens's novel, but also of the Victorian social landscape. The Copperfields live in a house haunted by commercial depredation, and Mary Anne initiates "a long line of Incapables; that include a washerwoman who pawns the clothes and "a young person of genteel appearance, who went to Greenwich Fair in Dora's bonnet. . . . Everybody we had anything to do with seemed to cheat us," David writes woefully (590). This chapter provides the legal and cultural context for the Mary Annes of the Copperfield home; for the avaricious servants of *Vanity Fair;* for Miss Matty's anxieties about followers in Gaskell's *Cranford;* and for the servants, cooks, and housemaids that maintain, and fail to maintain, the houses of the Victorian canon.

Professional Mobility

Although there were Tichbornes and Sadleirs in Victorian England, there were plenty of citizens who managed to accumulate significant wealth while maintaining at least some modicum of honesty. Class transcendence was both a lure and a very real possibility, so great that, by 1865, Lord Palmerston was able to present it as a given to the audience at a prize-giving ceremony of the South London Industrial Exhibition. The Prime Minister confidently assured his audience:

> you have all seen, in your own experience, men starting from the smallest beginnings, who have in this very city realised princely fortunes. In the manufacturing districts examples of this kind are abundant; for no man can go, even for a few days, into those districts without hearing of great wealth, acquired by men who started with little; but, by their talents and genius, raised themselves and their families to opulence. (Palmerston 1865, 401)

The "rise" of which Palmerston spoke was both material and social. The Industrial Revolution, the growth of the British Empire, the rise of professions, and the possibilities of the stock market made it feasible for men of no great fortune to "make themselves." For women, new opportunities for self-making were less overtly economic, but the role of homemaker offered possibilities for financial advancement through the dividends of marriage and other forms of domestic administration. "English society, hierarchical as it was, proved sufficiently adaptable to permit the wealthy merchant to buy a country seat and to have his children intermarry with the squirarchy; a fledgling industrialist might hope to do the same" (Willcox and Arnstein 2001, 192). At the same time, then, as one might purchase an estate, one might also purchase access to aristocratic company. Class status had become a buyable commodity. It had long been for sale in limited supply, of course, but moving on up became so much a part of cultural mythology that the bloodlines that previously governed access to power and influence seemed to have lost their sway.[2]

Class fluidity encompassed both promise and peril. As the Rev. J. Baldwin Brown remarked, "No man knows surely either his neighbor's [place], or his own. There is no sort of fixity in any of the institutions of society, no sort of continence in any of its orders. . . . All things are in constant flux; and above all things the habits, pursuits, callings and social status of men. We do not know where to find men, and large classes do not know where to find themselves" (1871, 278). These problems of location—of "finding" men (and women) in their proper places, and of what those places might be—made for a crisis in social topography. As Peter Bailey notes, "Mid-Victorian England appears remarkable not only for its volatile social order but for the plasticity of its human geography. . . . There were as yet no adequate physical *cordons sanitaires* to protect the assumptions and apparatus of class superiority" (1979, 345).

The domestic servant seemed to offer a key for charting the social terrain. For example, in his 1889 maps of London, Charles Booth literally gilded,

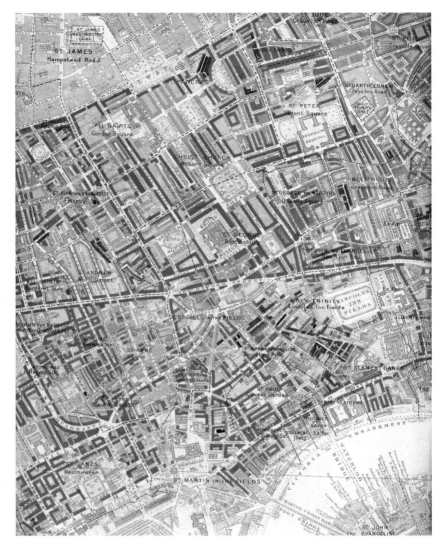

FIGURE 2.1
Charles Booth's Descriptive Map of London Poverty. [Original in color]

in goldenrod, a social distinction with which his culture had been living for decades: the golden sections of the map, concentrated around the West End parks, refer to the wealthy population of Victorian England, or the "servant keeping class" (a term Booth coined himself) (see figure 2.1).

—◌◦◌—

Booth's color-coding indicates visually that employing servants distinguished well-off families from their more remote neighbors whose black-and-blue hues in Booth's cartographic schema denote a bruised and hungry poverty.[3] These maps, alongside a wide range of earlier popular documents, illustrate the widely held opinion that, alongside whatever household chores they might perform, servants were markers of their employers' wealth and comfort. As Bruce Robbins writes, "the desire to be defined as middle class was a major reason for keeping servants" (1993, 15).[4]

Construed as symbols—indeed, as property—servants frequently appeared in popular images as useful props for distinguishing class status. However, they were ultimately rather problematic place markers because they simply did not stay put. As Thorstein Veblen snidely remarks, "The first requisite of a good servant is that he should conspicuously know his place" (1899, 56). Desirable as might be their active labor *within* the home, servants increasingly changed places *between* homes, regularly traveling beyond their places of employment. Furthermore, alongside the established discourse about servants not staying in their places professionally, there was increasing concern about their desires for social mobility. As Ellen Darwin observed, "No people contemplate so frequently and so strikingly the unequal distribution of wealth: they fold up dresses whose price contains double the amount of their year's wages; they pour out at dinner wine whose cost would have kept a poor family for weeks" (1890, 290). Thus, in texts produced for servants, one frequently finds attempts to curtail material aspirations. In *Jane Wright; or, The Young Servant*, young Jane's father tells her, "God has said there shall be differences of rank. The Queen is appointed to govern the country, and we ought to serve her. Masters and mistresses have their duty to do in ordering their servants, and they must serve their Queen and obey their rulers at the same time; and servants are doing their duty to God quite as much as to their masters when they obey them" (1865, 10). Jane's father calls in the big guns to reprove any servant's aspirations to join the class for which she labors, as *Jane Wright* establishes a Biblical injunction that servants not question their masters' rights to govern.

Whereas pamphlets *for servants* attempted, by cultivating humility, to redress the stress that arose from economic disparities, other texts with wider readerships were far more interested in playing on social tensions, making hay of servants' unruly behavior toward their employers and their property. The long literary tradition of servants figured as objects of scorn and ridicule testifies to this history of unease between domestic employers and the people who worked in their abodes—Shakespeare, Richardson, Defoe, and various other early authors include a solid stock of household servants whose scruples are far from scrupulous. Plots about plotting servants only multiplied in the Victorian period.[5] Because of their activity, mobility, and access to the emblematic trappings of middle-classness, servants metonymically signaled the vulnerabilities of the household. At the same time, then, as servants served as markers of class difference, they were also itinerant figures in the popular imagination, emblematic of the slippage between classes and of the commerce among spheres. Accordingly, the relationship between domestic and employer became a lightning rod for diverse anxieties about the unstable demarcation of ranks, and about unsavory market practices within the home.

Work That Is Not Work

Most middle-class establishments would not have had a large roster of servants. In *The Greatest Plague of Life; or, The Adventures of a Lady in Search of A Good Servant* (1847), a comic serial Henry Mayhew co-wrote with his brother Augustus before turning his eye to *London Labour and the London Poor*, the protagonist's resolution to hire a footman is the *ne plus ultra* of pretension. Mr. S—st—n protests to his wife, "He wasn't going to bring himself to the workhouse, he wasn't, for any of my fine fal-lal notions. As for his having a great, fat, lazy footman, sauntering about his house, and eating the very bed from under him, he wouldn't think of it for a moment; for the long and the short of it was, *he couldn't afford it*" (244; emphasis in original). The majority of middle-class households couldn't either: most did not keep decorative servants, and many modest homes relied on a single maid-of-all-work. Families that were slightly better off might have a cook and a manservant as well, but in the average home a small staff carried the heavy burden of domestic labor, which included cooking, marketing, dusting, emptying chamberpots, polishing silver and copper, beating rugs, and so on. It was hardly idle employment.

It is ironic, therefore, how much energy went into the effort to divorce the home from the commercial world of work, and how much anxiety surrounded their proximity. As various critics have demonstrated, the ideal of separate spheres instituted a gendered division of labor that buttressed the capitalist system: women's management of the home allowed men to pursue employment outside it.[6] However, a wife's work was not generally construed as labor. John Ruskin's (in)famous depiction of the sanctuary of the home alongside a debilitating public sphere, which I reference in the introduction, suggests that the move to eschew domestic labor *as* labor appealed, at least in part, because the idea of a safe haven was so seductive in a perilous world.

The man, in his rough work in open world, must encounter all peril and trial:—to him, therefore, the failure, the offence, the inevitable error: often he must be wounded, or subdued; often misled, and always hardened. But he guards the woman from all this; within his house, as ruled by her, unless she herself has sought it, need enter no danger, no temptation, no cause of error or offence. This is the true nature of home—it is the place of Peace; the shelter, not only from all injury, but from all terror, doubt, and division. In so far as it is not this, it is not home; so far as the anxieties of the outer life penetrate into it, and the inconsistently-minded, unknown, unloved, or hostile society of the outer world is allowed by either husband or wife to cross the threshold, it ceases to be home; it is then only a part of that outer world which you have roofed over, and lighted fire in. (84–85; emphasis in original)

In this most famous formulation of the doctrine of separate spheres, Ruskin strategically presents the Victorian home as a remedial locale removed from the bustle of the public domain and its concerns; home is a therapeutic sphere in which a loving wife provides an exhausted husband with draughts for his humanity, poultices for his morality, and sustenance for his body against the contaminating effects of the outside world. Yet one cannot help noting the fragility of the barrier between domains as the "outer world" presses at the threshold. If the doctrine of separate spheres figures the home as a site of melioration, as a sickroom of sorts to heal the ravages of the marketplace, it also marks that home's susceptibility to infection. It can, with perilous speed, become merely a "roofed over" extension of the world outside.

Ruskin was likely aware that his vision of discrete worlds was a pretty and appealing plea for an idyllic distribution of gendered powers and spaces. In contrast, alongside the powerful ideology of separate spheres in Victorian culture, nineteenth-century manuals of domestic administration *emphasized* that the home was a workplace. And servants were key to that more sophisticated understanding of how the household machine operated. As John Jordan observes, "Servants, by their very presence, call into question the homogeneity of the home. Guardians of the threshold, they bring with them across that barrier 'anxieties' and 'divisions' from the outside world, to use Ruskin's terms, that are inconsistent with the peaceful, orderly picture that domestic ideology seeks to paint" (1998, 80). In this respect at least, the home runs like a business, with the mistress at the head of domestic operations. Mrs. Beeton's famous *Book of Household Management* offers in its very first chapter so detailed a table of annual wages for servants, from house steward to stable boy, from housekeeper to scullery-maid, that it is difficult to overlook the "management" components of Mrs. Beeton's project.

In seeking to resolve the incongruity between home as refuge and home as place of employment, many domestic ideologues worked to transfigure the business of household labor into what Monica Cohen terms "busyness," whereby "housework can figure as a methodical, systematized engagement with the materials of the world" that nonetheless denies the explicit gain-seeking ends of business proper (1998, 91). As Poovey observes, "Despite the fact that women contributed materially to the consolidation of bourgeois wealth and political power, their economic support tended to be translated into a language of morality and affection" (1988, 10)—into, in other words, a form of labor roughly akin to the East Indian sense of *seva* (selfless service) that allowed women and those around them to ignore the economic components of their exertions.

Despite the undeniable facts of wages and management, many Victorian texts sought to deny a mistress's business relationship with her servants. This project was made easier by the history of servitude as a feudal arrangement in which the master held a custodial—indeed, familial—position in relation to his employees. Although, as Norman Feltes notes, "From the seventeenth century onward, both the extra-economic, legal compulsion to labour and the reciprocal rights which assured the servant some personal freedom were replaced by the forms of the 'free market in labour' necessary to industrial capitalism" (1978, 200), many employers clung to the vision of the impermeable home and imagined their servants as children or family members.[7] The author of *Domestic Servants* writes that "servants, like children, require to be treated with firmness and kindness" (Practical Mistress 1859, 4), and Mrs Blair, mentor to the eponymous Lily of Catherine Bell's instructional novel, *Lily Gordon; or, the Young Housekeeper* (1868), reminds our heroine that she is responsible for the moral well-being of her staff.[8] "Dear Lily," says Mrs. Blair,

> try to realise that each servant is a creature of God, one who has to give account to Him for all things done, or left undone, one whose character must be either improved or deteriorated by her residence under your roof. As the Christian mistress of a household, you are bound to see that the former be the case. As the Christian mistress of a household, it is sin in you to suffer without check or rebuke that wrong should be committed by any under your authority, whether that wrong be against God, against yourself, or against fellow-servants. (23)

In this particular system of checks and balances, the mistress's relation to her servants is explicitly parental. Likewise, many domestic manuals depicted the work of housekeeping as the supervision of servants' spiritual welfare, as much if not more than that of their labor in the home. These models not only cast the relationship between mistress and servant as more familial than commercial; they also disguised the explicitly economic arrangements by which servants entered the home in the first place.

While a familial model aptly described operations in some country establishments in which a servant might work a lifetime for a single family, it was less and less frequently the mode in urban centers. Harriet Martineau writes nostalgically about the old model's security for domestic workers: "Happier is the lot of the few old coachmen, butlers, valets, or housekeepers, whom one may now and then see in old houses, for they can never come to want, or waste their savings. They are not turned off because they are worn out, after spending their lives in the family service" (1862, 428). Yet Martineau neglects to mention the benefits for the employer in having an utterly dependent and familiar staff, or the ways in which the family's protection infantilized the employee. For all the safety of this old-fashioned arrangement, most servants wanted to spend (or "waste") their own money as they saw fit, and trouble arose frequently from employers' efforts to intervene in their servants' personal or spiritual lives. Although many servants' manuals struggled to instill in domestic employees an explicitly Christian attitude toward their work, selfless service was ultimately more the provenance of the housewife than of the member of staff who received wages.

Circulation and Professionalization

By the mid-nineteenth century, the same technologies that made it possible to rise from the working to the middle class had rendered the familial system of service decidedly outmoded, its attractive retirement benefits notwithstanding. George Henry Lewes's play *The Game of Speculation* (1851) emphasizes the new economic foundation of domestic employment: "As to servants, we change them every day. Attachment, indeed! pay them their wages regularly, and they leave you without regret; but owe them money, and you keep them devoted to the last" (1851, 6). Domestic labor was more and more a viable and real profession with opportunities for travel, competition, and advancement. As Frances Power Cobbe wrote in 1868, "Railways, registries, cheap newspaper advertisements, penny posts, and county courts, have between them rendered the change of service so perfectly easy, that the slightest cause of annoyance, or hope of improved position, is enough to provoke young and naturally change-loving men and women to give up their place" (1868, 130). These advances in various forms of circulation (transportation, publication, communication) made for a situation in which servants quite literally were no longer staying in their places.

Popular representations marked and exaggerated this shifting reality. For example, in *The Greatest Plague of Life* (Mayhew and Mayhew 1847), Mrs. Sk–n–st–n goes through roughly a dozen servants before she retires to the workhouse, and the eponymous heroine of G. W. M. Reynolds's immensely popular penny-dreadful *Mary Price; or, the Memoirs of a Servant-Maid* (1852) works for nearly a dozen families before coming into her surprise inheritance of thirteen thousand a year. The potential for both literal and abstract movement of place, of class, and of position made it possible for real servants to command negotiating power and to make careers of household work. Rejecting the Christian anti-commercial approach, and having learned to turn to their own account the laws of supply and demand, servants were becoming business agents, marketing and negotiating the terms of their own labor.

In response to these shifting power relations, Cobbe offered the consummately reasonable suggestions, first, that contracts be made more explicit, clear, and equitable; and second, that employers, rather than fighting the specter of the home-as-business, embrace it so as to bring to bear on the domestic servant the moral imperatives of an employment contract in an office or other professional establishment. However, in ceasing to envision their servants as feudal lieges, employers were forced to confront the market dynamics of a largely unregulated system of exchange. Cobbe imagines her results with hope: "A religion of faithful contracts might arise, and the idea of dishonesty in defrauding the other contracting party in labour might be esteemed as disgraceful as it is now felt to be to defraud the servant in wages" (1868, 133). Legitimate as her suggestions may seem, when Cobbe positions the servant as a sort of household clerk, she summons up more than the "religion of faithful contracts"; she points also to the many opportunities for fraud at home in the overlap between business and domestic management.

The Servant as Clerk

The business model was not comforting. There were rather nasty antecedents in the public sphere, where "real" swindlers were as likely to be clerks as CEOs. One of the more celebrated frauds of the century, Walter Watts of the Globe Insurance Company, was "not the manager with an income of £800 or £1000 a-year, but a simple check-clerk in the cashier's department, with a salary of something like £200 a-year," who instead of working his way steadily and slowly into a £1000-a-year management position, managed instead to fudge the Globe's books to the tune of £70,000 (Evans 1859, 77–78). D. Morier Evans notes that, although Watts had "great discernment" and "quick apprehension," he was "not over-burdened with moral principle" (78). Leading a double life, Watts was by day a modest clerk at the company he robbed. By night, however, he lived lavishly. Ironically, he floated other Globe-like prospects in the shape of two theaters, the Marylebone and the Olympic (both of which, like Watts himself, were doomed to failure). Watts's performance of innocence at work was sufficiently convincing to allow him to live in great style and respectability for six years before the Globe Assurance Company suspected him of any misdeed. "Walter Watts was, to all appearance, a kindly, free-hearted gentleman, who having infinite quantity of money at his command, applied it to the laudable purposes of patronizing art and making his friends happy" (83). He carried on the act after his arrest, responding to the charges with hauteur, declarations of innocence, and perfect sangfroid, which demeanors he maintained until, having been sentenced to ten years transportation, he committed suicide at Newgate.

It is telling that Evans registers more surprise at the *degree* of Watts's fraud, than at the actual deed:

> From time immemorial, clerks have been discovered embezzling the property of their employers; but when, save in the middle of the nineteenth century, could it be supposed a case such as that of Walter Watts would occur, who, not content with trifling peccadilloes, successively opened two theatres with money surreptitiously obtained from the Globe Insurance Company, and managed them in a style of undisputed magnificence in the face of empty treasuries. (1859, 3)

Taking as fact that clerks regularly skim from their employers' tills, Evans illustrates a general rule about employers' vulnerabilities, of which Watts was only an extreme example. An essay entitled *Business: As It Is, And as It Might Be*, published for the Young Men's Christian Association, declared that "Dishonesty has become epidemical. . . . Christianity is not carried into the counting-house or the shop; but a widely different code of morals is adopted there. . . . How absurd the notion, that a man can lead a double life and retain his uprightness of character! That he may cheat in the market and compensate for it by an increased goodness in the parlour!" (Lyndall 1854, 34–35). Yet British legal history establishes that one was as likely to encounter fraud in the parlor as in the counting-house.

In 1799, Parliament passed the Embezzlements Prevention Bill, designed explicitly "to protect masters against embezzlements by their clerks *or servants*" (quoted in Hawkins and Curwood 1824, 1: 157; emphasis added). To some extent, the conflation between clerks and servants was linguistic, in much the same way that earlier Master and Servant Acts generally legislated commercial, rather than domestic, employment and often specifically excluded household servants from their provisions. However, the two groups had parallel access to valuable resources and information—both clerks and servants were employees, trusted by necessity, with access to the goods of an establishment. Parliament worked to protect employers from forms of theft that did not require trespass, and religious leaders took up the cause at mid-century, producing a proliferation of texts for both groups. For example, in *Domestic Duties*, the Chaplain to the House of Commons, Reverend Thomas Garnier, urges servants to "refuse to defraud with the dishonest," but notes that even "the upright and conscientious servant must find it a difficult thing. . . . to resist the powerful temptations to peculation and dishonesty, which are so constantly placed before him by the unprincipled tradesman, who is but too ready to reward him in exact proportion to the waste he shall occasion in his master's goods" (1851, 78).

The dishonest disposal of those goods might include circulating the more fluid stuff of narrative, as well as literal property. Various mid-Victorian texts display a distinct paranoia about the employee's knowledge of the family's economic assets, and of the family's secrets. As Brian McCuskey notes, "Through servants' curiosity and gossip, the private affairs of the family become public knowledge: the master's business interests are disclosed, the mistress's confidences broadcast, the daughter's flirtations and the son's debts exposed" (2000, 359–60). The more social of these secrets had the potential to compromise the family's social solvency. Others, of checks and balances, of bills and salaries unpaid, of horses kept rather than bought, could compromise the family's fiscal well-being. The parallel between servant and clerk acknowledges the servant as a business appurtenance of the household, through whose hands passed the material on which the employer's security depended.

Ripe with the potential for exploitation through illicit exchange, both palpable and cognitive household property could exit the home through servants' access to it. Thus, despite the image of the devoted associate whose function in the office was akin to that of the dedicated family retainer, Cobbe's wistful hope for a "religion of faithful contracts" appeared unlikely and idealistic. Especially in popular representations, neither the clerk nor the servant was a terribly reassuring figure.

The Permeable Threshold and
the Fragility of Private Property

From the 1860s onward, the public was at least canny about the sources of conflicts between servants and their employers, and many popular narratives contain many tiny moments representing servants as deceptive agents bent on defrauding their employers. Mid-Victorian texts were particularly attentive to servants' potential to ferry money and property out of the home. The threshold, therefore, became a notable site of trouble. Jordan notes that servants "open up the middle-class home to the world beyond, . . . collaps[ing] the distinction between inside and outside, between the safe, orderly domestic world and the world of 'terror, doubt, and division' that hovers just outside its doorstep" (1998, 88–89). As this passage suggests, literal entrances into the home offered explicit and instructive thresholds across which to understand middle-class anxieties about servants in market culture, for through those doors passed the accoutrements of middle-classness: food, furniture, goods, gossip, and visitors. Servants quite literally functioned as conduits between the home and the outside world, in that they managed the purchase, preparation, and maintenance of familial property that made up the external trappings of middle-class identity.[9] They also had significant power over those portals, which, as Charles Dickens, Jr., observes, could lead to its own forms of trouble. "Too much caution cannot be exercised in regard to the admission of strangers, especially during the absence from home of the master of the house. Every kind of thief is on the watch for a favourable moment to gain admission, and after having induced the servant to leave unprotected the hall or room, into which he contrives to be shown, to lay hands on all the available portable property" (1888, 131).

Anxieties about "portable property" help to explain, at least in part, the common stipulation that servant girls have "no followers," or beaux. Followers might compromise household operations by introducing the marriage plot into the kitchen, as in Elizabeth Gaskell's *Cranford*, where Miss Matilda's "mysterious dread of men and matrimony" takes less hysterical form among the other women of the town, who "might well feel a little anxious, lest the heads of their comely maids should be turned by the joiner, or the butcher, or the gardener; who were obliged, by their callings, to come to the house: and who, as ill-luck would have it, were generally handsome and unmarried" (1853, 64, 65).[10] However, more often, the discourse on followers reinforces the fragile economy of the home and the difficulty of securing possessions more common than a good servant.[11] In "Kate's Young Man," a popular ballad, the grammar of ownership nicely sums up this anxiety about private property. Initially, said young man is a regular darling, and he is decidedly "Kate's." The early verses depict him as the universal object of desire, so charming that all the women want him.

> Some servant girls at Croydon fair,
> A dancing with young fellows were
> But there was none among the clan,
> So spruce and smart as kate's [*sic*] young man—
> They were seen home by kate's [*sic*] young man—
> And ask'd to tea was Kate's young man—
> And cookey prepared a sop in the pan,
> Next day to give to Kate's young man.

The ballad begins as a standard narrative of female competition for an eligible bachelor. "Spruce and smart," Kate's young man is quite a catch for any young woman involved in domestic labor. And he incites competition. In a later verse, the housemaid entices Kate's young man to play a game with the street door key: "romping round for the key he ran, / And take it away did Kate's young man." The ballad still retains the lexicon of romantic rivalry, as Kate confronts the housemaid: "Pray is he your or my young man? / Why don't you get your own young man? / And then they were within a span / Of scratching each other for Kate's young man."

Up to this point, Kate proudly modifies the young man who has the female housekeeping population so close to blows. The locus of desire shifts, however, in the next stanza when Kate suddenly realizes that she has more to worry about losing than her young man.

> 'Bout Kate's young man was all this fuss,
> When Kate cried out, "Why, where's my puss?"
> "And vhere's my vatch?" said Cook, and Ann
> Exclaim'd "Confound that Kate's young man!
> I've lost my brooch through Kate's young man."

"Kate's Young Man" sums up the general attitude toward followers. Although the women had initially played the young man between them as a prize to be won, their missing goods mock both their desire and their desirability. The young man redefines the terms of exchange, so that the game of courting a servant is only a means by which a young man might gain a purse, a watch, a brooch, and then some. The ballad continues, "That very night as sure as fate, / Some thief got in and stole the plate." As a follower, the cryptic young man without a name enters the home through a ruse of romance, only to exit it with material items of domestic value. The missing plate discovered, the staff forces the young man back upon the young woman who originally claimed him as her own: when the housemaid discovers the silver missing, she cries, "Oh Kate, I fear it's your young man!" and then calls the police. The young man doesn't stick around, however, to allow Kate to modify him socially or own him grammatically. Having played Kate and the household, the nameless thief reemerges only briefly before the law transports him to Australia, far removed from both Kate and the marriage plot he had briefly inhabited.[12]

Character Plots

Within the world of Victorian commerce, the rise of cities and technologies of transportation made it exponentially easier to commit and to get away with both small- and large-scale swindles. Employers, shopkeepers, and creditors rarely knew very much about the people to whom they entrusted their property or their confidence; financial and interpersonal trust, accordingly, was increasingly tenuous. As Peter Bailey notes, "Contemporaries were far from unaware that men might take advantage of the discontinuities of big city life to default upon their respectability" (1979, 346).

Because a bad servant might render the house a warehouse, hiring servants was serious business. But how was one to tell the bad from the good? Imposture on the scale of the Tichborne Claimant was rare, but respectability could be manufactured by consulting the wealth of conduct manuals that illustrated in minute detail how to perform the attributes of moral goodness. Through careful study of the exemplars offered in the works of Samuel Smiles and other moralists, one could learn to polish a corrupt surface into something bright and seemingly valuable. The threat of the actor who could perform respectability well enough to pass him- or herself off, as one might a false coin, brought home the ramifications of trading on a burnished exterior in order to obtain things, positions, or circumstances of value. The potential ramifications of the doctrine of self-help went beyond the promise of upward mobility, beyond the field of financial gain; as the Tichborne case demonstrates, they also included the menace of counterfeiting the self. Hence, even when Cobbe establishes a grown-up professional identity for the newly mobile servant, she rues the mobility that has effected the change. "What it [mobility] costs in time, temper, comfort, and money, is not to be calculated," she writes, "but its essential mischief is that, while it goes on, no true relations can possibly be established between employers and employed, and both parties learn to regard each other with no feelings save those of distrust" (1868, 130). Departure from the model of service that subsumed the worker's work under a benevolent familial fiction had the psychological consequence of a marked and marketlike household suspicion.

A servant's "character" was meant to be a means of regulating admission to the home, but it became a source of considerably anxiety. Within the lexicon of domestic employment, a character was a reference, a spoken or written testimony of a servant's performance at a previous post and hence of his or her promise for a subsequent one.[13] Intended to help employers "feel safe from the strangers they were taking into their homes," a character was what Bruce Robbins terms "a 'labor passport,' a means of policing the borders of respectable society by restricting the movements of class aliens" (1993, 36). As the Tichborne case illustrates, character and credit were intricately linked in popular consciousness; just as the more general concept of character was meant to regulate credit and credibility in the field of economic exchange, a servant's character ostensibly served to regulate rights of access within the household. Like bankers, merchants, and other creditors who sought to protect their assets, middle-class women strove to evaluate the capacities and moral fiber of the persons who would work in their homes.

To be released from a post "without a character" was generally considered disastrous, for it meant the potential annihilation of one's professional identity. For example, when Lydia Bennett (a character more demure, plain, poor, and hungry than Austen's girl of the same name) appears in Miss Poole's *Without a Character: A Tale of Servant Life* (1870), she is distraught when she must apply for a job: "Both my master and mistress got into trouble, and one morning they went out in a hired carriage and never came back," she sobs. "I don't know what became of the money. I never saw a halfpenny of it, though there was a twelvemonth's wages owing to me. . . . I say nothing about the wages, but they needn't have robbed me of my bread!" (14–16). Lydia's comparison of wages and "a line even that I could show to get me into another situation" establishes that line as more valuable than even her long unpaid salary. A salary was nothing to be sneezed at, to be sure, but nothing much alongside a "labor passport."

Nonetheless, many employers feared that a servant's character might prove a *forged* "passport" which could grant a fraud passage into the home. And characters regularly *were* forged, fudged, and otherwise counterfeited. The author of *Domestic Servants* overtly states the anxiety that governed many households:

If they came to us as they are, the case would be widely different. If they came and said, "I have sinned, I am penitent, and wish to lead a new life, take me into your home and I will repay you with good service," what heart that is not made of stone would refuse to melt at such an appeal, and the repentant wanderers would be welcomed and aided in their efforts to reform; but we have no opportunity of this sort. The criminal comes to us indeed, but under false colours, runs riot in our houses, and encroaches upon our hospitality. Why should we open our doors so freely to such characters, and yet close them to a class of persons who have real claims on our benevolence? (Practical Mistress 1859, 10)

The author, a "Practical Mistress of a Household," makes explicit how false characters summoned up the specter of other swindlers who manufactured convincing stories in order to get what they wanted. When the criminal enters the home, riot and violation ensue. The general implication suggests not only that the servant is a bad guest (one who "encroaches upon our hospitality") rather than an employee; it also suggests that this bad guest is one who renders the portals of the home perilously ajar.

Although there were legal penalties for manufacturing false characters, such manufacture was nonetheless rampant.[14] According to *Domestic Servants*, "It should be generally known that the recommendations received with servants which they call their 'character' are in general utterly without value; for when they are not actually 'false,' they are so *delusive* as entirely to mislead, with regard to the conduct and capabilities—or rather propensities—of the person recommended" (8; emphasis in original). An 1848 edition of *The Servants' Magazine* corroborates the particularly dodgy nature of the text in its "Useful hints to servants": "Never offer a written character: no prudent master or mistress, whose service is worth engaging in, will take it" (79). Mrs. Beeton recommends that a lady disdain the veracity of a written character in engaging a servant and "have an interview, if at all possible, with the former mistress. By this means," she suggests, "you will be assisted in your decision of the suitableness of the servant for your place, from the appearance of the lady and the state of her house" (14).

This crisis about characters had been going on since the late eighteenth century, as the middle class became more established and the employment of servants increasingly de rigueur. At roughly the same time as readers were growing increasingly attached to realistic characters in novels, both servants and their masters were learning the tricks of realism, manufacturing convincing narratives of character that were often far from real.[15] There was a general sense that characters might be concocted by servants themselves or, more often, by an employer's sense of obligation or guilt. Thus, as character plots made their way into popular culture as both comedy and tragedy, they focused on the risks of trust and the potential consequences of these fictions.

The comic ballad "The He She Lady's Maid," for example, gleefully records the escapades of a maid who turns out to be a "He." The impersonator's intimacy with his married mistress adds playful fun to the tune—"He us'd to take her stockings off and help her into bed"—perhaps especially because Lady B. seems quite well aware that her maid is no maiden. The play becomes more serious when "This slashing dashing lady's maid as was suppos'd to be, / Was caught stealing from his mistress some jewels do you see." Alongside the ribald implications of stolen jewels, the greedy maid finds himself shipped off to Newgate for the theft of real gems. The ballad closes with a warning that all ladies "beware / Or else perhaps you may be drawn into a woeful snare, / So ladies search your servants well, or else I am afraid / Like lady B—you'll have a man to be your lady's maid."

Lady B. has not only hired a man for a maid; she has also ushered fraud into her house. It is tempting to relegate the crime to simple theft, but the maid in question works with more nuance, persuading his employer to make ill-founded investments in him, so that he may make away with the jewels (the trust inherent in the implicit sexual liaisons between the married Lady and her "maid" only makes her "investments" all the more graphic).[16] In a less erotic but relevant scenario, the footman who absconds with the silver in *The Greatest Plague of Life* has a "fine, honest, open countenance" and "did appear *so* clean, and was *so* respectful and meek, and *so* willing and good-tempered looking, and was *so* fond of children" that Mrs. Sk–n–st–n feels she cannot do without him. In his initial interview, Thompson claims that he has left his last place with a bishop because "his poor master . . . got embarrassed in railway speculations, and [has] been obliged to break up his palace in the country" (Mayhew and Mayhew 1847, 276). Mrs. Sk–n–st–n does not take the reference to problematic speculation; furthermore, although she follows Mrs. Beeton's advice in investigating Thompson's character—she insists on meeting the supposed bishop's supposed wife—she overlooks some crucial signs of impending trouble. Mrs. Sk–n–st–n finds the woman "a perfect lady," despite the fact that "Her dress . . . was a little too showy for a person in her station; and (between ourselves) when I looked at her steadfastly in the face, I declare if the beautiful high colour she had got on her cheeks wasn't as artificial as a Grand Banquet on the stage" (ibid.). Notwithstanding these reservations, Mrs. Sk–n–st–n invests her trust in Thompson and deems him, for some time, a perfect treasure.

In line with the new legal regulations governing embezzlement, his subsequent larceny is the culmination of a larger and much more intricate scheme than any simple breaking and entering. Reminiscent of those railway kings who ruined many a person (including Thompson's former, albeit mythical, employer), Thompson uses personal misrepresentation, false backers, good manners, and a carefully managed appearance to seduce the Sk–n–st–n into investing in him. In the aftermath, Mrs. S. learns the lesson of many a reckless speculator, as her husband chastises her for both her blindness and the loss of the family plate:

> Of course, Mr. Edward made out that it was my fault, and would have it that if I'd had a grain of sense in my head, I might have seen that the character was false, and indeed the bishop's lady a common imposter—as, indeed, her reverend ladyship turned out. For when I went after her the next day, to give it her well, I learnt that she, too, had decamped from her lodgings the very same night as her inestimable treasure of a Thompson, without paying the week's rent, and leaving nothing behind her but an empty rouge pot, and a hair trunk full of brick bats. (279)

These "common imposters," with their appurtenances of rouge pot and "fine, honest, open countenances," are common fare in popular representations, in which swindlers are not only company directors and promoters in the public sphere, but also domestic employees intent on defrauding the Victorian home. In all these arenas, the servants who serve as signs of their masters' wealth also maintain the dangerous capability to undercut the monetary and moral value of the homes that employ them.

Invisible Fraud: Eye-Service

In reality, masters were most often the parties who violated economic contracts, shortchanging wages or failing to pay their servants altogether. The Victorian courts had a surprisingly complicated understanding of domestic economics, proving sympathetic to servants who took in property that which they were overdue in pay. For example, in the 1847 trials of Janet Rose, a cook, and Mary McIntosh, her friend, for stealing bedding, towels, and a carpet, "the goods of Charles George Noel, Esq., . . . the master of Rose," the women were exonerated when the lady's maid testified that "Rose was an honest respectable women—there was money due to her" (Central Criminal Court 1847, 285). In the milieu of popular culture, however, where middle-class producers and consumers dominated the market, battles between masters and servants tended to wage less in the courtrooms than on the field of representation. Although there were visual and literary texts about servants checking the characters of their employers, the majority of popular materials focused on the servant's potential to reward an employer's investment of trust with some form of fraud.

One particularly slippery venue was labor, which servants could appropriate by giving their employers little more than "eye-service." When Cobbe writes her wistful entreaty for "a religion of faithful contracts," she imagines a world in which "To shirk work and do eye-service, to neglect a master's property committed to his charge, might be felt to be as base for the well paid servant as it would be for the master to give him bad money for good service" (1868, 133). In this passage, she links fraud (here, in the form of counterfeiting) with a biblical expression often cited in tracts for domestic workers. The term derives originally from the Bible—"Advice to Servants" in *The Servants' Magazine* instructs servants to work "'Not with eye-service,' (that is to say, while your master or mistress's eye is upon you,) 'as men-pleasers; but as the servants of Christ, doing the will of God from the heart' (Ephes. vi. 6)" (11 [1848]: 238). Like the discourse on "busyness," the instruction to avoid eye-service dispenses with the business components of domestic work, so that the servant serves not the domestic employer, but God. An earlier edition of the *Servants' Magazine* lectures,

> Eye-service may with much truth be called sad-service; for its sole object is a present reward and present gain. It is earthly in its nature, low in its object, and brief in its satisfactions; it implies the existence of selfishness, for self is its motive and end; of impatience—inasmuch as it seeks its reward in this life; and of hypocrisy—for, although it may be anxious to derive the earthly advantages derivable from a profession of religion, it yet leads to the secret cherishing and indulgence of sins, rendered the more hateful in the sight of God, because artfully concealed from the view of the world. ("Eye Service" [1846], 17; emphasis in original)

Eye-service is problematic for its attachment to temporal reward, and for its implicit correlation with deceit. Reinforcing the housewife's need to watch her servants constantly, the threat of eye-service emphasizes the risk of employing un-Christian souls on the lookout to serve themselves, rather than the family who provides their salary, room, and board. In *Kind Words to Domestic Servants*, the author of *Lily Gordon* depicts a young servant named Mary receiving a scolding from her mistress. The unnamed employer explicitly trusts Mary not to steal from her in the exact sense of the term, but she finds that Mary nonetheless debases both her property and their contract:

> I know that in sending you to buy goods for me, I might put a purse full of
> uncounted money into your hands, and feel quite sure that you would not
> keep back one farthing of it. But Mary, could I feel equally sure that you
> would go to the particular shop to which I had bid you go, if it suited you
> better to go to another one, and if you knew that I could never find out to
> which you had gone? . . . I could send you to my room, where a hundred
> little things are lying about, or to my desk, full of papers, money, &c., and
> be quite sure that you would not take so much as a pin from the one, or a
> penny stamp from the other; but could I feel at all sure that, if you knew
> you were unseen, you would not try on my bonnet, cap, or collar, in the
> one case, or read my letters in the other? . . . Dear Mary, let me ask you,
> with affectionate earnestness, is such conduct perfectly honest, truthful,
> upright? . . . Is it such conduct as will stand the search of God's all-seeing
> eye? (Bell 1857, 48–50)

The mistress's definition of property encompasses obedience and information, as well as material goods. She demands that Mary respect the integrity
of her purse, but she also demands that she respect her privacy and her
authority. Calling on God's omniscience to protect the sanctity of her diverse
belongings, she frames Mary's actions within the language of exchange. "Dear
Mary," she asks, "are any of these things worth what you have paid for them?"
(52). Using the "price" of conscience to balance the cost of cloth, secrets, and
bonnets, she attempts to bring "Dear Mary" back into the fold of legitimate
commerce.

The effort to initiate an all-seeing eye into the household confirms the
Foucauldian paradigm that I mentioned in the last chapter and will develop
further in the next; it also remarks its human failure. The impetus toward
policing and self-policing here originates in the language of piety, but it
ought to remind us that the kindly Christian housekeeper, devoted to protecting her servants' souls, also conveniently protected her property and her
establishment. More than anything else, perhaps, the discourse on eye-service
articulated the inadequacy of human supervision. The servant who served
with an eye to "present reward and present gain," and a dedication to "the
secret cherishing and indulgence of sins, . . . artfully concealed from the view
of the world," defrauded the labor contract, regardless of the cleanliness of the
plate or the stables or the threshold, regardless of the servant's exactness with
regard to purses filled with uncounted money and desks full of penny stamps
(*Servants Magazine* 9 [1846]: 17).

FIGURE 2.2
George Cruikshank, "Oh ah! Let 'em ring again!"

The copious Victorian satires of the lazy servant accrue meaning under this rubric. "Oh ah! let 'em ring again!" Cruikshank captions one particularly lively sketch from *The Greatest Plague of Life*, in which servants laugh merrily around a cozy fire as they watch the household bells tinkle (see figure 2.2).[17] The outrage on which such images drew suggests a decided irritation that time and energy are not material objects and hence are rather difficult to track. The frontispiece to *The Greatest Plague* juxtaposes such invisible forms of property with more tangible stuff (see figure 2.3). On the left side of the illustration, Cruikshank shows servants happily ignoring a dripping candle, an overboiling teapot, spilling sauces, a smoking fire, and coals ground into the rug. These

FIGURE 2.3
Geroge Cruikshank, "Nearly 'Worried to Death' by the 'Greatest Plagues of Life.'"

latter instances depict active negligence, which, while not technically embezzlement of an employer's property, nonetheless effects an economic toll on the family. The other tiny servants, however, caper about with material goods: a manservant runs away with the silver, a page eats jam, a butler drinks the family wine beneath the table, a dusky shadow of a male servant rifles through a cash box, a maid hands unmarked bags to an unspecified gentleman, two cooks rummage the family stores, and a maid cavorts happily in her mistress's bonnet. In Cruikshank's satiric vision, servants render the home something quite different from the sanctuary Ruskin apostrophizes: it is a veritable playing field of fiscal liability. In the center of it all stands the mistress, literally up in arms, "worried to death." As if to mark how profoundly her diabolical servants have afflicted the poor lady, Cruikshank gives us a "Before" picture in her portrait, smiling demurely above the fray.

Gifts That Are Not Gifts: The Problems with Perquisites

Cruikshank's illustration offers various examples of the palpable depredations of the household on which I focus for the remainder of this chapter. Two forms of property, clothing and food, provoke particular anxiety. They do so because of their immediate relationship to the body and their ensuing capacity to make personal and visceral the threat of illegitimate domestic consumption. John Plotz argues that "certain belongings come to seem dually endowed: they are at once products of a cash market and, potentially, the rare fruits of a highly sentimentalized realm of value both domestic and spiritual, a realm defined by being anything but marketable" (2008, 15).[18] The class implications of this formulation are evident in the emotional attachment that both facilitates and masks the synecdochal function of one's belongings. Food had a primal relationship to the family meant to consume it, in that the servant-keeping family's consumption of goods was often intended to establish a sense of taste that would distinguish them from their neighbors (and, of course, from their servants). Likewise, clothing served as a marker of identity for the body that sported it. The perquisite system muddled legislation of these forms of property and was a primary site of contention within domestic administration.

Alongside the kinds of swindling that involved passing off a bad character, or eschewing the fair exchange of labor for pay, there were many means by which servants could corrupt the home. Cobbe observes that servants

> share the influences of the terrible commercial improbity of the times. The complications of town life especially expose them to a whole new class of temptations, from the briberies and percentages offered by even wealthy tradesmen, and the perpetual solicitations of the tribe of clothes vendors, hareskin buyers, et hoc genus omne, to sell as "perquisites" food and raiment belonging to their masters. (1868, 131)

The effects of "the perquisite and percentage system," like those that resulted from the dealings of dishonest financiers, money managers, and clerks, were so close to theft as to require "microscopic" differentiation from it. Hovering between the categories of present and plunder, the system to which Cobbe refers was a focal point for economic transgression within the home.

Now more commonly known as "perks," perquisites initially encompassed the leftovers of the household which, as G. W. M. Reynolds observes in *Mary Price; or, the Memoirs of a Servant Maid*, might include almost anything: "From the left-off garments of his lordship down to the lees of wine in a bottle—from a cast-away silk dress of her ladyship down to the contents of a dripping-pot in the scullery—these perquisites were incessant bones of contention, ramifying the spirit of bickering throughout the entire domestic organization" (1852, 1: 64). While it seems unlikely that the family would *want* the lees of their wine or their cast-off clothing, the anxiety surrounding perquisites suggests the effort to preserve middle-class power by controlling the circulation of material goods in the home. The perquisite system thus presented an avenue by which servants could appropriate to themselves the profits of domestic economy, thereby, like swindlers, subverting the trust fundamental to both capitalism and the household.

Assets with neither clear boundaries of ownership, clear markers of access, nor formal documentation of exchange, perquisites also brought the avarice of embezzlement to bear on the ostensibly munificent rituals of gifting. Various early scholars heralded the gift economy as an alternative to capitalism, wherein exchange occurs without reference to market value. As many others have observed, however, no gift comes without some form of debt— as Bourdieu writes, "Until he has given in return, the receiver is *'obliged,'* expected to show his gratitude towards his benefactor" (1977, 6–7; emphasis in original).[19] Perquisites further call into question happier constructions of gift theory because, first, as Mark Osteen notes of the potlatch, "these 'gifts' are obligatory" (2002, 4); and second, perquisite gifting is clearly an alternate method of commodity exchange, rather than an escape from it.[20] According to *The Servant's Magazine* for 1844, the perquisite system "creates a covetous, *money-making* spirit on the part of servants, proves a strong temptation to dishonesty, and prevents the exercise of that beautiful principle which should lead them to serve in love, not looking for reward" ("Perquisites" 1844, 9; emphasis in original).

No doubt in response to that "*money-making* spirit," various authors represent perquisites as stolen goods with explicit economic ramifications for the household. For example, *The Servants' Magazine* writes of the property to which many servants felt entitled:

There are those who, because they never go beyond little thefts, imagine themselves honest enough;—who, while they would neither take clothes out of a drawer, nor money out of a desk, think it no crime to help themselves to tea, sugar, wine, or spirits, or to any nicety which may be set aside for the family. A servant so disposed would be found to make great havoc in the course of a year, were the amount of all the articles she thus seizes reckoned up; to say nothing of the inconvenience to families, in being compelled to keep such things under lock and key, than which nothing is more unpleasant to generous feelings. (11 [1848]: 157–58)

As they equate clothes (which could be sold) and money with less fungible forms of capital (tea, sugar, wine, or spirits), the authors turn to the account books, where "the amount of all the articles she thus seizes" are "reckoned up" and converted into cash value. It was far more difficult in fact than in theory to "reckon up" the materials claimed as perquisites, many of which blurred the line between private and communal property, and many servants considered perks to be the rightful spoils of their jobs. A little flurry of print emerged at mid-century about the new wave of servants who demanded perquisites as conditions of their employment. Some employers actually lowered salaries and supplemented perks in an effort to bring the system more in line with the family budget, and to redress the problem of servants helping themselves beyond their employers' intended beneficence.

The authors' remarks about the compulsion to keep things "under lock and key" resonate with traditions that were still very much in place in the 1860s, when Harriet Martineau also remarked on the problems of the well-bolted home. "In Ireland," she writes, "the thing is insufferable. . . . One is warned on arrival to keep one's drawers and wardrobe locked, as the hostess can never answer for her servants." In this household, unsecured property has so great a propensity to "walk off" that even the food is kept under lock and key. In the morning, "The hostess, or a daughter, unlocks the larder door before breakfast, gets out the loaf, butter, and eggs, brings the loaf herself to the breakfast table, where she cuts off the due number of rounds, and sends them down to be toasted. The keys are never out of sight or hearing" (1862, 421). Martineau argues that the best course of action is do away with degrading locks and vigilance, even arguing that these practices will prove economical, for "when the stores are left open, they [servants] use what they need, and no more" (1862, 422). Nonetheless, Martineau creates a sense of domestic panic.[21] One wonders how many guests would be willing to leave their wardrobes unlocked after such instructions, for there were cases of "real" robbery within the household, and personal property could turn up in the servants' quarters or beyond the walls of the home.

Unlike the vague regulations that governed perquisite violations, there were explicit legal remedies for outright theft in the aforementioned legislation regarding embezzlement. When Kate's Young Man marches out the door with the plate, he finds himself on a ship to Australia; when the He She Lady's Maid helps himself to his mistress's jewels, he winds up in Newgate; and the real court of London sent both the avaricious Dearlove servant Jane Robinson and her mother to jail. Significantly, Jane and Eliza Robinson sought to deflect the charges against them by citing the unspoken system of perquisites, claiming the items were presents. "Jane told her that she [Mrs. Dearlove] had them given to her," the police-inspector reported Mrs. Robinson averring. However, the Robinsons went to prison, largely because such prodigious bequests were uncommon alongside the supposed donor's emphatic refutation. It was *not* okay to take off with the silver, the family jewels, or "a black silk mantle, a photographic portrait, 2 China crape shawls, a wool bag, a silk pocket hand-kerchief, a piece of glazed lining," and so on. Jane received one year for her accumulation, her mother four months for receiving stolen goods.

Nonetheless, perquisites were part of a gift economy within domestic management that was considerably more complicated than the easy conviction of Jane Robinson implies. Pettier instances of "larceny" generally passed with no more official correction than releasing the servant. Even when they gave away their goods happily and openly, middle-class employers had to confront the affective and subjective consequences of putting their property into circulation. In part, because social class was so strongly tied to material possessions, and in part because the middle classes were increasingly confronted with the master–servant relationship as a contract that might be exploited, fears of servants' impulses toward class subversion emerge with particular strength around the palpable stuff of property. Clothing and other personal items illustrate how the affectionate relationships Plotz cites, above, worked to invest property with sentiment: one would not want James traipsing about the house in the morning jacket his master sports in the portrait above the mantel, nor ought Sara to have her mistress's Christmas gown. Residues more concrete than memory might accumulate in the dried saliva about the mouthpiece of a pipe. In the absence of dry cleaning, a ball gown was likely to be steeped in the perspiration of the lady who had danced in it, while other varieties of bodily imprint might appear in the relaxed weave at the knees of trousers, in strained seams about the hips of a skirt, or in the pucker and sag of a bodice.

Most domestic manuals questioned the wisdom of gifting cast-off dresses to the servants and encouraged the lady of the house to serve her servants as model of ethical propriety, rather than fashion—in *Daughters of England*, for example, Mrs. Ellis asks her middle-class readers, "Shall we continue to compete with our servants in dress, . . . or shall we . . . compete with them in self-denial?" (1842, 130)—yet beyond seeking to instill moral fiber, these

FIGURE 2.4
Henry Heath, from *One With An Excellent Character.*

tracts ward off the threat inherent in the physical intimacy of clothing. Even in giving away one's "torn-up damask," one seemed to give away something of oneself along with thread and fabric.

Narratives about servants almost inevitably contain an edge of hostility about the dynamics of class aspirations. For example, when Henry Heath draws his servant "With an Excellent Character" preening before a mirror with the caption "There can't be any great harm in trying on other people's things," one sees instantly that the reverse is true (see figure 2.4). In this case, the raiment has *not* been gifted, so that the servant accesses her employer's clothes without recourse to the regulations that ought to govern her behavior in the household economy. Furthermore, her haughty countenance (she literally looks down her nose) offers an acerbic parody of her mistress's posture, and hence of her class identity. Repeating her employer's bodily attitude with the difference of class, the sneering servant visibly undercuts any essential basis for social privilege.

A different form of aggression occurs in a seemingly minor passage in *Vanity Fair*, when Jos Sedley's servant Isidor mentally appropriates to himself "the very articles with which he was decorating his master's person," collecting up Jos's "silver-essence bottles and toilette knickknacks, . . . the English cutlery and the large ruby pin, . . . the fine frilled shirts, . . . the gold laced cap and the frogged frock coat, . . . and the captain's gold-headed cane, and the great double ring with the rubies," and, of course, Jos's sleeve-buttons. "I long for sleeve-buttons," Isidor muses, "and the captain's boots with brass spurs, in the next room," and the musing continues (*Fair*, 303). Andrew Miller cites this passage to establish how "the desire of servants for their master's 'movables'" contributes to the "propulsive narrative energy" of *Vanity Fair* (1997, 16), a novel in which finance outshines romance and circulation best defines both economic and social operations. However, this form of circulation provokes more anxiety than many others in Victorian culture. When Jos prepares to flee to Brussels, Isidor does come to own much of Jos's portable property ("*Ne porty ploo—habit militair—bonny—donny a voo, prenny dehors*," Jos gasps to Isidor [*Fair*, 318]), but given Isidor's earlier ruminations and the seeming insatiability of his longings, we glimpse through Thackeray's deft humor a decided anxiety about the sanctioned system of perquisites by which servants take possession of their employers' property. As Miller observes, "The implicit violence of the servant's vision is firmly suggested by the presence of Isidor's razor along his master's neck" (1997, 17).

A later moment in the same novel offers further insight. Miss Horrocks, Sir Pitt's new housekeeper at Queen's Crawley, otherwise known as "the Ribbons," begins to fancy herself the next Lady Crawley. Sir Pitt encourages this illusion and "swore it was as good as a play to see her in the character of a fine dame, and he made her put on one of the first Lady Crawley's courtdresses, swearing (entirely to Miss Horrocks' own concurrence,) that the dress became her prodigiously, and threatening to drive her off that very instant to Court in a coach-and-four" (*Fair*, 400). Despite its humor, the specter of Miss Horrocks in her former mistress's dress takes on as much potential violence as Isidor with his razor on Jos's neck when we discover the extent of her sartorial capers: "She had ransacked the wardrobes of the two defunct ladies, and cut and hacked their posthumous finery so as to suit her own tastes and figure" (ibid.). Miss Horrocks's fashion of cutting and hacking certainly suggests neither self-denial nor a desire to emulate the previous Lady Crawleys; rather "the Ribbons" aims to replace them. And therein lies the rub.

As in Heath's engraving of the snooty servant, Thackeray illustrates how

—◈—

the potential for the servant to access her mistress's position by accessing her personal property cuts and hacks at the very structure of domestic management. As F. M. L. Thompson has noted, "Working-class girls . . . could and did marry upwards in the social scale in significant numbers, chiefly into the lower middle class, many of them no doubt making the transition via a spell in domestic service" (1988, 95). Although Thompson refers to a class decidedly below Sir Pitt's, it seems clear nonetheless that concerns about the family's property circulating amongst the servants speak to anxieties about the circulation of power and privilege within the household. The Ribbons's actions toward her dead mistresses' dresses are indicative of class violence, even though Sir Pitt has explicitly gifted the clothing to her.

In other homes, in which there were no dearly departed spouses, the wardrobes of live employers provoked other, more underhanded, forms of appropriation. *Mary Price* observes that

> A clever lady's-maid, with plenty of tact and cunning, will avail herself of all the extravagances and weaknesses of her mistress in order to suit her own selfish ends. She will affirm, for instance, "that her ladyship does not look at all well in the pale satin dress, but that the dark one becomes her admirably:" so the lady is set against the pale satin, which accordingly becomes the perquisite of the artful maid. Or if the coveted satin dress should not become a "cast-off" so soon as the maid thinks it ought, she will manage to soil it with a fruit stain or grease; and then with exclamations about its being "a thousand pities," will display the mark to her lady, who of course abandons the dress at once. Furs are purposely soiled, muslin dresses inked, silks and satins stained, bonnets bent, linen torn, and all kind of tricks thus put into practice, in order to swell the lady's-maid's perquisites with the discarded articles from her mistress's wardrobe. (Reynolds 1852, 1: 64)

Sacrificing the integrity of the property they coveted, Reynolds's maids soil, grease, bend, and tear their way to sartorial finery. More subtly aggressive than the Ribbons's cutting and hacking, these petty acts of violence bespeak not only hostility to the ladyships whose wardrobes the maids attack; they also cut both ways. So close to the bodies that sport them, gowns, furs, and bonnets signal the character of their wearers. These particular possessions, therefore, are no longer suitable to reflect on the Lady, but when the clothing trades hands, the artful maid who despoils the property she would own actually wears the stains of her triumph.[22] At the same time, then, as these marks take on nearly biblical significance, they also signal the polluted employment practices that haunt the home.

Cooking the Books and Other Kitchen Problems

Cooks, stewards, and housekeepers, more than any other group of servants, bore the brunt of the blame for domestic larceny. Because they transacted the family's business with tradespeople at the threshold of the home, Mary Price instructs her readers that "the steward and the housekeeper . . . enjoyed immense opportunities for peculation" in that "they had the appointing of all the tradesmen belonging to their respective departments, and compelled every dealer to make out his bills in such a manner as to afford a liberal discount for the behoof of the said steward and housekeeper when pay-day came" (Reynolds 1852, 64). The author of *Domestic Servants* calls the cook an "(evil) genius, who reigns lady-paramount, and has unlimited sway in the regions below!" (Practical Mistress 1859, 1: 12). In fact, the majority of Victorian ephemera depicts cooks as barefaced criminals who specialize in grifting cash and goods through the practices of bill padding, cooking the books, and selling the household surplus to illicit dealers.

Whereas taking cash from one's employer qualified for legal action—servants could be prosecuted for retaining even the small change of purchases made for their masters (as in the case of Cornelius Parr, who was indicted in 1847 for spending the change of a purchase for his master on skittles)—there were plenty of other opportunities for graft (Central Criminal Court 1847, 285).[23] The Practical Mistress lets her readers in on

a system which is but little known to heads of families, though carried on to a very great extent between servants and tradespeople, I mean a practice of falsifying the books. . . . These practices are not peculiar to any one trade. Grocers, bakers, butchers, &c., &c., all have the means if they are so inclined, and if the opportunities are allowed them by families, of performing these tricks. (1859, 15; emphasis in original)

Such transactions were so common that it was impractical for an employer to intervene in them without a significant expenditure of time and energy. Some authors recommend that the mistress demand and minutely check the books against the home inventory on a weekly basis, while others propose keeping a scale in the kitchen so as to ensure that the joint of meat one has ordered really weighs ten pounds, rather than eight. The larger one's household and concomitant diversity of commerce, the more cumbersome it became to ensure that one was not roundly cheated. Most upper-class and upper-middle-class homes simply gave up. Mary Price remarks of the wealthy Harlesdowns, "That [they] were perfectly well aware they were thus systematically and continuously robbed, there cannot be the slightest doubt: but they were equally conscious that it was part of an invariable system, and that if they were to discharge their present steward and housekeeper, their successors would pursue exactly the same course" (Reynolds 1852, 1: 64).[24] Although more average households had less commerce to oversee, it was nonetheless inconvenient and difficult to prevent the depredations of a savvy cook or steward.

In addition to inveigling spurious bonuses from tradespeople and running explicit numbers games with the books, cooks and other domestic servants also engaged in trade either at the door of the home or at shady establishments, known as marine shops. There, they sold commodities they had pinched from their employers, including clothing, silver, or most anything that would bring a price. In instances where the property was readily identifiable, as in the case of Jane Robinson, servants were liable for prosecution and often were convicted. However, when they sold butter, drippings, extra meat, sugar, and other goods lifted from the family's stores, it was nearly impossible to bring charges, and they might defend themselves as the Robinsons attempted to do, by claiming that the goods came to them rightfully, either as gifts or as job benefits.

In various ways, food was even more intimate a commodity than clothing. Whereas cloth might retain various intimate traces of its original owners, pilfered food has a hauntingly primal relationship to its initial or intended consumers. At times these traces might be literally manifest in bite marks on the remains of partially eaten meals; at others, more amorphous forms of attachment govern the relationship to food. In its most literal form, good taste takes the shape of those delicacies middle-class families put on their tables and into their mouths. This fare is meant for discriminating palates, and I intend the double entendre on discrimination—as Joseph Litvak writes, "The exercise of sophisticated taste rather horrifyingly involves the consumption . . . not just of those lesser animals that ordinarily pass for, or end up as, food, but . . . of other consumers. To be sophisticated, that is, is to be *more sophisticated than,* and to outsophisticate the other is to incorporate the other; to incorporate, at any rate, the other's way of incorporating" (1992, 9; emphasis added). Because cuisine helped to establish a family's place in the food chain, it helps to explain the terror that servants would consume it or otherwise put it into circulation, thereby subverting its social function.

The roast that "walks off" into the marketplace, the butter that enters the cook's home, the beer that descends into the groom's stomach, all suggest an anxious bodily proximity, a shared circulation among employers and servants that might make an employer queasy. Early engravings such as "The Cooks Rout, or High Life Below Stairs" are part of an enduring category of ephemera

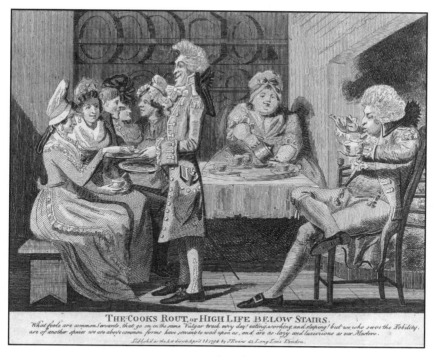

FIGURE 2.5
"The Cook's Rout; or, High Life below Stairs."

in which servants merrily consume their employers' fare (see figure 2.5). "What fools are common servants, that go on in the same vulgar track every day!" the caption begins, championing the better and more varied "tracks" of "we who serve the Nobility" and are "as lazy and luxurious as our Masters." The spread is luxurious indeed: one jolly footman serves cakes to a maid, while another eats jam from a pot, and the cook pours out what appears to be a hot punch. But "The Cooks Rout" depicts something more than downstairs luxury; here, culinary embezzlement compromises not only the household economy, but also the dignity of the Masters: as the term "rout" implies, the servants destabilize their employers' power by consuming their cakes and jam.

In other schemas, outside parties entered the circle through illicit culinary transactions. A plate from "One With an Excellent Character" illustrates our now-familiar servant handing food to a man in a top hat, whose apparent respectability is rendered suspicious both by his posture (he is stooping) and by the fact that he is reaching through the back gate for what appears to be a turkey leg (see figure 2.6). Even if she had legitimately obtained said poultry,

FIGURE 2.6
Henry Heath, from *One With an Excellent Character*

the servant's disbursal of her employers' goods brings undesirable characters to (or across) the threshold of the home. Furthermore, the caption for Heath's illustration ("And isn't it better to give things away than let em be wasted") references the simple fact that food was expensive and waste could pose fiscal problems.

Household Work; or, The Duties of Female Servants reminds its readers, "Food is property—property that, in a family, is of a very costly nature" (n.d., 4). The manual attempts to restore ownership rights over the crumbs and crusts of their provisions to the family that pays the bills, which makes good sense given the creative means other authors find to resurrect those crumbs and crusts. *The Cookmaid's Complete Guide and Adviser* counsels,

> A conscientious and well-disposed servant would never feel justified in wasting the smallest bit of any thing that might be turned to account; and if a cookmaid knows her business well, she can make good use of every morsel of meat, bread, vegetable, and in short, of every thing that may happen to be left.
>
> A good cookmaid will make many a nice little dish of mince or hash out of pieces that an extravagant one would give to the cat, or throw aside until they were spoiled. ([1846], 6)

Held to account even for household scraps, the cook could be a literal treasure, like Miss Pross in Dickens's *A Tale of Two Cities*, whose "dinners, of a very modest quality, were so well cooked and so well served, and so neat in their contrivances, half English and half French, that nothing could be better" (103). In *Miss Marjoribanks*, Margaret Oliphant offers a similar model in Nancy, "Dr. Marjoribanks's famous cook, who had spent a fortune on her gravy-beef alone, and was one of the most expensive people in Carlingford," who nonetheless resolves to stick by Lucilla when she has fallen on hard times. Nancy the gourmet insists on staying with her mistress, if only to roast a simple chop. "Me as would," she exclaims tearfully, "—if it was but a roast potato!" (424). Such women are prized for their sensitivity to the household budget, and their devotion to saving their employers unnecessary expense: *The Cookmaid's Complete Guide* advises that "a habit of economy is indispensable in a cookmaid, and should never be lost sight of, even in the most trifling things, for a number of trifles saved every day will amount to a considerable sum in the course of a year" ([1846], 6). Furthermore, their ability to transform even the most basic and modest fare—a simple chop, perhaps—into a gourmet dish denotes a most desirable combination of ingenuity, honesty, and economy. When Dickens writes that Miss Pross can take "a fowl, a rabbit, a vegetable or two from the garden, and change them into anything she pleased," he describes the very best kind of household sorcery in which the cook makes luscious food appear seemingly from nowhere (*Tale*, 103).

However, the history of culinary suspicion suggests how practitioners of darker arts than Miss Pross's might make a rabbit—or a simple chop, or a turkey leg—disappear. Even households that could well afford a rout or two often wanted the spoils, leftovers, and skimmed excess of their meals, for people hungrier than those below stairs. Neighborhood charity interrupted a cook's claim to perquisites: giving to the poor was a marker of social respectability, and therefore an invisible component of the household budget. Thus, even if a family did not intend to consume its culinary surplus, the household remnants were often earmarked for more impoverished diners, as is the case in *Susan Dering; or, A Cook's Perquisites* by "M. M.," in which Mr. and Mrs. Norton's new cook arranges to sell the leftover drippings for pin money. Shortly after Susan has begun her new enterprise, Mrs. Norton tells her she'd like the dripping for "a very poor family I have just heard of, who are in great distress" (1869, 19). Caught in a bind, Susan confers with an old family friend, who advises her that, although claiming perquisites without consultation "may have become a rule among many, . . . it is a bad rule, and not one that we ought to follow" (32). Susan can hardly argue to take food out of the mouths of the poor, and the drippings that may have seemed hers to sell revert to Mrs. Norton, along with the capacity to control the economic functioning of her kitchen.

The following chapter traces a different and more dangerous component of food fraud, namely, the problem of adulteration. The potentially fatal outcome of consuming adulterated food was, no doubt, more serious than the problems I discuss here, but I want to maintain nonetheless the psychological weight of fraud in transgressions against the nuanced, but often unspoken, exchange systems that structured master–servant relations. These affirm the vulnerability of the household to the very corruption, insurgence, and fraud that troubled the Victorian marketplace.

In "The Duty of Servants," Reverend Garnier reminds his readers "that to take *any* thing which is not their own, however insignificant in value, is an act of dishonesty, for which they will have, most surely, to give account. There are no *trivial* acts of fraud in the sight of God" (1851, 73; emphasis in original). Garnier expands the parameters of domestic property to include spoons, bonnets, crumbs, and the more amorphous stuff of labor. Because all of these belong to their employers, because those employers had paid for them, servants that attempt to take "*any* thing which is not their own" commit an act of deceit that threatens the honest functioning of the household, much as a clerk's embezzlement imperils the security of a company's stockholders. Garnier's turn to a holy ledger ("they will have, most surely, to give account") emphasizes the financial underpinnings of his argument. Representations of servants' depredations within the home; their violations of contract and property rights; and their mobility between places, spheres, and classes, made clear that the street door was not only a literal portal through which a servant might pass out with the plate, but also a metaphor through which duplicitous market practices really did enter, to become manifest in domestic space and in domestic representation.

3

Dangerous Provisions

Victorian Food Fraud

> Every article capable of adulteration is made a cheat. Your wine is
> nearly all spurious; your brandy is coloured whisky; your tea is mixed
> with sloe leaves, and coloured blue by poisonous dyes; your ground
> coffee is mixed with peas and chicory; your tobacco is made of mul-
> len, oak, and cabbage leaf; your beer is drugged with coculus indicus;
> your bread is made with alum, soap, lard, potash, and plaster of Paris;
> your salt is stone; your sugar is sand; your ground spices are anything
> that comes handy.
> —G. P. R. James, *The Smuggler* (1845)

A S THE PREVIOUS CHAPTER suggests, food proved a complicated haz-
ard for the servant-keeping household. Here I turn to food adulteration,
a gastronomic problem that potentially affected *all* Victorian households.
Chemists and merchants invented the processes of adulteration as a way to
increase sales and profits. What began as an indisputably human enterprise
to boost earnings resulted in mute merchandise that brought adulteration
silently into the Victorian home and, more noisily, into Victorian popular
culture. A startlingly prevalent problem, food fraud proved a popular topic
at mid-century when Parliament appointed the committee that attempted
to draft the first food safety laws in England. The Parliamentary hearings
produced a furor that initiated a national campaign to educate consumers and to warn merchants away from tampering with comestible products.
Those efforts cultivated a stringently paranoid approach to reading, perhaps
best epitomized by the scientific instrument the Parliamentary Committee
extolled, namely, the microscope.

That approach conflicts fairly radically with the pleasure-based consumption of narrative I discuss in chapter 1. To some degree, the difference in

attitude had to do with the fact that the capital at risk in food fraud was the consumer's own body. While various sardonic texts engage playfully with the perils of adulteration as a symbol of the country's pervasive market corruption, generally the pleasures associated with reading, and reading about adulteration, derived from the practices of detection. Christina Rossetti's "Goblin Market" offers a model for the complicated reading strategies "serious" domestic fraud promoted. At the close of this chapter, I turn to Mrs. J. H. Riddell's 1866 novel *The Race for Wealth* to discuss how food adulteration worked to signal the danger of fraud in more popular plots.

Commercial Poetry

Like many Victorian texts, "Goblin Market" offers salient critical commentary about the deceptions and seductions of the capitalist marketplace. However, its scholarly history is largely silent about the materiality of both the poem's luscious fruit and its clamorous market. Most early reviewers read Rossetti's fantastic parable *as* parable, interpreting the goblin merchants' remarkable wares as a bushel of Edenic apples, and the poem itself as a tale of sin and redemption. More recent critics again read the poem as metaphor, but as a more complicated fable of falling, in which Laura's appetite tells a story of sexual difference not only between genders but also between women, the fallen and the pure.[1] As Terrence Holt notes, "The emphasis in all of these readings has been on the goblins and the issues of gender and sexuality they seem to represent, while the 'market' of the title has received little attention" (1990, 51). Only recently have critics read "Goblin Market" as a tale *of* the market and, to the best of my knowledge, only three, Paula Marantz Cohen, Deborah Thompson, and Richard Menke, have heeded the goblins' cries and bought the goblins' fruit as actual food.[2] If, as most critics have argued, the poem is a parable, I want in this chapter to emphasize it as one that attends carefully to literal economic and cultural concerns. Reading the goblins' fruit as food allows us to cash in on the promise of the poem's original title, to have "A Peep at the Goblins" and the Victorian spaces they haunt.[3]

The luxurious inventory of the poem's opening passage overtly invites materialist readings. I quote it in full to underscore its profound fusion of domestic and corporate concerns, its melding of dangers among goblin and fiscal markets:

Morning and evening
Maids heard the goblins cry:

"Come buy our orchard fruits,
Come buy, come buy:
Apples and quinces,
Lemons and oranges,
Plump unpecked cherries—
Melons and raspberries,
Bloom-down-cheeked peaches,
Swart-headed mulberries,
Wild free-born cranberries,
Crab-apples, dewberries,
Pine-apples, blackberries,
Apricots, strawberries—
All ripe together
In summer weather—
Morns that pass by,
Fair eves that fly;
Come buy, come buy;
Our grapes fresh from the vine,
Pomegranates full and fine,
Dates and sharp bullaces,
Rare pears and greengages,
Damsons and bilberries,
Taste them and try:
Currants and gooseberries,
Bright-fire-like barberries,
Figs to fill your mouth,
Citrons from the South,
Sweet to tongue and sound to eye,
Come buy, come buy." (1–31)

As the goblins' chants of "Come buy" call attention to their wares, "Goblin Market" highlights the impact *of* the market on the lives of those denizens who lived in its thick and on its margins. Marrying fetishized foodstuff with the more amorphous machinations of economic development, Rossetti's first lines clearly link her fairy tale with the concerns of the modern world. Foregrounding the Victorian market's propensity for offering sensuous, indeed charmed, commodities, the vocabulary that frames the poem's pastoral story is, as Elizabeth Helsinger notes, "remarkably mercantile" (1991, 903).[4] Terrence Holt observes how "Economic language and metaphors, terms of finance and commerce ('buy,' 'offer,' 'merchant,' 'stock,' 'money,' 'golden,' 'precious,' 'sell,' 'fee,' 'hawking,' 'coin,' 'rich,' etc.) permeate the poem" (1990, 51).[5] Further, the lush adjectives the goblins assign to their catalog of fruit ("plump unpecked," "bloom-down-cheeked," "fresh from the vine," and simply "rare"), alongside its simple abundance and the hypnotic rhythm of their song, give this harvest an irresistible, mouth-watering appeal.

"Goblin Market" tells the story of two sisters, Lizzie, who abstains from eating the goblins' fruit, and Laura, who succumbs to the goblins' lavish, seductive voices and comes to buy and to eat. Although Rossetti encapsulates the prevailing wisdom of the period in Lizzie, the abstemious sister who advises suspicion, prudence, and a tight-lipped approach to the world of trade, she is clearly sympathetic to Laura's susceptibility as well, writing that she "heard a voice like voice of doves / Cooing all together: / They sounded kind and full of loves" (77–79).

Alas for Laura, the fruits of this market, though "Sweet to tongue and sound to eye," have markedly undesirable effects (30). Lured by the merchants' promises of rich delights, "sweet-tooth Laura" trades a golden curl for her fill of fruit only to fall desperately ill: "Her hair grew thin and grey: / She dwindled, as the fair full moon doth turn / To swift decay and burn / Her fire away" (277–80). Like the poem's cautionary figure of Jeanie, who had also eaten and then "dwindled and grew grey; / Then fell with the first snow" (156–57), Laura succumbs to a mysterious illness, one capable of bringing a healthy young woman to the grave: Jeanie "Fell sick and died / In her gay prime" (315–16), and Laura seems fated to follow her.

Although we might productively read this strange illness as metaphor for sin, sexual fall, or capitalism, I want to suggest the profits of a more literal reading. Specifically, the widespread problem of food adulteration provides an apt framework for this tale of a young woman sickened by the food she consumes. An 1855 pamphlet, *How to Detect Adulteration in Our Daily Food and Drink*, explicitly states that "traders have been proved to be the coadjutors of death, and it is not to be doubted that the physical strength, the stature, perhaps the moral dignity of our people, have all deteriorated under the steady action of impure food, impure water, and poisonous preparations" (3). Food adulteration was a serious problem in 1859 when Rossetti composed the poem, and still very much a concern in 1862 when it first appeared in print, accompanied by her brother Dante Gabriel's cornucopian illustrations. Throughout the 1850s, the numbers of people who ate seemingly nutritious food only to wither and die in consequence provoked both governmental and popular alarm.[6] Food poisoning was no longer a rare occurrence, and the story of a young girl eating beautiful food only to sicken unto death was not so unusual as one might imagine.

Thus, as the breadth and complexity of its scholarship suggests, "Goblin Market" is no simple pastoral story. In reading this tale of sumptuous fruit, dubious merchants, and near-fatal illness, I understand both "Goblin Market" and the literature of adulteration with which I contextualize it to be concrete and specific examples of a more widespread condition that equally infected food, economics, and social exchange. Through the story of Laura's illness and recovery, Rossetti makes overt and narrative the poem's subtext about the home and the market's operations within it—a point she emphasizes by making these merchants brothers who sell their wares to cohabiting sisters. Although the sisters live in bucolic space that seems well removed from the market and its interests, the merchant brothers' capacity to invade and infect that home life emphasizes the proximity of economic and domestic concerns.[7] Adulteration was a serious issue, touching actual material goods, but further, as the Victorian biologist Arthur Hill Hassall noted, it "is . . . a great national question, closely affecting the pocket of the consumer, the revenue, and the health and morals of the people" (*Adulterations Detected* 1857, 17). More than just an epidemiological problem, food adulteration entered the field of literature, thereby helping to shape private responses to public fraud.

In *Mary Price*, for example, one of Mary's many masters is a shopkeeper, whom she discovers chuckling to himself as he adulterates his goods. "There!" he says. "I have put the sloe-leaves into all that tea—the sand into this sugar—the turmeric into that mustard—the potato-flour into the arrow-root—the prepared starch into that cocoa—the chicory into the bean coffee—and the stuff out of the deal box into the ground coffee" (Reynolds 1852, 1: 43). Mr. Messiter compounds the horror of Mary's discovery by mixing it with religious deception. Mr. Messiter had

> declared that he was going down to the shop to *commune with himself in a pious manner,* [but] had in reality taken advantage of that leisure time on the Sunday morning to do, as he expressed it, "a pretty good hour's business." And what was that business? how had his Sunday morning been employed? In a pursuit which I should call the most wicked dishonesty, mixing improper things with his goods—in fact practising the most scandalous adulterations! (ibid., 1: 44; emphasis in original)

The adulteration of food accompanies an adulteration of both spirit and business, serving to mark Mr. Messiter's descent not only into the shop, but into a state of "wicked dishonesty." Food fraud serves a similar function in Tennyson's "Maud" (1855), in which it appears within the speaker's opening litany as a marker of widespread social corruption. "But these are the days of advance, the works of the men of mind," / Tennyson's speaker laments, "When who but a fool would have faith in a tradesman's ware or his word?" (25–26); three stanzas later, he observes that "chalk and alum and plaster are sold to the poor for bread" (39).[8] Alongside pamphlets, articles, and full-length books on the subject, literary publications of the 1850s testify to an established concern about short weights and measures and a new consciousness about the dangers of adulteration.[9]

Adulterations Detected

Food adulteration was already a popular concern in the eighteenth century and, by the early 1800s, various texts were available about spurious additions to the British daily meal. For example, in 1820, Frederick Accum published *A Treatise on Adulterations of Food . . . and Methods of Detecting Them*. Accum's premise was that, although it was only one small manifestation of a larger quandary within the British market economy, food adulteration was the worst of all schools of fraud:

> Of all possible nefarious traffic and deception, practised by mercenary dealers, that of adulterating the articles intended for human food with ingredients deleterious to health, is the most criminal, and, in the mind of every honest man, must excite feelings of regret and disgust. Numerous facts are on record, of human food, contaminated with poisonous ingredients, having been vended to the public; and the annals of medicine record tragical events ensuing from the use of such food. (iv)

Accum stresses food adulteration as a particularly virulent form of contamination because it crosses so many boundaries. This "nefarious traffic" drives into the consumer's body, destroying corporeal integrity as well as commercial trust. It is fitting, then, that his outrage focuses on fraud's incursion into the home, on "mercenary dealers" who taint health and hearth simultaneously by poisoning the private spaces of the body and the supper table.[10] Although Accum writes ostensibly in protection of "the public," he does so from a markedly private perspective.

Accum's treatise was still current in the mid-nineteenth century, when food adulteration became sufficiently prevalent to provoke action by an "Analytical Sanitary Commission."[11] The commission's discoveries, which appeared in the *Lancet* between 1851 and 1854, were so unsettling that Parliament formed a Select Committee in 1855 to inquire into the situation. The reports were horrifying. Arthur Hill Hassall, the committee's star witness and the author of the *Lancet* articles, details the extent of the problem in his 1857 text, *Adulterations Detected*:

> With the potted meats and fish, anchovies, red sauces or cayenne, taken at breakfast, [the average person] would consume more or less bole Armenian, Venetian red, red lead, or even bisulphuret of mercury. At dinner, with his curry or cayenne, he would run the chance of a second dose of lead or mercury; with the pickles, bottled fruits and vegetables, he would be nearly sure to have copper administered to him; while if he partook of bon bons at dessert, there is no telling what number of poisonous pigments he might consume. Again, in his tea, of mixed or green, he would certainly not escape without the administration of a little Prussian blue, and it might be worse things: if he were a snuff-taker, he would be pretty sure to be putting up his nostrils from time to time, small quantities of either some ferruginous earth, bichromate of potash, chromate of lead, or red lead: finally, if he indulged himself with a glass or so of grog before going to bed, he would incur the risk of having the coats of his stomach burned and irritated with tincture of capsicum or essence of cayenne. . . . This is no fanciful or exaggerated picture, but one based upon the results derived from the repeated analysis of different articles as furnished to the consumer. (22)[12]

To be fair, *fresh* fruit rarely produced such dangerous consequences as those Laura suffers, but potted fruits were perilous. As the author of *How to Detect Adulteration* notes, grocers had an "abominable practice of adulterating all *green* fruits with copper. Gooseberries, greengages, olives, limes and rhubarb are almost invariably coppered to give them a false colour. The purchaser of these fruits is advised to abstain from any that have a bright green look, for it is impossible to preserve greenness in preparations of this kind without the use of copper; but a bad colour is preferable to poison" (1855, 22–23). Further, a particular danger to "sweet-tooth" girls like Laura was colored sugar confectionery, which proved to be the most toxic food source of all. According to Hassall, candy was so powerfully and so frequently adulterated that it might be considered straight poison.

> The principal colours employed are yellows, reds, including pink and scarlet, browns, purples, blues, and greens. Of the yellows it appeared that 59 were coloured with chromate of lead; 11 with gamboge; while the colour of the majority was confined to the surface, in many cases it was diffused equally throughout the whole mass of the sugar used. . . . In four samples, the colours

used were painted on with white lead, or carbonate of lead. . . . Scarcely a year passes without very serious accidents happening from the employment of poisonous pigments in confectionery; there are instances of persons who have been killed by them, and many more of persons who have been taken seriously ill. The chief consumption of such confectionery is among children, upon whom the effect of adulteration is likely to be much greater than upon a grown person. I remember the instance of a public dinner in Essex, in which a person died in consequence of eating some of the confectionery thus adulterated; and several other cases are recorded in the Lancet. (*Adulteration of Food, Drink, and Drugs* [1855], 25–26)

Although Rossetti's Laura suffers from delirium, nausea, and hearing and visual problems, I don't know that it's necessary to link her malaise directly to lead poisoning: the dangers associated with sweets led to a plethora of perils.[13] *How to Detect Adulteration* notes, "A sweetmeat shop is a juvenile paradise, where all the elements of human happiness are sold in cake, rock, comfit, and bolus; happiness, alas! but temporary, and to be paid for dearly, in spoilt appetites, ruined stomachs, pale looks, intestinal worms, and a long catalogue of ills, to which the termination is sometimes a coroner's inquest" (1855, 19–20). Even the Sadleir inquest commented on the dangers of sweets. When the chemist defended himself against his sale to Sadleir, he noted that "essential oil of bitter almonds was sold by every confectioner in the kingdom." The coroner replied sardonically, "A pleasant reflection for those who eat confectionery. (A laugh.) Some custards that I have seen I know have contained the essential oil of bitter almonds in poisonous quantities" (Evans 1859, 247–48).

Paranoid Reading

As the consumer seeking to purchase happiness, Rossetti's hungry girl renders allegory actual: because food is a commodity one literally consumes, food adulteration makes material the grossest fears about capitalist corruption and thus justifies the most paranoid attitudes toward market culture in general. Many popular Victorian texts on food adulteration overtly linked comestible consumption with commodity consumption as a way of representing fraud as a pandemic problem. Adulterated food thus worked as a signifier that *all* commodities and people that vended them were potentially poisonous.

For example, popular cartoons like this one from *Punch* articulate an increasingly skeptical consumer class (see figure 3.1).

FIGURE 3.1
John Leech, "The Use of Adulteration." *Punch* (4 August 1855).

The incongruity between the child's youth and her canny request forms the basis of both humor and social commentary: "If you please, sir, Mother says, will you let her have a quarter of a pound of your best tea to kill the rats with and an ounce of chocolate as would get rid of black beadles." She asks for what she is likely to get, and the grocer's stock of bole armenian, lead, and nux vomica testifies to his easy ability to fill such a bill. Other popular forms carried a similarly perspicacious tune; one ballad entitled "London Adulterations" lilts,

> London tradesmen, 'tis plain, at no roguery stop;
> They adulterate every thing they have in their shop:

You must buy what they sell, and they sell what they please,
For they would if they could sell the moon for green Cheese.
    Sing Tantarumtara, what terrible rogues!

Imitation, 'tis well known, is now all the rage;
Every thing imitated is in this rare age;
Tea, Coffee, Beer, Butter, Gin, Milk—and in brief,
No doubt they'll soon imitate Mutton and Beef.

The Grocer sel[1]s ash leaves and sloe leaves for Tea
Ting'd with Dutch pink and Verdigris just like Bohea,
What sloe Poison means slomon has now found out,
We shall all to a T. soon be poison'd no doubt.[14]

The ballad endorses what it frames as a healthy mistrust in response to the marketplace. As a commentary on consumerism, "London Adulterations" works from the specific—cheese, tea, coffee, beer, butter, gin, milk, mutton, and beef—to draw conclusions about the general state of the market: "*Every thing*" is adulterated or imitated, and "We shall *all* . . . soon be poison'd." The market here seems limitless, without either physical or moral boundaries; the tradesmen "at no roguery stop," poisoned goods pass from shop to kitchen to body, and even the moon may be brought to sale, not glowing and desirable in its own right, but rather as false cheese. Furthermore, because "imitation . . . is now all the rage," one can never be quite sure what one is getting—or, perhaps, one can be pretty sure one is getting poisoned—hence the embedded tragicomedy in the *Punch* girl's request for "tea to kill the rats with."

The ballad figures this tea as "ash leaves and sloe leaves . . . Ting'd with Dutch pink and Verdigris," which references another important aspect of adulteration. The Parliamentary Committee discovered not only that bread, flour, milk, and other such staples were cut with adulterants such as alum, chalk, and sawdust, but also that additives for the enhancement of appearance were contributing a new and different venue for corruption. In other words, the issue was no longer simply one of increasing quantity by cutting "pure" substance; it had grown to include a primary feature of merchandising, namely, that of increasing *apparent* desirability or value. Not only were merchants treating their bottled fruits and vegetables with copper and other metals (as in the example, above, of greengages, gooseberries, olives, limes, and rhubarb); but, in the attempt to make their wares more marketworthy, they added brick dust to cayenne, Bole Armenian and Venetian Red to anchovies, lobsters, shrimps, and tomato sauce, and Chromate of Lead to custard, egg powders, and, as we have seen, colored sugar confectionery (Hassall 1857, 11–17).

Rossetti's poem reflects this emphasis. The fruit is "bloom-down-cheeked," "full and fine," "Bright-fire-like" and "sound to eye," yet its substance is rather problematic. Laura claims, "I ate and ate my fill, / Yet my mouth waters still" ("Goblin Market," 165–66); and indeed she gets less satisfaction and more trouble than she had bargained for. Behind its apparent wholesomeness, the goblins' fruit proves decidedly sinister. Testifying before the Parliamentary committee, the chemist Alphonse Normandy commented on such deceptive appearances within the context of capitalism:

> At present competition, instead of being what it ought, a competition of skill as to who shall produce the best article at the cheapest price, is now really a competition as to who shall adulterate with the greatest cleverness. What a tradesman tries to do now, is not to gain a victory over his neighbours by supplying either a better article or the same article at a cheaper price, but his endeavour is, "How shall I take my neighbour's custom from him by *offering an article which will look as well, but which will cost me less?*" (*Adulteration of Food, Drink, and Drugs* [1855], 85; emphasis added)

Within the tiny space of "Goblin Market," we find many "article[s] which . . . look as well" but are far from what they promise to be. In fact, nothing is quite what it seems. This is strange fruit; the merchants are "cat-faced," "rat-paced," "obtuse and furry," and prone to disappearance; and the maidens are more desiring and knowing than your average girls. In both hermeneutic structure and content, "Goblin Market" discourages faith in appearances, primarily through the vehicle of the canny Lizzie, who cautions Laura not to "peep" at goblin men. Even Laura asks early in the poem, "Who knows upon what soil they fed / Their hungry thirsty roots?" warning her sister not to trust the goblins' fruit, and promoting a healthy measure of doubt in the face of market seductions (45–46).

Rossetti emphasizes the soundness of suspicion in a series of menacing mimicries. To begin, the "Apples and quinces, / Lemons and oranges, / Plump unpecked cherries—/ Melons and raspberries, / Bloom-down-cheeked peaches, / Swart-headed mulberries, / Wild free-born cranberries, / Crab-apples, dewberries, / Pine-apples, blackberries, / Apricots, strawberries" and so on repeat surfaces that look good and wholesome, but their poisonous contents radically contradict those appearances. This sense recurs in the goblins' dissimulations when Lizzie finally condescends to visit the market with "a silver penny in her purse" to purchase fruit for the "dwindling" Laura. The goblins greet her with apparent amiability:

Laughed every goblin
When they spied her peeping:
Came towards her hobbling,
Flying, running, leaping,
Puffing and blowing,
Chuckling, clapping, crowing,
Clucking and gobbling,
Mopping and mowing,
Full of airs and graces,
Pulling wry faces
Demure grimaces, . . .
Hugged her and kissed her,
Squeezed and caressed her:
Stretched up their dishes,
Panniers, and plates. (329–39, 348–50)

As if Laura's fate isn't warning enough, this passage contains a cadre of very red flags. The goblins are "Full of airs and graces" and they put on wry faces and demure grimaces: these are not "natural" spontaneous expressions, but rather *pulled*, performed in the interests of profit and exploitation. When Lizzie refuses to eat with them, the goblins' mimicry of fellowship quickly breaks down and they turn abruptly from alacrity to aggression: "They began to scratch their pates, / No longer wagging, purring, / But visibly demurring, / Grunting and snarling. / One called her proud, / Cross-grained uncivil; / Their tones waxed loud, / Their looks were evil" (390–96).

As "purring" becomes "demurring," and "civil" finds its echo in "evil," "Goblin Market" offers a cautionary tale about the perils of mimicry.[15] Both goblins and goblin fruit call into question the value of appearances. The poem certainly valorizes some construction of truth in nature, but it does so by expressing powerful misgivings that nature may be just as susceptible to construction as anything else. Rossetti sets up two valences of repetition: one imitative in innocent replication of wholesome tasks and values, the other decidedly unwholesome, threatening the very concept of innocence. Although the poem seems to construct one space of apparent safety in the agrarian home in which the girls "Fetched in honey, milked the cows, / Aired and set to rights the house, / Kneaded cakes of whitest wheat, / Cakes for dainty mouths to eat, / Next churned butter, whipped up cream, / Fed their poultry, sat and sewed" (203–8), one cannot help noting that this space is not necessarily any more genuine than the goblin market. Domestic life participated as well in strategically calculated repetitions, a dynamic underscored, perhaps, by the very acts of milking, kneading, churning, and sewing which depend on reduplications of the same actions over and over again. Even Lizzie's articulation of market peril is reiterative: "'No,' said Lizzie: 'No, no, no; / Their offers should not charm us, / Their evil gifts would harm us'" (64–66). Setting the "natural" domain in contradistinction to the sinister deceptions of the marketplace, Rossetti appears to posit the country/home as the site of originality, realness, and guilelessness, but the poem's entire plot emphasizes that the pastoral home is not safe from the threats inherent in mass production and cheap reduplication. The poem delivers an almost wistful apotheosis of integrity at the same time as it suggests that such realness is a hot commodity only because it is so rare.[16]

The Pleasures of Paranoia

"Goblin Market" manifests no simple nostalgia about prelapsarian gardens, however, nor are its enjoinders to suspicion uncomplicated. Rossetti's market poem thus offers up valuable fodder for modern critics, given that paranoia has acquired rather a bad scholarly reputation in recent years. As Eve Sedgwick observes ruefully in her introduction to *Novel Gazing*, paranoia has become so much a part of current critical methodology as to preclude nuanced readings that might explore more than surveillance and transgression. "Subversive and demystifying parody, suspicious archaeologies of the present, the detection of hidden patterns of violence and their exposure: . . . these infinitely doable and teachable protocols of unveiling," she writes, "have become the common currency of cultural and historicist studies" (1997, 21). Sedgwick has a point: certainly, the tenor and tendencies of Foucauldian scholarship ought not to circumscribe our sole critical options. However, as these reading practices testify to the critical pleasures of detecting moments of ideological exposure, and of policing the police in Victorian texts, there is something to be said for tracking down earlier incarnations of those pleasures.

First of all, for our nineteenth-century readerly counterparts, a "hermeneutics of suspicion" was entirely appropriate at times—for example, in the efforts to define, regulate, and prevent food adulteration. Lizzie's just circumspection—and the prevalence of frequently suitable wariness among Victorian "goblins"—suggests that paranoid reading was immediately relevant to many aspects of Victorian culture.[17] Furthermore, as I note above, "Goblin Market" is not simply a paranoid text. It also *delights* in the dynamics of apprehension: Laura's fall into bad shopping bespeaks undeniable fascination with a dangerous market, just as Lizzie's valiant prudence demonstrates the satisfactions of rightly placed suspicion. "Goblin Market" reminds us that we are often right to detect a predilection for detection, yet it encourages us also to see how often pleasure accompanies paranoia, and how diverse were Victorian responses to the hazards of a complicated market. Fresh perils in Victorian culture facilitated an ideological shift that frankly encouraged commercial anxiety, and authorities attempted, on a variety of fronts, to fortify consumers against the goblins of the modern economy. Teaching people to protect themselves (economically, physically, personally) meant engaging them in a defense against fraud, both at home and at large. That project could be more or less playful.

The illustrative context of food adulteration encapsulates the spirit of a larger conceptual change, as public activists scrambled to establish clearinghouses where the lower classes could bring their food to be tested; and scientific texts, newspaper articles, and home economics manuals encouraged middle-class consumers to protect themselves by acquiring the accoutrements of home laboratories.[18] Hassall's *Adulterations Detected* is classic, carefully instructing the middle-class Victorian customer how to suspend, incinerate, evaporate, and utilize an exhaustive supply of chemicals to prepare samples for microscopic examination at home. That rhetoric of sampling resonates with both Rossetti's poem and with more general cultural perspectives.

To illustrate: in the climax of "Goblin Market," Lizzie provides an antidote to her wasting sister. In entering the market, Lizzie does not want to eat, but rather to carry home the goblins' wares: "One waits / At home for me" (383–84), she says, declining their offer to "Sit down and feast with us" (380), and ignoring their claim that "Such fruits as these / No man can carry" (375–76). Lizzie's refusal either to engage the integrity of her body in trade or to eat with the goblin men leads to an assault that famously allows her to carry home to her sister what Richard Menke refers to as a "free sample" (1998, 128). "Tho' the goblins cuffed and caught her, / Coaxed and fought her," Rossetti writes, Lizzie "Would not open lip from lip / Lest they should cram a mouthful in / But laughed in heart to feel the drip / Of juice that syrupped all her face, / And lodged in dimples of her chin, / And streaked her neck which quaked like curd" ("Goblin Market," 424–25, 431–36).

In fact, Lizzie enters the market much like the members of the *Lancet* commission, feigning innocent engagement, offering to pay quietly for her food, but refusing to consume it. Arthur Hill Hassall found this method immeasurably superior to an aggressive seizure of goods practiced by the Excise commission. He preferred the dual methods of science and publicity, of purchasing goods incognito, and educating the public about the results of his committee's analysis. Consumers would then know from whom they might safely "come buy," while dishonest shopkeepers would be encouraged to mend their ways (the commission planned to release new results every three months). Hassall writes,

> The Excise has . . . been driven to adopt a system of espionage, . . . the rude and inquisitorial proceeding of entering forcibly upon suspected premises, and of seizing on any adulterated articles or substances employed in adulteration, and which, perchance, they might find in the course of search. The method adopted by "The Lancet" Commission was in striking contrast to this. It simply purchased the different articles as sold in the ordinary way of business, and applied to their analyses all the resources of science, especially the microscope and chemistry. By this proceeding it was not necessary, as in the case of the Excise, to maintain an Army of "4000" Excise inspectors, neither was it requisite to violate the sanctity of men's private dwellings. (1857, 33)

Little Lizzie returns triumphant from her trip to market, drenched in "samples" in the form of nectar. While I am reluctant to dismiss the frank sensuality of the passage in which she bids Laura, "Hug me, kiss me, suck my juices / Squeezed from goblin fruits for you" (468–69), I do want to suggest that it reverberates with biological approaches: the sample prudently brought home acts to remedy the foolish purchasing habits of the ailing sister. This reading breaks down as literal analogy, of course, when we consider that Laura *does* suck those juices, does again consume the fruits of the market, and that, as Hassall observed, both lead and copper "collect and accumulate in the system,—so that, no matter how small the quantity of them introduced at one time or in a single dose, the system, or particular parts of it, are at length brought under their influence, and certain diseases are induced, characteristic of poisoning" (1855, 34). However, within the context of public education about food adulteration, it seems significant that Laura's experience, mediated through the wary Lizzie, is markedly different: she suffers what seems like a seizure, then collapse, and then release. The following morning, "Laura woke as from a dream, / Laughed in the innocent old way / Hugged Lizzie but not twice or thrice" (537–39). Restored and moderate, Laura never again frequents the merchants whose wares proved so poisonous.

The principles of sampling and self-protection—in short, of *caveat emptor*—accurately describe the only recourse most consumers had. There were no effective laws to regulate, discipline, or discourage food adulteration, and the attempts of the Parliamentary Select Committee to pass legislation indicate the larger legal climate. An 1869 essay, "The Adulteration of Food and Drugs," recalls how those laws in place "were both at once too troublesome and too expensive to be at all generally adopted. . . . The committee, therefore, recommended that a change should be made in the law, with the object of placing within the reach of every one a cheap and expeditious legal remedy" (1869, 191). However, the general principles of laissez-faire economics impeded any such legislation. The bill was found to interfere with free market competition, to privilege unfairly those merchants whose goods weren't sampled, to be too vulnerable to the corruption of inspectors. In short, the bill went through three drafts before it became an Act in 1860, at which time it "was speedily seen to be almost totally useless, and further experience has only made its uselessness the more abundantly apparent" (ibid., 193–94). Hassall found the Act to be "weak, diluted, and itself adulterated" (quoted in Searle 1998, 93). Hence the importance of bringing suspicion home. There were some laws on the books to discipline the worst offenders, but general governmental indifference and free-market ethics suggested that individuals were responsible for their own protection.

Detecting Fraud

It is difficult to regard this responsibility without thinking of Foucault's argument that modern discipline operates not through force but through coercive cooperation. Although the Victorian period institutionalized the work of policing, alongside that institution existed a far more pervasive dynamic that emphasized the centrality of individual accountability. As D. A. Miller has argued, the power of discipline "cannot be identified with an institution or state apparatus, though these may certainly employ or underwrite it. . . . The mobility it enjoys allows precisely for its wide diffusion which extends from obviously disciplinary institutions (such as the prison) to institutions officially determined by 'other' functions (such as the school) down to the tiniest practices of everyday social life" (1988, 17). The practices surrounding food adulteration demonstrate in microcosm that the disciplinary regulations designed to discourage fraud concerned individual and private practices, far more than any state institution. Herein we find the work of private and self-policing made material, literal, and specific.

Mercantile fraud did not compromise the success of capitalism as an economic system. Rather, the potential for financial corruption set up alongside capitalism—indeed, within it—an ideological paradigm based in prospective guilt and the need for caution. Private forms of assessment are basic components of the capitalist system, as fraud (and/or its potential) is inherent in it. Ironically, this presupposition of materialist methodology supports rather than limits fiscal power. As Foucault notes, "If the economic take-off of the West began with the techniques that made possible the accumulation of capital, it might perhaps be said that the methods for administering the accumulation of men made possible a political take-off in relation to the traditional, ritual, costly violent forms of power which soon fell into disuse and were superseded by a subtle, calculated technology of subjection" (1979, 220–21). A penchant for scrutiny evolved alongside the development of capitalism and its abuses. In the context of food fraud, we find this strand of inquiry encapsulated and magnified, both, in the Victorian fascination with the microscope.

A quieter, gentler technology than the often clumsy interventions of actual police work, the microscope is literally and marks metaphorically a shift in perspective on vision and authenticity. The literature of food fraud celebrates the microscope as a key to all mythologies, a mystical instrument capable of disclosing Truth and vanquishing sin. Far more capable than chemistry in detecting sophistications of substance, the microscope seemed to offer a solution to the problems of adulteration. While chemical properties might be mimicked (sugars and starches often registered identically in chemical tests, and it was nearly impossible to tell coffee from chicory), the visual appearance of each substance was unique under the lens. "Until the microscope was brought to bear upon the subject," Hassall notes, ". . . no means existed whereby the great majority of adulterations could be discovered; and the parties practising them little dreamt that an instrument existed capable of bringing to light even these secret and guilty proceedings. . . . Now this feeling of security has been destroyed, and the adulterator knows that at any time he is liable to discovery" (quoted in "Adulteration of Food and Drugs" [1869], 189).

Satirizing the analytical chemist's inefficiency, the *Westminster Review* parodies Wordsworth ("The starch within the crusty rim / Is but a grain of starch to him, / And it is nothing more") to revel in the capacities of the microscope to reveal chemical deceptions. "But to the microscopist," the writer observes, the grain of rice "is something more." The microscope operates as a magical instrument that can unmask authentic identity and thereby empower the individual through the power of scrutiny. "Armed with [illustrations of cellular structure] and a small microscope it is possible for any who are so inclined to assure themselves of the purity or impurity of most of the articles of their ordinary consumption," he declares. Furthermore, he emphasizes the benefits of revealing individual characteristics and the truth of their origins. Under the microscope, "Each grain of starch has a well-defined individuality of its own, bearing upon it the legible impress of its history, and announcing in no dubious terms, by its size, shape, and superficial tracings, the particular source whence it was derived" (ibid., 189). Stressing each cell's difference from its brothers, the *Westminster Review* trumpets the microscope's ability to "announce" an ontological fingerprint. As Hillel Schwartz observes, despite the fact that the technology itself was far from perfect, subject to illusions from diffracted light, "the cultural *sense* of the microscope was that through its eyepiece one could see the inner truth" (1996, 184; emphasis in original). Authorities promised that, faced with the technology of the microscope, "the puny efforts of human fraud are rendered powerless to deceive" ("Adulteration of Food and Drugs" [1869], 188).

Of course, social life and biology operate differently. Microscopic technology pledged, by establishing appearance as the site of authenticity, to reveal the simple, clear, uncomplicated truth of things. However, not only were microscopes expensive investments, but, as an array of swindlers and scams affirmed, the market at large was a visually tricky place, and most of its subjects would not fit under a slide.[19] The microscope, in other words, offers tenuous ideological cognates. Thus, even as government authorities and popular texts advocated interpersonal observation, inquiry, and suspicion, these strategies hardly amounted to so precise a science as biology. In this tension between scrutiny and futility, one finds a dynamic that approaches, but has not yet become, modern cynicism. Despite the hopelessness of establishing uncontestable *social* ontology, of shoring up a place of surety, truth, and realness within a market that had given over its dedication to such values, Victorian texts continued to invest in investigation.

That investment signals two key aspects of Victorian paranoid reading. First, many texts that associated economic dishonesty with individuals rather than institutions, with specific moments rather than epidemic conditions, had little interest in minimizing the scope of public risk, even as they worked toward its reduction.[20] Rather, they stressed the toxicity of their contemporary culture to incite their readers to desire the perspectives (outrage, humor, suspicion, sarcasm) they offered on that world. For example, a popular ballad, "The Chapter of Cheats," uses the logic of synecdoche to signal the larger community for which each individual stands:

> The first is the lawyer, he will bother you with jaw,
> He knows well how to cheat you with a little bit of law;
> And in comes the doctor, who to handle you so rough,
> One guinea he will charge you for a shilling's worth of stuff.
>   And we're a' cheating, [cheat, cheat, cheating

And we're a' cheating through country and town.]

The next is the pawnbroker, with his ticket in his hand,
He well knows how to cheat for the interest of his pawn;
And the grocer sands his sugar, and sells sloe leaves for tea,
As for the dusty miller who is a bigger rogue than he[?]
    And we're a' cheating, &c.

The lawyer, *the* doctor, *the* pawnbroker, *the* grocer, *the* dusty miller—as this ballad comically laments the practices of the day, it also personalizes those practices, linking "a' cheating" to actions and identities that are singular and personal, but are also indices of widespread conditions. Like Rossetti's goblins ("*One* had a cat's face, / *One* whisked a tail, / *One* tramped at a rat's pace, / *One* crawled like a snail" [71–74]), the ballad's frauds are specific and individual, yet even as each cheater is a "one," each nonetheless functions to describe a much larger group.[21]

Like many Victorian texts, "Goblin Market" reads national suspicion through local instances, registering capitalist peril as a problem of individual corruption and vulnerability, and its detection as individual responsibility.[22] Yet, Laura says to Lizzie, "We must not look at goblin men, / We must not buy their fruits" (42–43), not "We must not go to market." In other words, the impetus toward paranoia maintained its share of pleasures. Hassell's handbook offered serious warnings, but it also demonstrated the ways in which self-defense could be fun—and not only for those who could afford a home laboratory. While many documents about fraud in general promoted apprehension as both demeanor and activity, those texts functioned to entertain as well as to warn. Scare tactics, whether delivered through scientific reporting or creative narrative, stressed the wisdom of suspicion, encouraged consumers to keep a wary eye out for trouble, and fed a growing interest in the play of detection.

However much they may have shaped popular rhetoric, in other words, the ideological principles of microscopy ultimately did little to restore stability or security. Certainly, fraud closed the garden gate on easy trust, leaving warier consumers in its wake; but if popular texts sought to stimulate and represent a suspicious citizenry whose attitudes toward consumption had changed, so too did those texts stimulate and represent a change in demand. Considering the number of popular Victorian texts that include mysteries to be solved, and considering that detective fiction became increasingly popular after the 1840s, it seems clear that these and other related narrative forms were not simply "about" paranoia. Rather, they whetted their readers' appetites for the opportunity to discover surprises, bad and otherwise.[23]

"Goblin Market" closes with its domestic securities marked with doubt, much like securities in the "real" market. The sample brought home, comfort and constitution restored, Laura and Lizzie grow to marry and have children of their own. Many critics have read Rossetti's closing lines as a fantasized withdrawal from the market, and the poem's concluding domestic scene may indeed seem hermetic.[24] However, although Lizzie and Laura "both were wives / With children of their own /," Rossetti emphasizes that "Their mother-hearts [were] beset with fears, / Their lives bound up in tender lives" (544–46). Lizzie and Laura have become savvy shoppers, and the poem promotes a powerful economic message, one that seeks to educate about, rather than to avoid, the perils of capitalism. The women warn their own children of "wicked, quaint fruit-merchant men, / Their fruits like honey to the throat / But poison in the blood" (553–55). Like the growing propensity for home examination that echoed a larger national cry of *caveat emptor*, like the plethora of texts that cautioned against both urban and individual risk, the poem's happy conclusion emphasizes the happiness that ensues from suspicion.

In other words, while Lizzie's militant caution defines one reigning ideological response to the "real" market, the power of Laura's appetite cannot be ignored, and here we find additional support for Sedgwick's argument that paranoia ought not to mark the end of our reading, but perhaps the beginning. Like the many consumers who entered the market despite its goblins, Laura's desire sends her sailing into peril, "Like a vessel at the launch / When its last restraint is gone" (85–86).[25] Her illness brings her domestic body into the financial field, literally as a singular case of food poisoning, and metaphorically as a victim of a larger syndrome in which many individuals were ruined by fraudulent market practices that affected investments as well as goods.[26]

Yet, if Laura's poisoned body is another metaphor for the kingdom, for a country poisoned by fraud, it is also a body that persistently craves that poison even as it decays. Laura's enduring "passionate yearning" bespeaks an incontrovertible taste for that which defiles (266). Hence, "Goblin Market" and the literature of food adulteration not only signal the prevalence of culinary fraud within Victorian England, but also comment on the larger social implications of adulteration for the self, the community, and the relationship of both to a growing range of commodities.

Adulterating Plots

One of those commodities was the narrative of domestic fraud itself, in which food adulteration often operated as shorthand for broader forms of deception, as it does in "Goblin Market," and in the aforementioned examples of "Maud" and *Mary Price*. As I've been arguing, these texts use food fraud to consider the ramifications of pervasive market dishonesty for sacred domestic relationships (between sisters, between lovers, between a man and his god).[27] The following passage from Wilkie Collins's *Man and Wife* (1870), in which Sir Patrick Lundie references adulteration to quiz his niece's suitor about courtship, plays in this same mode:

> You go to the tea-shop and get your moist sugar. You take it on the understanding that it is moist sugar. But it isn't any thing of the sort. It's a compound of adulterations made up to look like sugar. You shut your eyes to that awkward fact, and swallow your adulterated mess in various articles of food; and you and your sugar get on together as well as you can. . . . You go to the marriage-shop and get a wife. You take her on the understanding—let us say—that she has lovely yellow hair, that she has an exquisite complexion, that her figure is the perfection of plumpness, and that she is just tall enough to carry the plumpness off. You bring her home, and you discover that it's the old story of the sugar over again. Your wife is an adulterated article. Her lovely yellow hair is—dye. Her exquisite skin is—pearl powder. Her plumpness is—padding. And three inches of her height are—in the boot-maker's heels. (38)

Collins's inventory of adulterated articles offers a comic commentary on the deceptions inherent in attraction and courtship, on the design of stimulating appetite with the knowledge that one will leave one's target unsatisfied (you must simply "get on together as well as you can"). While Sir Patrick's commentary on Blanche remains within the genre of humor, the potential adulterations involved in courtship can also be serious business, especially in mid-century England when the "mess" of fraud takes center stage with regard to marriage, rather than food, as I discuss in the following chapter.

As a general rule, food fraud keeps to a supporting role in the novel, and it makes just a brief cameo in *Man and Wife*. In closing my discussion here, I turn to Mrs. J. H. Riddell's *The Race for Wealth* (1866), perhaps the only Victorian novel to feature an adulterator as protagonist.[28] In its way, *The Race for Wealth* is an Übernovel of Victorian fraud. Addressing a multitude of commercial and domestic depredations, the novel works through a series of horsy metaphors, to develop complicated arguments about market deception and about the fantasies of class transcendence that kept that market going. It maps the undesirable social consequences of modern commerce, it offers long soliloquies about servants who function like bad clerks, and it begins with an extended exploration of the science behind food adulteration. Across its many plots, the novel insists that the ethics of swindling seep between categories, so that nothing separates market fraud from domestic fraud. That formulation becomes particularly concrete in a painful anti-marriage plot that traces the disintegration of domestic bodies, trust, and relationships.

Published nearly a decade after the Parliamentary hearings, however, *The Race for Wealth* offers less opportunity for and maintains less interest in detection than its earlier popular counterparts. Its general tone is decidedly more mordant than exhortatory, testifying to a switch of lenses, as it were, to an acceptance of the fact of fraud, even as readers continue to suffer under it. In one scene late in the novel, for example, Riddell remarks that

> The cholera and Limited Liability reached a point at about the same period. The same post that brought newspapers containing the Registrar-General's report to quiet country districts brought likewise unwonted-looking letters inclosing samples of all manner of new fabrics, prospectuses of wonderful companies, forms of application for shares, moderate calculations of the thousand per cent. returns to be expected, and such flourishing statements, combined with such lists of names, as caused Paterfamilias to place his spectacles on his honored nose and peruse the document with much interest and astonishment. (132)

Stock fraud enters the home like the tainted food that provides the protagonist his financial start in the world. The daily mail to the breakfast table brings not only news but also invitations to speculate. Significantly, Paterfamilias's spectacles don't allow him to see that all the "declared schemes which promised such returns without trouble, or large individual expenditure, contained of necessity the germ of failure, and bore on their faces unmistakable marks of jobbery and fraud" (133). In other words, the paranoid reading practices that authors like Rossetti, Reynolds, and Hassell advocate have had little efficacy in a culture so thoroughly saturated in fraud.

The novel begins on Lower Thames Street, "where the air is literally foul with the smell of foreign fruits, . . . and the side paths are lined with open shops, that seem overflowing into the dirty gutters, with nuts, and shaddocks, and lemons" (5). In the sensory overload that characterizes the food of the East End market, oranges mix with "big baskets of fish" and filth to produce an effect of commercial nausea made literal (5). Riddell then establishes how flimsy is the boundary that separates this working-class street from the upper-class home:

Yes, my dear madam, it is indeed from Thames Street, by Billingsgate, that many of the fruits you have at dessert, and the delicate lemons wherewith you season your puddings, are originally procured; . . . that the cod-liver oil which the great Doctor Belgravia declares your consumptive daughter must either take or die is to be had in its integrity; . . . that the lemon juice and the lime-water which you find so valuable in a sick room make their way into genteel society; . . . that the bloaters the Londoners eat at breakfast, and the oysters they swallow for supper, and the salmon milor has at a fabulous price per pound, and the turbot you order from your suburban fishmonger, are all had "first hand," as it is called. (ibid.)

Conjoining vile market and cozy home through the conduit of food, Riddell sketches a world in which the comestible delicacies of the West End dining table and the accouterments of the West End sick room emerge from a "Babel where the Easterners congregate together to cheat the Westerns if they can," and where the look of the wares "are enough to make one loathe the sight of food for a month" (6).

On Thames Street, the reader meets Lawrence Barbour, an honest young man of a good but fallen family, who arrives in London with the project of earning sufficient funds to buy back Mallingford End, his familial estate. "I saw a vulgar, illiterate snob buy the place where we had lived for centuries," Lawrence tells his patron's partner, Mr. Sondes, "and then I saw that snob sell Mallingford End to a worse snob; and I saw the whole country-side bow down and worship Mammon" (17). By initially juxtaposing Lawrence against the corruptions of a corrupt marketplace, Riddell establishes the stakes of his fall: he starts the novel as an embodiment of just and righteous principles, an adversary to the capitalist ethic that has allowed a family of "snobs" to displace his own.

Lawrence crosses the miasma of Lower Thames Street to join the business of Josiah Perkins, a middle-class relation of the Barbours who offers him a place. Perkins proves an immediate disappointment, however, for his manners are crass, and his trade turns out to be a suspicious side-field of chemistry—as Riddell writes, "Mr. Perkins was less a manufacturing chemist than a manufacturing grocer" (10). The novel sardonically presents the creative side of food adulteration; it is, at the least, a profession that rewards evasive invention. "'I try to cheat nobody but the analytical chemists!'" Perkins claims. "But then," Riddell notes, "Mr. Perkins was continually trying to cheat those gentlemen; and it may safely be affirmed that he felt as proud of inventing any new process likely to delude them as Watt did of his condensing steam-engine or Arkwright of his spinning-jenny" (10). Of course, Perkins's milieu will never grant him the accord of a Watt or an Arkwright. Relegated by circumstance and class to a much lower innovative field, Perkins contents himself with the smaller triumph of keeping the analytical chemists on their toes.

One of the first signs of Lawrence's demise is his natural talent for adulteration: soon he too "delights in cheating the analyzers. He adds and he takes away, and he keeps them in a continual ferment" (100). His propensity for the trade is so impressive that Mr. Perkins actually rues Lawrence's professional fate. "Pity he had not gone in for regular chemistry. . . . He might have made a name and a fortune to talk about" (100).[29] Of course, a career in "regular chemistry" would not produce money enough to buy back Mallingford End anytime soon, requiring that Lawrence's domestic aspirations ironically compromise his range of professional choices. Here, the novel displays a surprisingly sophisticated moral perspective on food adulteration. Earlier, Perkins's partner, Mr. Sondes, explains to Lawrence, "It is the rage for cheapness that induces a trade like ours: people would rather pay twopence for an inferior article than threepence for genuine goods. . . . The consequence of which is, grocers must adulterate, and the grocers must be able to procure the wherewithal to adulterate from a firm like ours, where every ingredient used is perfectly pure of its kind and harmless" (18). Riddell throws blame back on the consumer, suggesting the larger context in which commercial corruption occurs. The purveyor of pure adulteratives signals the complexity of her vision, which becomes even more knotty as the novel loses its focus on food, and Riddell directs her energies to exploring other venues for fraud, including that form of domestic commerce that ultimately completes Lawrence's ruin, namely, the business of marriage.

Shortly after he begins his adulterating career, Lawrence suffers a sort of moral amnesia that erases his original motivations: the desire to buy Mallingford End effectively evaporates from Lawrence's consciousness. The novel shifts its focus from adulteration to adultery, as Lawrence expands his business prospects, finding new venues for fraud. In typical Victorian fashion, the novel features a pair of women of the familiar fair and dark variety. Sondes's angelic daughter, Olivine, sums up blonde innocence and domestic desirability, while the brunette Henrietta Alwyn, daughter of the current "snob" owner of Mallingford End, "was a flirt; not an innocent, harmless flirt, like many a girl who settles down after a time into a sufficiently sober and discreet matronhood—but a flirt ingrain, a flirt who did not care at what price her success was purchased, what tears flowed, what wounds were inflicted, so as she was satisfied—she triumphant" (35). Riddell underscores the domestic consequences of Lawrence's professional choices by opposing not simply the women's "types" but the relationships of their families to Lawrence. There are no heroes here. Sondes is an adulterator, but he positions himself to help Lawrence, while Alwyn has gained possession of Lawrence's family estate and is an unrepentant capitalist who "did not make his money over honestly" (18). Brought into contact with the Alwyns, his declared adversaries at the start of the novel, Lawrence continues in his personal life the departure from the moral high road he has already begun professionally: he falls in love with the beautiful Etta, who encourages his attentions only to jilt him for Mr. Gainswoode, a rich man considerably older than herself.

Lawrence's subsequent engagement to Olivine Sondes offers a brief moment of light in the novel's otherwise bleak landscape. Olivine radiates potential salvation in her simple devotion to Lawrence and to her father, and in her general kind regard for others. "Far away down in the natures of most," Riddell writes, "I suppose there is some well of purity that bubbles up to the surface rejoicingly when touched by a hand which is still perfectly unstained and unconscious of evil" (113). But the ambitious adulterator has no taste for purity, and he finds neither value in Olivine's charms, nor salvation in her wholesomeness. "Honey-moons, he decided, were mistakes," Riddell writes. "He ought never to have married Olivine Sondes" (101).

After the marriages, Lawrence turns his attentions to dubious business ventures, replacing the poisonous East End market with which the novel opens with the toxic Victorian stock market. As Lawrence's trade shifts from one form of poison to another, he begins a long, sordid, and surprisingly explicit affair with Etta Alwyn Gainswoode. Like the contagion of cholera that characterizes the perilously seductive stock prospectuses, the lexicon of financial and culinary fraud reframes the language of infidelity to characterize adultery in fiscal terms, and to suggest that the diseased morality of Lawrence's work cannot help but infect his domestic practices. Even pure Olivine, when she begins to suspect her husband's infidelity, expresses her moral and emotional responses in the language of the stock market. "Mrs. Barbour had now her stake in the national proprieties. She owned a husband whom she should not like to see on his knees before Etta Gainswoode or any other woman living" (114). Olivine has a more sophisticated understanding of her own race for wealth than might appear on the surface. Her "stake in the national proprieties" involves keeping her property, namely, the husband that she "owns." Although she is ready and willing to put her money where her heart is, that strategy keeps Lawrence only briefly, and she refuses Etta's own advice to "Let him imagine you have something else to think about occasionally. . . . What is had cheaply is rarely prized highly" (117). And Etta is right: Lawrence sells Olivine's charms short.

The novel balances its devaluation of pure womanhood with a wry commentary on the attractions of such rare commodities as rich widows, when Etta's husband dies. The novel offers little redemption. Olivine discovers her husband passionately kissing Etta, she offers him a divorce, and he offers to marry Etta. But Etta Gainswoode discounts his affections as just so many bills. His attempt to cash in on passion fails as miserably as will, shortly, his creditors' attempts to collect from him. "Marry indeed! . . . when every shilling I have in the world goes from me if I take to myself a second husband," Etta exclaims. When Lawrence assures her he has money "enough for both," she retorts, "I like something more substantial to depend on than shares in all sorts of companies. It is very profitable while the companies are good for any thing, doubtless; but I have seen so much of business ups and downs that now I am independent of trade I should like to keep so, thank you" (165). Canny about the fluctuating values of both the stock market and the marriage market, Etta Gainswoode knows enough to keep a tight hold on her assets. Independence has both economic and relational valences. On the one hand, Etta's appraisal of Lawrence's offer figures her as a decidedly unfeminine, cold woman when one considers the general value of romance, but it looks very much like reason given the state of the Victorian stock market and the laws governing women's property around 1866. When Lawrence's notes are unexpectedly called in, it is hard not to give Etta the credit of wisdom: his affairs are in "such a state that failure in one venture meant failure in all" (165).

The novel closes as Lawrence goes smash physically as well, falling into a delirium that obliterates all but his happy childhood. Olivine returns to nurse him, as "the long years of his struggling youth and unhappy manhood faded out of his recollection as breath fades away from the surface of a mirror, and the only things which remained fresh and unchanged as ever were the bright, idle, sunshiny days, spent in boyish pursuits, filled with folly and joy" (166). Returning to prelapsarian idylls, Lawrence's end echoes the close of "Goblin Market" both in its nostalgic construction of "the simple pleasures, the trivial distresses of his earlier life" and in its powerful deconstruction of that very vision. Lawrence, Riddell writes, "departed with the leaves, poor as the day when he first entered London. And yet not so. He was rich in love" (167).

Transforming the measure of Lawrence's success from economic to moral to emotional capital, Riddell juxtaposes family and finance as competing fields in which a man may transform his worth. On the surface, it seems that Lawrence would have done well to give over his pursuit of money and to exchange his interest in the assessments of speculators, capitalists, clerks, and "plodding business folks," for that in the "honest men and women . . . in whose eyes most of all he desired to stand well" (160). However, *The Race for Wealth* suggests family as the solution to finance only fleetingly. Although Riddell positions Olivine's pure simplicity as a redemptive alternative to the market, the novel nonetheless emphasizes how thoroughly affairs of the heart are implicated in economic ventures. If Lawrence is "rich in love" at the novel's close, he is so despite his best efforts to defraud the institution of marriage; if he learns, finally, how to cash in on the goods of the heart, we must note that he has been trading on Olivine's affections throughout, speculating on the constancy of her devotion, and his death finds him still a Midas, only in a different guise. "The wealth he once coveted the Lord in mercy took away; the wealth he once despised the Lord in mercy gave him in his hour of need" (167). Lawrence's frail redemption is little more than a shift in economic contexts, a short hop from one field of speculation to another.

The Race for Wealth works on a variety of fronts to foreground the relationship between domestic and corporate markets. Although the novel is unique in its extended focus on food adulteration, its ultimate concentration on marriage brings it into a much larger family of Victorian novels that speak romantic engagement in the vocabulary of market investment. The following chapter takes up that business, and the tenor of capitulation and play that characterizes its plots.

4

Speculating on Marriage

Fraud, Narrative, and the Business of Victorian Wedlock

> This subject I cannot conclude without a caution to females possessed
> of property. There is always a class of men pretending to be respect-
> able, and who perhaps are so till they have the means of leading a
> life of idleness and pleasure at the expense of others, and who make
> it their business, under colour of love, and by the kindest and most
> diligent attention, to win your affections, and so to induce you to
> marry them. But such a man's kindness will at longest but last till he
> has spent the whole of your property; or which, one way or another,
> by fraud or violence, he will be sure in the end to plunder you.
> —T. H. Rose, *The People's Important Guide* (1847)

> There is only one kind of marriage which makes good
> the assertion that it is the right and happy condition for mankind,
> and that is a marriage founded on free choice, esteem, and affec-
> tion—in one word, on love.
> —Frances Power Cobbe,
> "What Shall We Do With Our Old Maids?" (1862)

I T HAS BECOME SOMETHING of a critical commonplace to attribute the
mid-century rise of failed marriage narratives to the Matrimonial Causes
Act of 1857, which made divorce more readily available to the average person.
Similarly, many critics have contended that the proliferation of bigamy plots
in the early 1860s derives from the Yelverton marriage case, which sought to
determine whether Major William Charles Yelverton had married Maria Theresa Longworth once or twice or, as he insisted, not at all. In this chapter, I
read the Yelverton trials in light of the heated debates about sexual equity and
property rights that the Matrimonial Causes Act prompted. I mean thereby
to establish that fraud is a crucial subtext to the increasingly blighted marriage

plots that captivated mid-Victorian popular culture, and that to understand those plots without reference to their economic underpinnings is to understand them only partially.

❦

In 1857, Major William Charles Yelverton married Theresa Longworth. Twice. Or, at least, he participated in two marriage ceremonies with her. Apparently, the major had a penchant for weddings: despite the sheer redundancy of rites that would seem to make him more than a little married, Yelverton pledged his troth once again in 1858, this time to Emily Forbes. The Forbes marriage precipitated the wildly popular hearings that began with a jury trial in Dublin in 1861. By the time Parliament intervened to settle the case in 1864, Yelverton and Longworth had become names familiar to most every reader in the nation.

The trials were a sensation, so captivating the public that John Sutherland indexes them under the heading of "Bigamy Novels." "The bigamous marriage was taken up as a vogue by the sensation novel," he writes, "after the much-publicized Yelverton trial, in 1861–4, [which] had the whole country agog" (1989, 63). Sutherland suggests that the case influenced Mary Elizabeth Braddon, Wilkie Collins, and Thomas Hardy, as well as those novelists who basically transcribed the case (most notably Longworth herself).[1] Jeanne Fahnestock makes a similar argument, that "bigamy would have remained one of the stock of occasionally used conventions, along with infant swapping and the missing will, had not a real-life sensational case brought it from the ranks of the far-fetched and improbable to the pages of every newspaper in 1861. The notorious Yelverton case was the cause célèbre of the season" (1981, 50).

The first Yelverton trial *was* "a sensation," but it captivated the Victorian public for reasons both more familiar and more complex than bigamy.[2] To begin, the trial was not for bigamy; it was for debt. When Longworth attempted to sue for bigamy in Edinburgh in 1858, the case was dismissed for lack of proof. She then turned to the newly formed Court for Divorce and Matrimonial Causes in England, which refused the case because the major "pleaded that he was not a domiciled Englishman" (*Yelverton Marriage Case* [1861], 15). Issues of jurisdiction repeatedly stymied Longworth's attempts to obtain recognition of her marriage until an Irish court agreed in 1861 to hear a civil suit brought by Longworth's friend and landlord in Hull, Mr. Thelwall, "to recover a sum of £259 17s. 3d. for board and lodging, and

❦

necessaries supplied to the defendant's wife and her servant" (ibid., 9).[3] Fiscal responsibility would, due to the laws of coverture, establish Yelverton as Longworth's husband. Thus, although the primary object of the suit was to ascertain the legitimacy of the marriage ceremonies, the vehicle by which the action proceeded was explicitly economic.[4]

The records, popular materials, and events that contextualized both the Yelverton trials and the more general discourse of bigamy repeatedly articulated Victorian romance within the language of finance, rendering bigamy less a crime in and of itself, than an act of fraud upon a domestic contract. Insofar as the concerns of the Yelverton story coincided with concerns within the mid-Victorian novel, both reflect a tendency, which developed alongside the rise of capitalism, to understand romantic affiliation within the larger contexts of sexual, financial, and emotional risk. In 1810, for example, the minister Thomas Jackson bluntly called the seducer "a kind of swindler, who practices the same stratagems to get the possession of a woman's person, as the swindler employs to get possession of his neighbour's goods or money" (26). Another early sermon reminded married couples to fulfill their conjugal duties to one another, interpreting the imperative in 1 Corinthians "as a strong charge to the married pair, against defrauding one another," which is so called, he explains, "on account of the power, or right which the sacred contract of marriage gives to each over the other; and it is to guard against this fraud, and the impurities to which it may lead, that the apostle . . . charges [the couple] to come together" (Sandeman 1800, 39). In God's eyes, it seems, even abstinence counts as fraud.

By the mid-nineteenth century, most all marriage plots referenced, at least tangentially, the potential for fraud. Britain's appetite for narratives of marital corruption was no longer simple: the reading public craved sophisticated and complex storylines, and it seems little wonder, given the wide array of social corruption both at home and abroad.[5] Victorian readers grew hungry for narratives that explored human depravity, and, given the imbrication of marriage and money, they developed a decided fascination with nuptial fraud. When Queen Victoria wrote to her daughter Vicky in 1858, "I think people really marry far too much; it is such a lottery after all, and for a poor woman a very doubtful happiness," she illustrates the proclivity to emphasize the speculative nature of marriage. Because there were no guarantees of anything but doubt, Victoria's analogy suggests, marriage was a gamble entered into "far too much" for the dubious rewards it offered.

The play on marriage-as-lottery also underscores how, as the Victorian market operated according to an increasingly laissez-faire agenda, it multiplied both the opportunities available to investors and the odds of such ventures being fraudulent. As I note in chapter 1, buying shares was a gamble not only on a company director's competence, but also on a venture itself being genuine. Within the discourse of troubled speculation, the Queen's comment on marriage establishes that this paradigm was sufficiently capacious to include the dubious nature of speculating in love as well as stocks. The marriage market, like the stock market, was akin to the lottery in that both were risky venues for investment.

Most immediately, Victoria's attention to the plight of the poor woman, who would generally not have settlements made for her, was relevant to those forms of Victorian legislation that regulated divorce and married women's property. Written on the heels of the Matrimonial Causes Act, the Queen's letter makes implicit reference to the crisis that Act provoked about the value of and the values within Victorian middle-class marriage. Most simply, the Act secularized divorce, making it possible (or at least more so) for the common person to obtain legal separation from his or her spouse without the prohibitive expense of parliamentary legislation. More complexly, it provoked debate about the economic and sexual inequities within Victorian marriage. The new law made a wife's adultery sufficient grounds for divorce while a husband's infidelity remained inadequate cause without the additional ingredient of cruelty. Further, by refusing to draft legislation that would grant property rights to married women without recourse to Equity, Parliament endorsed by omission married women's financial impoverishment. Complicated and heated, the debates surrounding the Matrimonial Causes Act exposed popular Victorian anxieties about socioeconomic relations within private life.[6]

In bringing the Divorce Act and the Yelverton case together, I want to shift the terms of the critical conversation. Contrary to established wisdom, that the proliferation of troubled marriage plots at mid-century is largely due to the inception of the new divorce laws or to a spectacular bigamy trial, it is clear to me that neither these plots nor their method of articulation was actually new. I do not mean to argue that these plots did not multiply in this period, for they did. As Frances Power Cobbe lamented,

> The Divorce Court . . . has revealed secrets which must tend to modify immensely our ideas of English domestic felicity. . . . It has always been vaguely known, indeed, that both husbands and wives sometimes broke their most solemn vows and fell into sin; but it was reserved for the new law to show how many hundreds of tragedies underlie the outwardly decorous lives, not only of the long-blamed aristocracy, but of the middle ranks in England ("Celibacy v. Marriage" 1862, 82)

It would nonetheless be a mistake to attribute the tragic marriage plots of this period too completely to the secrets, sins, and tragedies that the Divorce Court made public and popular, or to any narrative of bigamy qua bigamy. Indeed, many of the novels that filled out the stock of railway bookstalls and circulating libraries after 1857 carried on well-established narrative trends from previous decades and bear the earmarks of earlier economic legislation.

While the Act was certainly legendary, the marriage plot already had an established history of trouble well before legislation in the 1850s precipitated debates about bigamy and other forms of matrimonial suffering. Breach of promise suits, for example, were significant forebears to the concerns about and interest in the precarious negotiations of marriage that came to dominate texts in the 1860s. Understanding betrothal as a contract that might be breached or defrauded, British law demanded monetary compensation for emotional and social losses. As Ginger Frost writes, "The engagement was considered a contract to marry and was legally binding on both parties. However, unlike most contracts, it could not be enforced because the civil courts would not coerce marriage, but the party breaking the contract was liable to damages" (1995, 17). In punishing financially parties who betrayed ostensibly romantic contracts, breach of promise trials articulated explicitly the anxieties about social, sexual, and fiscal capital involved in engaging marriage.[7] And the marriage market had more than its share of confidence men and women who abbreviated the security of its contract even as they bolstered the appeal and sustained the familiar motifs of the Victorian family romance. As I've been suggesting, these characters made for compelling narrative: even as Victorian lawmakers struggled to write proper mandates to protect the institutions of marriage and of the stock market, respectively, creative writers easily filled reams of paper with plots of their undoing.

In that light, the institution of limited liability in 1856 was as important as the Divorce Act of 1857 in stimulating public anxieties about familial security. Many feared that limited liability would simply legitimize irresponsible economic behavior by diminishing the potential consequences for frauds and swindlers, and given the propensity of diatribes against the stock market to accentuate its impact on wives, children, and widows, the family was a powerful site of anxiety.[8] Of course, no one piece of legislation shaped the narrative trajectories of mid-Victorian England: one could as easily cite revisions in the Master and Servant Acts, or the parliamentary inquiry into food adulteration, as sources for the increasing tension in marriage plots. My point is that economic contingencies provided a salient context and vocabulary for talking about the perils inherent in interpersonal relationships. Given the financial crises that marked nearly every decade of the Victorian period (1837, 1839,

1847, 1857, 1866, 1878), and the wide scope of domestic fraud, it is not surprising how many texts promoted caution on the matrimonial market, as well as in other fields of investment.

Romance without Finance Is a Nuisance

Plots *against* marriage structure and sustain the plot *toward* it, tacitly establishing the value of legally sanctioned, religiously blessed, monogamous heterosexual commitment by citing those plotters who seek to manipulate or corrupt it. The very earliest of marriage plots explicitly associate monetary concerns with affective values. As Nancy Armstrong has noted in *Desire and Domestic Fiction, Pamela* set up the gold standard for the assessment of the domestic woman, and for the middle-class values she embodies.[9] Further, though, it also opens a tradition by which those values are consistently threatened, by which narrative pleasure ensues from the friction of corrupt insurgencies on the chaste, marketable body. The marriage plot thus depends as much on characters that seek to unsettle its stability as on those who seek to close the deal on nuptial bliss.

And the language of romance is often explicitly economic. From Lizzy Bennet's coy remarks that she "must date [her love for Darcy] from [her] first seeing his beautiful grounds at Pemberley" (Austen, *Pride*, 332), to Rosamond Vincy's distracted difficulty in fixing her wedding date because "she was going through many intricacies of lace-edging and hosiery and petticoat-tucking," and "thinking of her evening dresses for the visit to Sir Godwin Lydgate's" (Eliot, *Middlemarch*, 330) to the enormous wealth that makes Marie Melmotte in Trollope's *The Way We Live Now* such a very appealing catch, the careening and various expectations of the classic Victorian novel makes it nearly impossible to disentangle fiscal avarice from amorous attachments.

While it may be rather callous to analogize seeking a life partner with the process of, say, shopping, popular texts consistently played on the notion of the "marriage market" as a form of consumerism. George Cruikshank, in fact, seems to have been fairly obsessed with the likeness. His illustration "Flying Artillery" (figure 4.1) offers a tableau of men and women pierced by the arrows of an army of cupids, among whose victims cupidity figures prominently.

The belle at the center wears a placard advertising her "10,000 a Year," which causes various mature young men to swoon; at the same time, one ready archer aims to strike a female victim with the arrow of "£500 per annum pin money."[10] The malleability of domestic values on which Cruikshank

FIGURE 4.1
George Cruikshank, "Flying Artillery."

focuses here reappears in his "Matrimony by Advertisement," a short essay that appeared in *Our Own Times* in 1846. Arguing that the ball is an occasion upon which "parents and guardians often advertise for husbands for unconscious and innocent young ladies,"[11] Cruikshank cites other, more direct versions of the matrimonial advert, reminiscent of current personal ads, to make clear the economic motivations for contracting marriage:

> We met, the other day, with a very candid proposal of this kind, the author of which was a young gentleman, who not only sought a consort, but also an heiress, as he frankly declared in the first place. He had fallen upon evil (rail)ways, and it was necessary that he should retrieve his position. In return for a hand with a purse in it ample enough for his purpose, he promised a faithful heart, and an introduction in the best society. We trust this straightforward young Stag has met with a doe—and a dowry—to his mind. In the meantime, we strongly recommend his example to persons who, from financial difficulties, are about to commit bankruptcy. (1846, 106)

Cruikshank subverts the conventions of romantic narrative, suggesting how the innovation of the "(rail)" has changed the allusion of evil ways, so that the traditional exchange of heart for hand requires, in "our own times," a hand with "a purse in it ample enough for his purpose."

Another bit of ephemera—a small illustrated pocket book entitled *Mr. Timothy Wiggins*—lays out the potential pitfalls in advertising for love, as the eponymous bachelor places an advertisement for matrimony and finds the results disastrous. Woman after woman proves decidedly unfit: a number are ugly or old, one is black ("oh horrors"), one has eight children, two are pranks, and one is lovely but engaged. Poor Timothy Wiggins "determines not to try any more but goes home, & consults with his Landlady who advises him to look at home. He takes the hint, and pops the question they get married! And live very happily" (JJC The Social Day 2). The general message of these satires is that the medium of advertisement is unsuitable for the pursuit of marriage. As a business form associated primarily with vending products, advertisement is not only rather gross; it also invites into romance the same dangerous corruptions that one encounters in business.

Of course, those corruptions were already established risks in and around Victorian romantic relationships. Due to the laws of coverture and the economic inequities between unmarried men and women, marriage was already both a form of business and an established venue for fiscal exploitation. There were even balder, related "street" scams that didn't require an extended courtship: a most basic and old-school trick was a version of ring dropping. *The London Spy* notes that ring droppers "most commonly exercise their villainous art upon young women." The trick is to get the dupe to purchase a "found" gold band "for what you have got in your pocket, and what else you can give me" (Barrington 1832, 79). The transaction made, the ring dropper disappears into the night, leaving the young woman to discover that the found "gold" ring is "only brass gilt" (80). In *London Labour and the London Poor*, printed some thirty years later, Henry Mayhew records how the con has morphed in a marital vein: the ring in question was now a wedding band. According to the Street-Seller of Rings, "The public are now too wide awake" for traditional scams to achieve wide success (1861–2, 1: 351). He notes that ring droppers have developed a new matrimonial ruse to prey on servant girls, in which one writes a letter. "This is the style:—'My dear Anne, I have sent you the ring, and hope it will fit.—Excuse me not bringing it. John will leave it with you.—You know I have so much to attend to.—I shall think every minute a year until the happy day arrives. Yours devotedly, JAMES BROWN'" (ibid.). The ring dropper wraps the note around the ring, to establish the truth of its metal, and waits for a likely target.[12] The gist of this scam is, of course, different from one involving full-on seduction (whether into false marriage or simple consummation), but its underlying combination of avarice and romantic idealism dovetails with more serious forms of matrimonial fraud.

—⚭—

Broadsheets and newspapers had been reporting on those more serious cases for some time. These texts emphasize the risks inherent in marriage, even after one gets past the altar. For example, an 1830 broadside on George Miller, a.k.a. "the matrimonial deceiver," describes a man

> possessed of a remarkable fine figure, . . . [who] endeavoured to get by fraud, and imposing on the weakness of the female sex, to supply his extravagance [*sic*]. His first attack was upon an amiable young woman of the name of Fanny . . . ; he imposed himself upon her as the younger son of a nobleman of distinction, but failing in his attempts to seduce her, he at last married her, having got two hundred pounds with her: in a few weeks he deserted her . . . He next . . . assumed the title of a baronet; being at a ball at Warwick, he there selected a young lady, whose personal charms chiefly lay in her fortune; . . . their marriage took place in a short time, and my lady was very proud of her newly-acquired titles; but he did not let her enjoy it long, having received her fortune, and sold all the furniture and equipage to a broker privately, he left my lady nothing but her sighs and tears, instead of titles and honours. (JJC Crime 1)

By the time of Miller's early death at the age of thirty-five, "he had nearly a wife for every year that he was old." His style of seduction proved enduring—the *Records of Whitecross Street Prison* remark on the inmate whose "taste in female charms . . . entirely depends upon the length of their purses, or the amount of Consols standing in their names at the Bank. There is not much difficulty about the age of the charmer; neither is deformity any objection; his heart being soft and flexible, [his] philanthropy being of such extraordinary latitude, he is not particular; but, in return for the flattery—extracts from the purse the precious metal" (1866, 234). The author seems particularly concerned that, although women have plenty of warnings about them, they seem only too confident in the power of their own charms. As he notes, "They feel a power within themselves of altering the natural propensities of some men, and by an amiable, but fanciful weakness, conceive that love and affection on their part will cure the most abandoned and wicked from a course of degradation and vice" (252). The tendency of female consumers to buy into the legend of the exceptional woman who could transform a scoundrel into a prince made them perilously easy marks.

Yet the game wasn't restricted to male swindlers. The tale of Mrs. Cooper, reported in the London *Times* in 1860, remarks on her "Extraordinary Swindling." Using male avarice in her favor, she made one Mr. Taylor quite willing prey, informing him that she was a widow, with two children . . . and that she had lately received a communication from the Court of Chancery, informing her that she was heiress to an immense property in Scotland, and that a few preliminaries were necessary, which would cost a few hundred pounds, before she could take possession of her property. The trap was so well laid that the victim fell into it at once, offered her his hand and heart, telling her he had about 100l., which was at her disposal. (5 January 1860)

After the couple were married, the new Mrs. Taylor took her husband for all he was worth and more, disappearing only when his fortune was gone and she had him well in debt. Like the previous tales, this escapade in matrimonial deception lends an explicitly monetary valence to the concept of romantic investment.[13]

These chronicles of fraud are the stuff not only of broadsheets and court reports but also of the sensation fiction Sutherland and Fahnestock cite. Trading on the typical British fascination with birth, title, and estates, Miller and Taylor embodied the types of matrimonial swindlers who seduced their victims into marriages that were both expensive and false. Stories of this ilk—artfully rendered in Wilkie Collins's *The Woman in White*, for example— exposed the economic risks of romantic entanglements, even as the outrage they elicited seemed to deny the legitimacy of mercenary lovemaking. Given the popularity and the profusion of this line of narrative, however, it clearly raised important issues about delicate interpersonal negotiations in "real life." The figure of the matrimonial deceiver makes productively (and often comically) visible the intricate amalgam of material, emotional, social, and erotic desires inherent in contracting romantic alliances.

Of Desire and Fraud

Alongside those matrimonial schemers who sought to defraud their potential spouses of money and property, there were other kinds of plotters after other forms of plunder. In other words, the "goods" at stake were not solely economic. Various comic forms promoted the careful shopping that featured so prominently in the purchase of food because, in seeking to cash in on the game of matrimony, many men and women brought to the marriage market "goods" that were not so good as they seemed.[14] For example, in the poignant ballad "The Virgin Only 19 Years Old," the speaker marries after a quick courtship a "fair damsel, . . . [who] said she was a Virgin, yes a Virgin only 19 years old." On the wedding night, the "19 year-old" bride removes various bits of her body in a Swiftean striptease, to reveal a "Virgin not nineteen, . . . but 99 years old."

> When she wiped off her eye-brows I thought I should faint,
> And scraped from her thin cheeks a cart-load of paint;
> When she pulled off her black wig then her bald pate soon told,
> That she was an old Virgin, an old Virgin, more than 19 years old.

The ballad's comedy derives from its emphasis on the social and physical con-structions imbedded in courtship. The romantic desire to present one's best self takes on a more mercenary and sinister cast here, as the suitor becomes shopper/investor, duped by the good appearance of the wares he finds so seductive (rather like pots of green vegetables or a box of gorgeous lead-painted candy). The ballad makes its consumer analogy explicit in the pun on buying and selling in its final cautionary refrain:

> Now young men take warning ere to church you go,
> Be sure your Bride's perfect from the top to the toe,
> Or you'll pay for your folly, and like me be sold,
> By some patch'd up old bit o' stuff, cruel old Virgin, 'bout 99 years old.
> (JJC Street Ballads 20)

"Oh, Crikey! Oh, Good Gracious!" (1850) is a similar ballad in which a pretty maid dupes a young suitor. In this instance, Betty Giddy-goat neglects to inform her generous fiancé that she is already a married mother of half a dozen children. If the refrain, "love oft proves a grand mistake, / So never trust in women," is rather broad, the tale of the ballad is specific in its refer-ence to the Victorian market. The narrator's lament is less one of heartbreak than that he has spent his "tin" on Betty "in manner, most splendacious"; in other words, he has invested monetarily in a woman who reveals her true sta-tus to him only after he has "laid out all the blunt [he] had, / Which warn't a little ochre." Having invested badly, the suitors in these ballads sing out their cautions to their compatriots on the marriage market.

Ballads render efficiently and consisely the matrimonial stings that novels work out at length.[15] These, among many other examples that preceded the famous Yelverton case, offer a window into the lexicon of marital fraud and establish a tradition of reading marriage as a venture subject to emotional, erotic, and economic deceit. If tales of marital fraud multiplied in nov-els, melodramas, ballads, and newspaper accounts, in the wake of the 1857 Divorce laws, they did so as part of a well-established trajectory.

Meet the Yelvertons

The Yelverton case was complicated and compelling—complicated because both parties seemed to be plotters; compelling because the case so explicitly articulated the incursions of fraud on romantic life. Yet the story of their courtship was appealingly romantic: the couple met on a steamer crossing from Boulogne to London in 1852. The evening was chilly and the major offered to share his plaid with the pretty young woman. Thus warmed, the two sat on deck and talked all night. Although they then lost touch for nearly two years, the pair reestablished contact when he was serving in the Crimean War and she was a Sister of Mercy in Galata. Over the subsequent years, they carried on a passionate correspondence that became an infamous part of the trials: the letters were racy by Victorian standards, both coyly flirtatious and surprisingly blunt in their declarations of desire. The visits that Yelverton interspersed with his letters culminated in the first of the dubious wedding ceremonies, which occurred in Scotland in April 1857, seeimingly against Longworth's wishes. According to a record of the 1861 Dublin trial that made him famous, the major

> induced her [Longworth] to hear him read the marriage ceremony from a Church of England prayer book. . . . He told her that, by the law of Scotland, marriage by a priest was not necessary—that mutual consent and promises made persons man and wife—and, having read the marriage ceremony, he proposed that it should legitimise their position as husband and wife. . . . She refused to be bound by it, and fled from him. (*Yelverton Marriage Case* [1861], 10–11)

This first wedding, which potentially produced what was known as an "irregular marriage," posed for Longworth two significant problems, beyond those it later put to legal minds. First, because she was a Catholic, Longworth claimed that the absence of a Catholic priest made the ceremony inadequate for her to "legitimise their position as husband and wife"—Yelverton, in short, immediately sought consummation, which, she testified, motivated her quick flight from him. Her second problem derived from the absence of witnesses, a circumstance supposedly due to Yelverton's need to keep the marriage secret from his family. Although he had made his sexual attraction to Longworth quite clear, Yelverton told her "that he could not then marry, and he had given a promise to his relations not to marry any lady who could not pay his debts. . . . He said that about £3000 would be sufficient" (ibid., 16).[16] Because Yelverton was in line for the Barony of Avonmore, he was invested in maintaining happy relations with his family. Longworth was equally interested in establishing happy relations with his noble relatives, but she apparently had sufficient mistrust of his integrity to suspect the absence of witnesses to the Scottish ceremony—and popular etiquette books would have warned her to take care. *Routledge's Etiquette of Courtship and Matrimony*, for example, cautioned that, "A clandestine marriage should be the last resort, the more so, because in too many instances it is a fraud committed by an elder and more experienced party upon the inexperience of one whose confiding tenderness he should rather protect, even from himself" (1852, 34).[17] Because Longworth was sufficiently capable of protecting herself to know when to flee the scene, the terms of negotiation between the couple became overt: she brought to the table the potential for sexual gratification, an interest in aristocratic alliance, and a demand for legitimate union. He brought his (in this case, competing) desires for sex and money, and his potential to confer title and respectability. The Scottish rite, easily repudiated due to the absence of witnesses, was Yelverton's play for conjugal rights without firmly conjugating marriage.[18]

Longworth's departure seemed to win the contest: Yelverton consented to a second ceremony, which occurred at a small chapel near Rostrevor, Ireland. In August 1857, Father Bernard Mooney, a Catholic priest, consecrated the couple's previous marriage vows. Prior to the nuptials, Yelverton claimed to be something of a Catholic ("I am no Protestant," he said), which was necessary due to the still-operating provisions of the 1745 statute, which decreed that any marriage "between a Papist and any person who hath been or hath professed him or herself to be a Protestant at any time within twelve months before such celebration of marriage, or between two Protestants, if celebrated by a Popish priest, shall be and is hereby declared absolutely null and void to all intents and purposes."[19] Yelverton did manage to carry his stipulation of secrecy, however, so that if Longworth seemed to win the battle, Yelverton won the day. There were no witnesses and the ceremony was never entered in the parish register. Both parties agreed that they had sex regularly after this event, although the major suggested that intercourse had already been going on for some time.

From August 1857 until April 1858, all was felicitous.[20] The couple traveled together under the names "Mr. and Mrs. Yelverton." When they parted in Bordeaux in April, she was ill from a pregnancy that would never come to term; he had been called back to his unit in Scotland but promised to return as soon as he was able. But he didn't. Instead, he married Mrs. Forbes, a wealthy widow worth at least £3000.

As I note above, Longworth's various attempts to sue Yelverton for restitution of conjugal rights failed, but Thelwall's suit for debt did the trick, initiating the Irish trial, which was the only one of the various Longworth–Yelverton suits to involve a jury. It was by far the most colorful of the hearings. In Dublin, Yelverton testified before a packed courtroom that both the Scottish and the Irish marriage ceremonies were false, the first because it was never meant to be a marriage, the second for various causes, most famously that he was *not* really a Catholic and therefore could not legally be married by Father Mooney. Beyond what appeared in Ireland as irrefutable religious blackguardism, Yelverton was also scandalously unrepentant about cashing in on his conjugal rights during (and, he claimed, prior to) the period in which he performed as Longworth's husband. According to *The Yelverton Marriage Case*, an "Authentic and Unabridged Account" of the trial put out by the popular publisher George Vickers in 1861, "His purpose, he swore, was from the first dishonourable. He resolved to make the young, beautiful, and gifted orphan his mistress" (vi). The major further enhanced the case's sensational appeal by engaging the Irish hatred of the landholding class when he attempted to justify his deceptive behavior by noting that Longworth was not of "gentle blood." Thus class discrimination, in combination with his status as a fake Catholic, cemented Yelverton's role as a stage villain in what one pamphlet referred to as the "romantic drama, which has just been performed in Dublin" (*Full Report* 1861, v).

Given his triple transgression of religion, class, and virtue, Yelverton's chances before an Irish jury were not very good at all. In the end, Thelwall won his £259 17s. 3d. with relative ease, and Longworth won her vindication: she was declared to be Mrs. Yelverton. Her triumph was brief, however, for Yelverton appealed immediately. An Edinburgh court heard the appeal (significantly *without* a jury) and overturned the Dublin ruling, only to reverse those findings once again on Longworth's appeal in 1862. When, at Yelverton's behest, the House of Lords took up the case in 1864, they produced the final decision on the case, nullifying the Irish verdict and asking that the Scottish court overturn its earlier ruling in favor of Longworth (it did).[21] Longworth's appeal to the Lords in 1867 went nowhere and, in the end, she emerged a single woman. She made the best of it, largely by refusing to acknowledge the legitimacy of the court's decision: she kept Yelverton's title until her death and established a career as an author, writing a number of novels and travel narratives.

∽

∽

The Irish trial was easily the most popular moment in the long history of litigation between Longworth and Yelverton. That was in part because it came first, in part because it occurred before a jury, in part because of its sensational content, and in part because of the timeliness of its concerns. It received nearly daily coverage in both *The Times* and *The Manchester Guardian* throughout its duration from 21 February to 4 March 1861 and also spawned illustrated "complete coverage" accounts, ballads, cartoons, pamphlets, a play, and at least three explicitly derivative novels, including Longworth's own *Martyrs to Circumstance.*[22]

Until recently, however, scholarship on the case has focused exclusively on the conflicting marriage laws of England, Scotland, and Ireland that came to a head in the House of Lords hearing.[23] As I note above, any marriage between a Protestant and a Catholic performed by a Catholic priest was deemed invalid, although a Protestant minister could perform the same ceremony without penalty. In addition to providing an opportunity to modernize outdated anti-Catholic legislation (redressed in Ireland's Matrimonial Causes and Marriage Law Amendment Act in 1870), the Yelverton case also offered an opportunity to reconcile the divergent marriage laws of England, Ireland, and Scotland. The issue of the "irregular marriage" provoked considerable debate, so much so that the Chief Justice mocked George H. Pattison, "more than twenty-six years a member of the Scotch bar." During his testimony, Pattison laid out the provisions of marriage in Scotland:

What constitutes a regular marriage in Scotland? I am afraid I must begin by stating the general law, and the distinction betwixt regular and irregular marriages. Marriage is contracted in Scotland by interchange of mutual consent, freely, unequivocally, seriously, and deliberately given, with a genuine purpose of immediately becoming husband and wife, without reference to any further ceremony, and so expressed and evidenced as will be recognized by the law. When such consent is given after proclamation of banns and before a clergyman it is a regular marriage. . . . An irregular marriage may be contracted by mutual writings accepting each other as husband and wife, or mutual declarations and acknowledgements of marriage; or by a series of letters passing between them, which from their own contents, as well as from the mode in which the parties address each other and subscribe themselves, will create a clear and unequivocal recognition of a marriage. It may also be expressed by mutual declarations or acknowledgements before witnesses called in for the purpose, such declarations being serious, not casual or transitory. There is a third mode—

Chief Justice—I wonder you are not all married. (laughter)

Witness—I do not say it is a good law. I am merely stating what is the law. (*Full Report* 1861, 81)

Many shared the Chief Justice's sense that Scotch marriage law was a joke and had been for some time. Most British popular culture accords the Gretna Green marriage little more than a derisive nod toward legitimacy. Legislation enacted in 1856, prior to the Yelverton hearings, remedied the loose construction of Scotch marriages at least in part, by making a three-week residency in Scotland a legal prerequisite for legitimate Scotch marriage. As legal historians have shown, the Longworth–Yelverton suits raised important questions about the different countries' constructions of marriage.

Yet the Lords who sat in judgment over the Scotch and English hearings were considerably more concerned with the issue of competing jurisdictions than were the judge and jury who decided the outcome of the Irish trial, or the consumers of the popular media that interpreted their findings. However significant the idiosyncrasies of Commonwealth marriage law may have been, in other words, they fail to explain the case's enormous popular appeal. With the exception of Wilkie Collins's *Man and Wife*, published in 1870, the texts that responded to the Yelverton hearings barely addressed Great Britain's conflicting marriage laws at all. And yet, most historical readings of the public dimensions of the trials have argued that those conflicts were the source of the trial's social significance.[24]

Literary studies buck this trend, however. The aforementioned assessments by Jeanne Fahnestock and John Sutherland link the case to the narrative attractions of the bigamy plot.[25] More recently, Ellen Rosenman has argued that the case's popularity derived from Theresa Longworth's impressive faculties of narrative self-invention, which emerged in the private letters that the case made available to the public. In these letters and on the stand, Rosenman argues, "Longworth raided the stock of gender norms to fashion new and unconventional personas, finding subtle resources for sexual subjectivity and, in the end, a libidinal life beyond the heterosexual dyad" (2003, 125). Following on Rosenman's reading, I want to suggest that the case's engagement with the more general crisis of value and values in Victorian domestic life made it an unusually powerful and appealing story. "The Yelventon [*sic*] Case, or The Major in a Minor Key," for example, casts the Irish trial as a contest of costs and confidence:

His liberty he tried to keep,
As in the case it does appear,

To do a marriage *on the cheap,*
But its [*sic*] like to cost him dear.

. . .

But for the army's honour,
And to the Major's shame,
They look'd with credit on her,
And on him cast the blame. . . . (emphasis in original)

Playing with the language of credibility and credit, the balladeer celebrates the "cost" to Yelverton, which is situational rather than fiduciary (although Yelverton *would* have lost access to Mrs. Forbes's fortune if the verdict had held). In the complex moral economics behind a case that was ostensibly for debt, "to do a marriage *on the cheap*" means cheapening not only the bride but the act of matrimony too.

Casting the Yelvertons

Many popular renditions of the first Yelverton hearing struggled to cast Yelverton as a matrimonial charlatan and Longworth as his only-too-trusting dupe. For example, a verse from "The Lady Beat the Soldier" runs,

He was a Major, a Lord's son,
　　As evil as a monkey,
All the religion that he cared about,
　　Was who had got most money;
The fool was of no creed at all,
　　The Church of Rome defied a sad way,
He could swear a lie through a nine inch wall
　　And cover his nob with pipeclay. (Bodleian; Harding)

The line that accuses Yelverton of caring for no religion but money makes clear how popular authors linked financial avarice with the corruption of religious values (a sentiment one might expect in an Irish ballad). Further, though, the implication is that Yelverton defied the Church of Rome, defrauding Longworth, his ostensible wife, and, through her, the general value of marriage. The man who "could swear a lie through a nine inch wall" was a man whose passionate stories were socially dangerous.

　　It is profoundly tempting to read Yelverton as a consummate rake who went to great lengths to take advantage of a pretty young woman, especially when one reads the accounts of the Irish trial. Most renditions depict Yelverton as a villain whose game was a variation on male marriage-plotting in which the booty was "booty." Yelverton's open admission of his plan to seduce Longworth only makes him seem all the more the villain in a melodrama or mid-century novel in which she plays the injured maiden.[26] His testimony regarding a steamer trip in 1857, just prior to his departure for Leith Fort, certainly made it quite clear that he was no gentleman. His account famously caused the judge to insist that all ladies exit the courtroom, as the major detailed the steamy scene on the ship.

> Did any familiarities take place between you on that occasion?—Yes.
> What were they, and where?—Sitting on the raised poop of the vessel. I put my arm round her waist, and kissed her, and attempted to take further liberties with her.
> Chief Justice—Of what description?
> Witness—I attempted to take possession of her.
> Chief Justice—In other words you attempted her virtue?
> Witness—I did (after a pause), but I should explain that the attempt did not go to a very great extent.
> Chief Justice—Explain how far it went—...
> Chief Justice—If ladies wish to remain in court during this examination I cannot help them. [The ladies depart.] . . .
> The examination of the defendant was then resumed. He stated that whilst sitting on the poop of the steamer, with his hands round her waist, with the lady, he became very excited, and that she did also; he then described certain liberties which he said he took with her on that occasion, the details of which are unfit for publication. (*Yelverton Marriage Case* [1861], 71–72)

Much of the press attempted to turn the racy tone of this passage to the advantage of "the young, beautiful, and gifted orphan" by depicting Yelverton as a wealthy rascal who sought to tarnish the virtue of a good-as-gold motherless girl. For example, the infamy of Yelverton's testimony reached across the Atlantic, where *Harper's Weekly* portrayed him as a sensational rake:

> Thus says the defendant in his argument—"I have added hypocrisy and profanity to deception and profligacy. I am not bound to pay for the sustenance of this woman. I am not her wedded husband. I stand before you her profligate and heartless seducer. I found her young, I found her virtuous." What is she now, gentlemen? Innocence defiled, virtue lost, beauty spoiled,

and the hopes of life fled forever. Better the hand of death had swept her to an early grave. ("Great Yelverton Case" [1861], 5)

This narrative format followed the lead of Longworth's attorney, Mr. Whiteside, whose closing speech called on the jury to

> do justice to that injured woman. You cannot restore her to the husband she adored or to the happiness she enjoyed. You cannot give colour to that faded cheek, or lustre to that eye that has been dimmed by many a tear. You cannot relieve the sorrows of her bursting heart, but you may restore her to her place in society. You may, by your verdict, enable her to say—"Rash I have been, indiscreet I may have been through excess of my affection for you, but guilty never!" You may replace her in the rank which she would never disgrace—you may restore her to that society in which she is qualified to shine, and has ever adorned. To you I commit this great cause. (*Yelverton Marriage Case* [1861], 164)

For all the appeal of casting Longworth as the stereotypical wronged woman, the actual evidence in the case seriously compromised her status as the unsuspecting victim of a wily scammer. She had indeed been rash and indiscreet, and Yelverton furthermore accused her of being a sexually hungry social climber. Her scandalously amorous letters suggested a woman who was both erotically wide awake and quite canny about the game she was playing. In her letter of 22 July 1857, she writes, "'I scarcely dare believe I am going to see you again, and have *bon bons* given to me!! *Quel bonheur*. . . . You can't suppose for a moment I mean real ones? Your pockets are only figurative of course" (ibid., 106).[27] Furthermore, Longworth's subsequent use of the title Baroness of Avonmore, which she exploited until her death, made clear that she was hardly without guile. Sergeant Armstrong, Yelverton's council, named her "the most artful woman that ever captivated and enslaved a man who tried to flee from her. . . . Nothing would satisfy the ambition of this artful woman but the cornet of Avonmore," he continued. "Let us not be led astray by the artifices of as charming an actress as ever played on the stage of life" (*Full Report* 1861, 85). If Armstrong's superlatives perhaps exaggerate the case, he does seem to have some credibility in claiming that Longworth was no ingenue. Her letters to Yelverton depict a knowing woman whose desiring language and subsequent actions suggest that she, like the Major, was speculating on the powers of attraction to gain the satisfactions she wanted.

Her general tone in addressing Yelverton appears in her letter to him, following the episode on the ship: "This time last Saturday night, Carlo mio,

MAJOR YELVERTON'S FIRST THOUGHT OF DISHONOUR.

FIGURE 4.2
"Major Yelverton's First Thought of Dishonour." *Yelverton Marriage Case* (1861), 72.

was our *second* steamer scene. God grant the third not be far distant—and the consummation of all. . . . As I know the length, depth, and breadth of your wickedness now, you need have no fear of losing my good opinion—*comprenez vous?*" (*Yelverton Marriage Case* [1861], 72). Her frank longing for "the consummation of all"—to say nothing of her oblique comments about the "length, depth, and breadth" of Yelverton's "wickedness"—were hardly compatible with the role of wronged innocent.

Furthermore, the illustration that appears on the same page as this letter in the Vickers "Authentic and Unabridged Account" suggests a collaborative iniquity (see figure 4.2).[28] In the plate, a wily and mustachioed Yelverton regards a miniature Longworth who stands amongst the cordial glasses on a table set with candles. His full lips, tousled hair, and sly glance (need I note the cigar?) all cast him as the stereotypical seducer, especially in relation to the doll-like, hyperbolically diminutive Longworth. However, the illustration also suggests that the tiny woman is whispering into her seducer's ear, which is particularly problematic in light of the illustration's title: "Major Yelverton's

First Thought of Dishonour." On the stand, Yelverton claimed that the Irish wedding was merely a "conscience saving ceremony" which Longworth suggested herself, "something . . . to save her conscience, which should leave me free" (ibid., 91). Although Longworth vehemently contested the charge, Yelverton claimed that she knew there was no marriage, and that she simply wanted a more legitimate form to cover her desire for erotic experience. The posture of the demurely dressed, tiny woman conveys confidence in both its trusting and its dodgier denotations, neatly summing up the contradiction that Theresa Longworth seems to have been. The figure that emerges from the full testimony suggests that she gambled that the marriage would "take," or would at least hold up in a court of law.

When Yelverton averred that "this young lady was very well able to take care of herself"—a remark that drew hisses from the gallery—it seems fair for modern readers to concede him at least some credence (*Full Report* 1861, 62). In the Irish trial, however, Longworth's performance as defiled innocent clearly trumped the more complicated reality, despite the fact that that reality was visible even then. As Rosenman observes, "Longworth was obviously a dedicated reader of popular literature, patterning her fantasies and expectations on its conventions just as conservative commentators feared women would do" (2003, 130). Drawing on established novelistic conventions to shape her self-presentation at the Irish trial, her appearance on the stand was carefully stylized. She reveled in the dramatic circumstances of the case, playing her part in the box with such spirit, delicacy, and gentility as to easily win over her audience—among the more impressive moments was her swoon at first seeing Yelverton (*Full Report* 1861, 93). Popular reports of the case note her "exceedingly agreeable *personnel*" and that "She gave her evidence with a distinctness, an apparent absence of reservation, and with a dignity and candour that elicited the hearty sympathy, and very frequently the loud applause, of a densely crowded court" (*Yelverton Marriage Case* [1861], 18–19).

Longworth's performance on the stand did not receive universal acclaim, however. Some spectators registered her demeanor as too conscious, too theatrical. One such was Sergeant Armstrong, one of Yelverton's attorneys, whose distaste for his own client's actions and attitude did not prevent him from denouncing Longworth's shrewd self-presentation:[29]

> In his day, he had seen the greatest actors, Vestris amongst the rest, but Mrs. Yelverton was superior to any one he had ever seen. [The jury] should not imagine that the clever explanations given by the lady in the witness-box were impromptu. . . . She was the wooer and pursuer, and he the fleer. Was ever this net of artifice cast about a man with such consummate tact?

... Whatever might be thought of Major Yelverton's conduct towards this woman, he fearlessly contrasted his credit with hers on any matter of fact in the case. (*Full Report* 1861, 86–87)

In using theatrical metaphor to foreground the issue of artifice, Armstrong directly references the category of melodrama that so powerfully influenced how the respective players' accounts "played" in the Dublin courtroom. Melodrama was, among its various properties, a vehicle for addressing class conflict, expressing anxieties about money and power, and critiquing the imbalance of access to both. It was a genre explicitly concerned with aristocratic deception, financial misdealing, and interpersonal fraud.

The double-entendre within Armstrong's choice of words, "He fearlessly contrasted his credit with hers," emphasizes the economic underpinnings of the battle of credibility in the case. As Walter Bagehot remarked in "The Transferability of Capital,"

> a very great many of the strongest heads in England spend their minds on little else than on thinking whether other people will pay their debts. . . . The mind of a man like Mr. Chapman [one of the partners in the esteemed firm Overend, Gurney, and Co.], if it could be looked into, would be found to be a graduating machine marking in an instant the rises and falls of pecuniary likelihood. Each banker in his own neighbourhood is the same; he is a kind of "solvency meter," and lives by estimating rightly the "responsibility of parties," as he would call it. (1876, 72)

Obviously, not only the nation's strongest minds and local bankers were "solvency meters"; the process of "estimating rightly the 'responsibility of parties'" extended well beyond the workings of the savings and loan. Bagehot's conception of the banker as "solvency meter" applied equally to the work of the jury, and to the consumers of a popular culture whose project it was to learn how properly to accord authenticity (of anecdote, of letters, of rumor, of appearance). The Yelverton case, in its competition for narrative credibility, played within familiar generic fields with regard to class, corruption, and the difficulty of evaluating where one might safely bestow credit.

In the period during which the Yelverton trials took place, questions of individual value were peculiarly molded by gender, largely due to the gross inequity in population between men and women (to say nothing of the inequities of economic opportunity open to each gender) and the predicament that that inequity prompted for women in the British economic system. As Rosenman observes,

[Longworth's] abandonment would also have taken on public significance in the context of the female redundancy crisis, particularly acute in Ireland because of extensive male emigration and widespread poverty. . . . By the 1860s, the collision of ideology and demographics suggested that the patriarchal promise had been broken: it could no longer be claimed that middle-class women needed no economic power because men would always take care of them. What could symbolize this crisis more directly than Yelverton's refusal to take Longworth as a wife? The jury had the choice of siding with the forsaken middle-class woman or the callous aristocrat who had left her vulnerable and unprotected in order, it was said, to marry money. (2003, 146)

W. R. Greg's essay on female redundancy famously proposes voluntary transportation to Australia as a solution to the lack of suitors at home. It also, however, proposes a challenge to British women to maintain chastity, so that men will not just take sexual pleasure without paying for it with proper coin. "Few men," he writes, "would not purchase love, or the indulgences which are its coarse equivalents, by the surrender or the curtailment of nearly all other luxuries and shadows, if they could obtain them on no cheaper terms. In a word, few—comparatively very few—would not marry as soon as they could maintain a wife in any thing like decency or comfort, if only through marriage could they satisfy their cravings and gratify their passions" (1862, 162). Greg's argument lays at least some of the blame for the female redundancy crisis at the feet of women, especially of those loose gals who make it "perfectly feasible" for men to "satisfy their cravings and gratify their passions" without recourse to marriage. If only women would unify to force men to *marry* for sex, there would be plenty of proposals to go around, and no economic crisis for middle- and upper-class women.

Longworth's account of the case trembled most precariously because she seemed not to hold up her end of the Gregian deal. Her amorous letters, with their not even coy allusions to size, "*bon-bons*," and consummation threatened to unravel her image as wronged woman, and her credibility as a dupe. As Sergeant Armstrong asked the jury, "Did ever a woman fling herself into the arms of a man as the woman who in this case had been paraded before a crowded court as a paragon of purity and excellence? In the name of God, what could be expected upon any ordinary principle of human conduct, to be the result upon a young officer, receiving these suggestive, these burning letters?" (*Yelverton Marriage Case* [1861], 139). However, the most problematic letter to emerge in the Irish trial was not one that she had written, but rather one from Yelverton in which she had clearly altered his words.

The forged document Longworth presented at the trial contains the words "petting *sposa bella mia*," while the original seemed to refer to "some petting *possibilmente*" (ibid., 142). The two versions of "petting" neatly sum up the tension between wife and mistress, wherein the form Longworth presented as evidence renders "petting" as a gentle act bestowed on a respected spouse who appears as a beloved and beautiful treasure. The original words, however, allude to the heavier version of petting, in which the touch implied is more erotic than tender. Longworth's choice to tamper with the letter and present it as evidence in her favor ultimately helped the defense to portray her as a con in her own right, one who attempted to persuade a jury to award her a status she had never rightfully obtained. In the Scottish hearing, the Lord Ordinary observed

> that the pursuer's agents say that the words at the close of the letter were "Petting sposa bella mia"—most important words if they were really there. In point of fact, however, no such words were there originally. It is obvious from examination of the letter, and it is provided by the testimony of Professor Penny of Glasgow, that this letter has been tampered with, and altered in different ink. The original words were—"Some petting possibilmente." It is not proved by whom that alteration was made, but the letter is addressed to the pursuer; it was produced by the pursuer; and, in its altered state, it was founded on by the pursuer. (*Cases Decided* [1863], 110–11)

Although her falsification of the "petting" letter did not turn the Irish jury against Longworth, it did turn the tables in the implication of fraud, ultimately imputing to her as well as to him the scheming character of the swindler. In other words, the vision of Longworth that emerged in the subsequent trials—a less ladylike, more avaricious, and decidedly more designing character—was readily available at the Dublin trial to those who wished to see it.

As I note above, the illustrations for the Vickers account of that trial suggest that at least some interpreters were attending to the major's defamatory comments about Longworth. In this edition, Sgt. Armstrong's condemnations of her appear opposite an illustration entitled "Visions of Gentle-Blooded Life" (*Yelverton Marriage Case* [1861], 145) (see figure 4.3). The central panel depicts a well-appointed dining table at which a pretty woman watches a haughty gentleman examine the plate while an anxious serving steward looks on. The smaller surrounding scenes offer "visions," respectively, of a gentleman having his wig powdered, a couple visiting the theater, a duel, two bewigged heads, and the pretty young woman standing before a writing man.

FIGURE 4.3
"Visions of Gentle-Blooded Life." *Yelverton Marriage Case* (1861), 145.

Interestingly, the major's famous mustache decidedly does not adorn the face of the male protagonist in these scenes, suggesting either that this rendition of the major has undergone a radical shift in facial fashion, or that this male protagonist is not the major—that Longworth has, perhaps, neatly excised Yelverton in favor of a less hirsute swain once she has attained access to the society of Avonmore.[30] In any case, the apparently disposable reality of Yelverton's body within the illustration's romantic visions of aristocratic life suggests that Longworth's passion had as much to do with the man's ability to admit her to gentle society as with the man himself.

Gentle Blood

The cartoon's title references Yelverton's assertion that Longworth did not have "gentle blood." This statement was one of the most notorious aspects of the case and likely summoned up much of the melodramatic vocabulary in which it was popularized, but it also sought to estimate Longworth's credit by the value of her bodily contents. This component of his defense held that, because she was not of gentle lineage, the seduction did not merit much attention. The worth of what he had got by his false marriage vows (which he never contested) was not very much at all. Whiteside's interrogation pressed this point.

> Do you think the fact of a lady not having gentle blood makes the seduction better or worse: I do not think it makes any great difference.
>
> Does it make any in your opinion? Well, it does, a little. May I explain my reason.
>
> Certainly. Well, because the one has more to lose than the other (hisses).
>
> And that as regards the woman herself, makes the seduction better or worse—as the case might be as regards the woman's own feelings?
>
> As regards herself and her position. There is a greater loss of position in the one case than in the other. (*Full Report* 1861, 60)

The public reacted fiercely to Yelverton's logic that it was acceptable to defraud a middle-class woman of the twin jewels of her virginity and respectability. His testimony clashed with contemporary Victorian ideology about honor in both business and love, but it also raised larger questions: What made up gentility? What made a woman valuable? What was the merit of a wedding ceremony? Do vows have actual meaning, or are they subject to subsequent interpretation? And what should marriage be about, money or love? fiduciary security or honor?

Beyond his claims that Longworth was not wife material because she lacked gentle blood, the major's financial difficulties also defined a woman's worth by her economic assets; in contrast with Mrs. Forbes, Longworth fell short in her ability to pay Yelverton's debts. This mercenary attitude toward marriage received condemnation from a variety of sources, perhaps most notably J. R. O'Flanagan's novel *Gentle Blood; or, The Secret Marriage*, published just after the trial's end in 1861. O'Flanagan transforms Yelverton into Rodolphus Silverton, and does away with the acrimonious reality that marked the Yelvertons' relations after the Irish trial. Whereas Yelverton never acknowledged Longworth as his wife, and was eventually successful in having the Irish decision overturned, O'Flanagan's Silverton reunites with his Theresa (here dubbed Sybilla Longsword), whom he rewards with nuptial bliss and £15,000. Sybilla playfully reproaches him:

> "Though I have no GENTLE BLOOD, perhaps I have something, which, in the eyes of worldly-wise people, is better. You have got a fortune with your wife, Sir."
>
> "My wife is a fortune in herself," replied Rodolphus smiling.
>
> "Oh! of course; but a matter of fifteen thousand pounds won't make her less attractive, I suspect, Rodolpho mio." (380)

O'Flanagan's revision is surely meant to be instructive. With the logic that the novel as a genre invents, he grants Rodolphus an impressive fiscal reward for dispensing with his acquisitive perspectives on marriage. O'Flanagan changes the currency in which "fortune" may be estimated, so that Sybilla becomes "a fortune in herself," whose value cannot be measured in pounds. However, this heroine is unequivocally pure from the start, is firmly established as a gentlewoman (though not of family so high as Silverton's), and shows no inclination for litigation. O'Flanagan's romantic corrections to the inequities and nonformulaic components of the actual case, then, reinforce how the complicated reality forced a jury, various judges, and a diverse reading public to articulate in ways that were often uncomfortable with the values that comprised both marriage and gentility.

While some authors tried to establish Longworth's own noble lineage, most dismissed the validity of blood, opting instead to reinforce the system of moral values that more broadly dictated the ascendancy of the middle classes over the nobility.[31] Shifting the terms of gentility, they constructed a more accessible definition of worth that explicitly excluded Yelverton. The one-penny pamphlet *A Complete History of the Yelverton Family*, for example, begins with two quotations. The first is from Sir Thomas Overbury: "The man who has not anything to boast of but his illustrious ancestors, is like a potato—the only good belonging to him is under the ground." The second is by Bruce Burton: "True nobility is derived from virtue, not from birth. Titles, indeed, may be purchased; but *virtue* is the only coin that makes the bargain valid" (n.d., 3). The passage from Burton inverts the ratio of currencies within the major's discourse so that gentility derives its value not from historical lineage, but from present acts, reflecting the more general mindset of mid-Victorian readers. Weighed in *that* scale, the major comes up light, lacking the virtue capable of "mak[ing] a bargain valid." If "true nobility" in the 1860s derives from virtue, the major has little claim to his coronet.

Nonetheless, Yelverton's use of the term "gentle blood" accurately summed up Victorian hierarchies of both gender and class: some women's bodies *were* more valuable than others (as he remarked above: "one has more to lose [in seduction] than the other"). In constructing different systems of worth for different classes of women, Yelverton tapped into a central Victorian anxiety. Arguing that it was acceptable to seduce a woman of a lower class because she had less to lose was as good as suggesting that it was okay to defraud a poor investor on the same grounds. In a culture busily confronting fraud on mani-fold fronts, it would hardly do to argue that some women were fair targets of matrimonial swindling.

Arguing against Yelverton that all women were equally valuable and deserved equal treatment, not just legally but romantically, Longworth's sup-porters were able to construct a far more appealing vision. As the *Full Report* put it, "if 'gentle blood' does not flow through the veins of the lawful but ill-mated wife of the accomplished 'rue,' a purer quality courses through them, which she has shown in the moral principle which has always guided her conduct—that love of virtue which is the brightest jewel in the casket of woman's greatness" (*Full Report* 1861, vi). Suggesting more broadly that all women's "brightest jewels" deserved protection from Yelvertonian "rues," the major's adversaries argued for more general rights of protection.

Defending the honor of all women proved central to a larger project: defending the honor of marriage as an institution. Mr. Whiteside's closing remarks in Dublin elucidate the strategy and the stakes of this line of argu-ment.

No matter who or what this woman was—if instead of being, as she was when first she was met by this man, a young and attractive woman, and, as far as any evidence appears in the case, an honourable and a virtuous woman,—suppose that, instead of being all that, she were the commonest outcast of society,—suppose she had been the mistress of many, a common street-walker—yet, if a man will enter into a marriage with a woman of that description, there is not the least doubt that she is as much his wife as the purest and most virtuous woman that ever entered into such holy bonds. (*Yelverton Marriage Case* [1861], 167)

As I note above, Yelverton's most egregious act proved not so much his unrepentant seduction, but his defamation of the marriage contract. Whiteside's insistence that "there is not the least doubt" that any two people who enter into marriage are married, even the most extreme of social differences notwithstanding, seeks to reinforce the stability, reliability, and integrity of the marriage contract.

The Business of Marriage

The Yelverton case made visible how very vulnerable marriage was to deceit and trickery. Yelverton's own attorneys highlighted this issue, Sergeant Brewster arguing that

> Some parties looked upon marriage as a mere temporal contract, binding upon them nevertheless: others as a holy rite; whilst a third class considered it a most solemn sacrament. But no matter in which category a marriage was placed *in for conscientia,* it ought to be equally sacred in all. . . . The question the jury had to try was not whether the defendant's conduct was justifiable or not, but whether he had, in point of fact, contracted a valid or unvalid [sic] marriage, according to the law of the country. (*Full Report* 1861, 52)[32]

At the heart of this case, that is, was a fundamental question about what constituted "a valid or unvalid marriage." Given the culture of fraud in which the Irish case emerged—Armstrong bluntly conceded to the jury, "We live in a world where immorality is rampant, crime common, seduction, unhappily, too frequent"—it is little wonder that the jury, a packed courtroom of spectators, and an avid reading public chose to hold Yelverton to the arrangement he had contracted, despite the powerful counterarguments against Longworth (*Yelverton Marriage Case* [1861], 143–44).

The notion of a defrauded marriage was ultimately the most salient element of both the hearing and popular materials on it. A report published by the Penny Newsman's Office states bluntly that Yelverton "profaned the ceremony of marriage to make this woman his more confiding mistress" (*Newsman's* [1861], 3), while the poem opposite the frontispiece suggests that Yelverton has committed "Such an act / As blurs the grace and blush of modesty; / Makes virtue hypocrite; takes off the rose / From the fair forehead of an innocent love, / And sets a blister there: Making / Marriage vows as false as dicers' oaths" (5). Recalling through the specter of gambling the logic of marriage-as-lottery with which I began this chapter, the poem articulates the malleability of vows: vows may be false, and virtue hypocritical. Rather than constructing a simple opposition between vice and virtue, however, these lines suggest their potential overlap in the propensity of the vow to become an oath, and of a proposal to become mere profanity.

Cyrus Redding's *A Wife and Not a Wife*, an 1867 triple-decker based on the Yelverton case, carries the metaphor still further in narrating the story of the reprobate Captain O'Brien who courts the young and beautiful Mary Fitzwalter. Mary's mother is quickly suspicious of the captain and warns her daughter to beware his attentions. She is particularly worried that there will come a "moment when the female heart is given away, and the supposed exchange is on one side a pretence, or to use a vulgar but faithful term, a mere 'swindle'—a selfish game played by dishonesty upon the susceptibility of the female heart" (81). Mrs. Fitzwalter's perspective is another rendition of the advice given to investors, employers, and consumers: be on your guard, and be quite sure, before you give up your heart (or any other part of your body), that you are not buying into a con. To deduce properly is a tricky game that involves careful, methodical investigation beyond the level of appearances. Mary's mother instructs her daughter to "Remember that love-feigning and love-feeling are all, externally, the same. You have only the manners and mode of expression of your lover to guide you. Men continually address us under false pretenses, and the detection of such ill-doing is only facile with those of the sex who have been long familiar with society" (87). Mrs. Fitzwalter's worldly suspicions are confirmed when O'Brien pulls a Yelverton on Mary. The captain then attempts to reunite with his estranged and disowned wife after his version of Mrs. Forbes disposes of him, but Mary's father intercedes: "Captain O'Brien has failed, so I learn, in his new matrimonial speculation, for he has shown himself a speculator, I too much fear, because he was never otherwise" (238). The Fitzwalters decline to "invest" again in the dashing man whose capacities for "love-feigning" have already burnt them once. The novel's overt didacticism closes with a wiser, if sadder, Mary who has learned a few things about the market of love.

In the Dublin trial, Yelverton used the unwritten "law" of *caveat emptor* to argue that Longworth had refused to be on her guard against him, that she had ignored obvious signs of his impending betrayal. One of his attorneys told the jury that "[Longworth] had got from him as fair a warning as could be conceived, but did not take it" (*Full Report* 1861, 88). The judges that heard the original 1862 Edinburgh case also suggested that Longworth had plenty of notice to be wary in any form of exchange with Yelverton. The Lord Ordinary stated explicitly that Yelverton "has certainly given her no encouragement to expect marriage, but on the contrary has said enough to put her to some extent on her guard" (*Cases Decided* [1863], 96).[33] In particular, he mentions one of Yelverton's letters, which reads, "'[K]nowing I cannot gain on your terms, I will not try on mine.' Lord Ardmillian construes this to mean, 'I cannot marry you; I will not ruin you.' This construction he considers to be quite consistent with the defender's other letters, and particularly with many of the other warnings given to the pursuer" (ibid., 102). In summing up his findings that Longworth is not the major's lawful wife, Ardmillian writes decisively,

> For the conduct of the defender there can be no excuse. But he was not the seeker, the seducer, or the betrayer of the pursuer. The story of the pursuer,— her charms, her talent, her misfortune,—even the intense and persevering devotedness of the passion by which she was impelled,—must excite interest, pity, and sympathy. But she was no mere girl,—no simpleton,—no stranger to the ways of the world,—no victim to insidious arts. She was not deceived. She fell with her own consent. (ibid., 116)

In other words, the court went beyond invalidating the Scotch and Irish ceremonies; it also dwelt on the evidence that Longworth was complicit in the false marriages she contested.

When the Scottish board found in Longworth's favor on appeal, Yelverton petitioned for a hearing by the House of Lords, which took up the case in 1864. They focused on rudiments of matrimonial law by which they established once and for all that Yelverton and Longworth had not contracted marriage.[34] Ironically, Longworth's persistent contention that she did not give up "the goods" until after the Irish ceremony ultimately undermined her petition. The Lords determined that, because she did not consider the Scottish marriage valid *and* had not consummated that marriage in Scotland, she was not in fact married. The Irish blessing of vows did not constitute a marriage, and in the end Theresa's claim to the name of Yelverton was deemed null and void.[35] Despite her appeal, in which she spoke on her own behalf to the House of Lords in 1867, the findings stood and the Yelverton marriage case finally ended in 1868.[36]

All three of the courts focused on the sanctity of contracts, even though the English attention to the specific arrangements between Yelverton and Longworth trumped the earlier findings. Even the event in Dublin, though, raised the specter of the wronged contractee or investor, summoning up the wider context of fraud by which to interpret the case. Despite the fact that each subsequent hearing shifted the blame a bit further from Yelverton, the centrality of fraud to the case's cultural impact is unmistakable.

Lord Ardmillian's ruling in the Scottish trial makes clear that this case was not simply about bigamy, nor simply about resolving the diverse marriage laws of Great Britain. His comments on the Irish ceremony, which proved a particularly problematic event for all three jurisdictions that heard the case, suggest how much anxiety the contest between Longworth and Yelverton provoked about the authenticity of marriage vows and the value of marriage in general. Lord Ardmillian remarks especially about how grossly the Rostrevor ceremony compromised the marital contract.

> [T]he scene enacted in the chapel at Rostrevor, stripped though it be of all validity as constituting marriage . . . is a very serious and distressing incident in this case. . . . The pursuer and defender did, on that occasion, in the chapel, at the altar, and before the priest, distinctly and unequivocally, amid the most solemn attendant circumstances, declare in words that they mutually accepted each other as husband and wife. The defender's plea now is, and has been so put, that he did not intend to deceive, and that he actually did not deceive the pursuer; for that neither of them meant this proceeding to be really a marriage, or to be more than a device to satisfy her conscience. He says that the solemn words then uttered at the altar were intentionally untrue, and that the whole proceeding in the chapel was an empty form, and a mere mockery. It is sad that such a plea should be maintained, and should be required. It is still more sad that there is too much room for believing that the plea is well founded in fact. (*Cases Decided* [1863], 108)

Even in releasing Yelverton from his marital obligations, Lord Ardmillian relies on terms like "intentionally untrue," "empty form," and "mere mockery." Far from emphasizing the question of bigamy, and equally far from speaking the language of competing jurisdiction, he finds *both* parties culpable of defrauding the sacred institution of marriage. In this regard, it is all the more noteworthy that the challenge in the Irish trial was about financial responsibility. As the Vickers account remarks, "He married her in a way that she believed to be sacred and binding, and though, for his sake, she consented that it should be secret, she was conscious that it invested her with all the rights of a wife" (*Yelverton Marriage Case* [1861], vi). The desire to establish matrimony as a space of safe investment accords the case much of its pathos. In the end, Longworth v. Yelverton, in all of its many guises, proved a contest of values, an interrogation into which sorts of values merit legal protection, which merit punishment, and which fall beyond the provenance of the laws of a laissez-faire government. The English court in particular rued the actions of both the man and the woman they ultimately decided was *not* his wife.

It seems significant, in closing, that Ardmillian's language distinctly lacks the dramatic tenor of earlier accounts. When he deems it "sad" that this sham marriage should have taken place, he enters a different realm of representation, one that regards the range that fraud has achieved and finds in it, not outrage, but rather the lament of acceptance that is "sadness." The mid-Victorian period was an era in which fraud could no longer be deemed exceptional, in which the threshold to marriage proved as vulnerable to depredation as the threshold to the home. As Lord Ardmillian carries the growing popular cynicism about the world of finance into his pronouncements about romance, he reflects how powerfully the dynamics of fraud had touched the domestic life of Victorian England.

Conclusion

Child Rearing,
Time Bargains, and the
Modern Life of Fraud

———— ⌒ ————

I N CLOSING THIS BOOK, I turn to two pasts and two futures. The pasts
are those of the pages that precede this one and of the historical moment
those pages consider. The futures are the oddly domestic permutations of,
first, the Victorian futures market and second, the emergent forms of fraud
that continue to fascinate consumers of twentieth- and twenty-first-century
popular culture.

I have been arguing that fraud was a vital component of the Victorian
home, basic to its daily operations and to its contours in the imagination.
In reviewing influential legal contexts for imposture, domestic employment,
food, and marriage, I have sought to establish the complexities of duplicity
and of the diverse forms of capital that were at risk within even the most
secure household. Further, I have been suggesting various of the structures of
reading that popular culture offered for the consumption of its own goods.
Pleasure, danger, possessiveness, detection, play, and rueful detachment all
emerge as salient perspectives in Victorian texts, although they hardly exhaust
the possible modes by which Victorian subjects might engage the proximate
valences of risk. I return to the past to consider how, sometime around 1860,
Victorian mothers became responsible for the economic future of England.
I then turn from that past to its futures, in part to note the endurance of its
principles (the home produces the nation), and in part to remark how powerfully recent incarnations of swindling work to invest the con with a startlingly
cozy and *ethical* family life.

————— ⌒ —————

The future is almost inevitably a space of investment in which one may hedge one's bets, speculate with measured optimism, or venture full hope that the harvest will be good. It is also, as Lee Edelman has argued, "kid stuff" (2004, 1). Childrearing is a future-oriented pursuit, a sustained practice that engages with time both concretely, in the often rigorous schedules of children's daily activities, and speculatively, in the hopes that motivate those schedules—namely that the measured disbursement of hours and energy will equip the home's future adults with desirable sets of skills, attitudes, and ethics. The abstract temporality of investment emerges with particular clarity in a European television spot that won a Silver Lion award in Cannes in 2003. Originally produced in Belgium, the ad depicts a handsome young father shopping with his son in the supermarket. The child is young, perhaps six years old, but he is already very much his own person, at least in the consumer sense of things. Walking to a shelf, he selects a large bag of candy and, looking hopefully up at his father, places it amongst the leeks and celery and oranges in the cart. His father removes the bag and replaces it on the shelf. The child again picks up the bag, returns it determinedly to the cart, and crosses his arms, regarding his father impudently. The father only raises an eyebrow in response and undauntedly subtracts the bag of candy from his groceries. With a defiant gleam in his eye, the boy begins to scream. "I want those sweeties!" he insists in French, "I want those sweeties!" Running through the aisles, the child throws merchandise from the shelves, throws himself on the floor, and makes such a scene that the other customers look reprovingly at the father. The shot closes in on his exhausted face, as the tag-line for the ad appears below: "Use condoms."[1]

Not surprisingly, this commercial sets up a very different perspective on the future than one finds in Victorian England, but it nonetheless helps to define the terms of the argument I'll be advancing here. In the logic of the brand (Zazoo condoms), to spend in the present is to look forward to profits that accrue deductively, as both libidinal and economic savings in the future: with the wise purchase of condoms, there will be no need to buy big bags of candy, no need to engage with the personal costs of exhaustion or public humiliation. Depending on a logic of regret to promote an investment in the future, Zazoo advocates spending a little money now so as to circumvent a potential tomorrow characterized by shame in the supermarket and the unreasonable (and significantly commercial) demands of a child.

While Victorian popular materials were significantly less contraceptively oriented, the Zazoo ad's emphasis on quality of life factors into much mid-Victorian discourse about financial and reproductive futures. In fact, throughout the 1850s and 1860s, there was a marked spike in conversation about the risks involved in both fields and the urgency of policing them. Bringing together the language of economic futurism with the discourse of childrearing, various advisors urged and sometime pleaded with Victorian parents to consider England's future as they tended their tender crops. The rhetoric in childrearing manuals stands in radical contrast to the message of the condom ad: for the Victorians, the life to be protected was that of the nation, rather than the potential parent, and the savings that might ensue depended on properly dedicated (that is, unselfish) investments in raising up children who would have a similarly unselfish perspective. Mid-Victorian popular culture also regarded the child as a problem, but its vision of a profitable British future depended on properly managing these little crops, not on avoiding planting them in the first place.

The financial futures market also encouraged speculation on as yet unharvested crops. Futures in cotton, for example, were particularly popular and profoundly risky in the 1860s, when the American Civil War produced a cotton famine in England and prices went through the roof. Futures trading was already well established by then and had in fact been in place almost since the stock market was in its infancy. One of its most popular forms was the time bargain, a promise to buy stock at a specified price on a specified date.[2] As Stuart Banner observes, futures trading was largely virtual, in that "one did not need to transfer any stock, or indeed to own any stock, in order to speculate in the market. . . . Neither [party] even needs to be wealthy enough to buy any shares, because the most either could lose from the transaction is the difference in share prices between the two dates" (1998, 28–29).

Despite, or perhaps because of, its uniquely democratic access to speculation, the futures market was riddled with fraud—as Banner notes, "Stock jobbers soon discovered [that] the price of stock was much more easily manipulated than the price of anything previously known" (30). It was remarkably simple to drive prices up or down by forming consortia of speculators who would either puff worthless shares, or buy or sell large numbers of them, in order to skew the stock price for the moment of settling. Apparently the state of affairs was quite bad quite early, for in 1734 Parliament passed Sir John Barnard's Act, which prohibited trade of stocks that a person did not already own; forbade contracts for trading stock in any time other than the present; and finally, refused to protect, and indeed imposed fines on, those who violated these prohibitions.

The Act was ambitious, but not entirely effective. Futures trading continued but gained the reputation of being the riskiest field for speculation. Over a hundred years later, John Francis's *Chronicles and Characters of the Stock Exchange* warned readers away from the market and the jobbers who ran it. "The great mass of their transactions are without the pale of the law," he cautioned. "All their time-bargains . . . are illegal. . . . The tricks which are resorted to are numerous. . . . The public cannot be too decidedly warned against the dangers to which they may be exposed [even] in legitimate transactions (1850, 329–30).[3] Despite the continued relevance of such warnings, Parliament repealed Barnard's Act in 1860, and futures trading ceased to be illegal. In some senses, the repeal functioned as a kind of surrender to the existence of fraud—which is not to say that fraud became acceptable in 1860, but rather that it was sufficiently commonplace to be set aside in favor of the practicalities of the modern exchange. The rollercoaster of price indexes and price fixing that characterized the 1860s futures markets—most notably in cotton but in myriad other commodities as well—reminded the public of the dangers involved in futures investing, and of the continued presence of sharp characters in what was now a legitimate field of exchange.

Speculation, Hope, and the Future

As I have been arguing throughout this book, speculation involved more intimate forms of capital than just money, and angled at profits that were social as well as economic. Dreams of the good life generally took shape against happy domestic backdrops, in which perfect families might caper among perfect furnishings with perfect upholstery. Varieties of perfection were individual, of course, but these fantasies were key elements of both economic and libidinal investing. Such dreams, however, were not always so wise, and Victorian popular culture worked to reinforce that point. In Richard Redgrave's "Waking Dreams," for example, the pretty maid's reverie, coupled with her complete inattention to the eggs at her feet, suggests how irresponsible and self-centered flights of fancy might muddle one's focus on the present, and hence, make a mess of one's future (see figure C.1).

The young woman's desire for upward mobility appears in both the direction of her gaze and her overly pretty attire, the latter contrasting explicitly with the humble condition of her surroundings (note the spider web and the visible shovel and broom). The broken eggs resonate with the notion of smash suggested by the handbill for the lottery on the wall behind her, and suggest too that the engraving offers a double message about wasted assets. To read the broken eggs within the context of reproduction is, admittedly, something of a stretch, but her languid, open posture suggests a susceptibility to seduction that portends a potentially tragic childbearing future, reminiscent of the fate of Hetty Sorrell in George Eliot's *Adam Bede*. It is, I think, fair to say that

FIGURE C.1
Charles Heath, etching after Richard Redgrave, "Waking Dreams."

those eggs dictate the viewer's perspective on the young woman's dreams, by suggesting her inattention to the impact of her present actions on the profits or losses of her future.

In contrast, I'll offer another image, Arthur Boyd Hilton's 1862 woodcut for the monthly magazine *Good Words*. Entitled "My Treasure," the tableau signals a more appropriate system of feminine investing (see figure C.2). The treasure in this image is not suspended, virtual, or unlikely; rather, it is very much present, filling the lap of the pretty young mother. These are expensive children, if their grasping hands tell true; but, the title suggests, they are decidedly valuable. That value, of course, is affective, rather than monetary—the young mother is not planning to sell her children. Their worth is an abstraction of "treasure" rather than a specific figure in pounds and pence.

Our own culture, too, generally thinks of children as expensive little creatures, rather than as means of accruing economic profit. We are in that way indebted to the nineteenth century's various movements to reframe the child in the popular imagination. The Victorian period witnessed the birth of an imperative to cease thinking of children as so much working capital and to

FIGURE C.2
Arthur Boyd Hilton, "My Treasure." *Good Words* 3 (1862).

conceive of them instead as investments in, and beneficiaries of, the nation's future. Child labor laws and education bills recontextualized the economics of and investments in childbearing, anticipating Lee Edelman's theory of "reproductive futurism," which locates the Child as the embodiment of the expectant logic on which Western capitalist society depends, and by which it reproduces both its structures and its subjects. Sustaining and rationalizing the suffering of the present with the promise of a better future, the Child, Edelman argues, "remains the perpetual horizon of every acknowledged politics, the fantasmatic beneficiary of every political intervention" (2004, 3). The political potential behind the implicit nihilism of Edelman's theories merit more and different discussion than my work in this chapter allows.[4] Here, I draw far too briefly on his notion of reproductive futurism to articulate how Victorian market anxieties found their way into the discourse of childrearing. The title of Edelman's current project, *Bad Education*, allows me to begin that work.

Bad Education

As Susan Zieger notes in her reading of *Nicholas Nickleby*, "a child can only signify as a desirable commodity when it becomes expensive" (2006, 12).[5] There were monetary expenses to Victorian childrearing, of course, but it more crucially involved investments of time and energy in the interests of producing a desirable product. As Edelman's work would suggest, that product might better be termed a subject or, within Victorian discourse, a pupil. Surprisingly, then, sources such as *Eccles Household Guides*, popular in the 1870s, figure children as stocks, and their education a form of futures trading in which present costs are sustainable because they promise deferred profits: "No time, expense, or zealous care is too great to bestow on the culture and correct training of our children. There is no office higher than that of a teacher of youth, as there is nothing on earth so precious as the mind, soul, and character of a child" (1877).[6] That child was to be profitable not in and of himself, but as part of a larger community: the nation. However, investments in children could prove rather a bad bargain. *Nicholas Nickleby* nicely illustrates the rationale behind this logic: in the sadistic passages of Dotheboys Hall, the boys are supposed to receive education; instead, the Squeers family abuses them, starves them of both food and information, and forces them to work. As Zieger notes, these boys present an ominous glimpse at a blasted and potentially violent future. In a moment of odd agriculture, late in the novel, Ralph Nickleby passes a burial ground: it is "a rank, unwholesome, rotten spot, where the very grass and weeds seemed, in their frowsy growth, to tell that they had sprung from paupers' bodies [who] lay thick and close—corrupting in body as they had in mind; a dense and squalid crowd" (750). The weeds that symbolize the harvest of a neglected pauper class correspond with a thornier plant in the novel, namely little Wackford Squeers, son of the one-eyed schoolmaster who runs Dotheboys Hall. Explaining why he has hired Nicholas Nickleby as an assistant, Wackford Sr. contends that he needs a second, a "man under him . . . till such a time as little Wackford is able to take charge of the school."

> "Am I to take care of the school when I grow up a man, father?" said Wackford junior, suspending, in the excess of his delight, a vicious kick, which he was administering to his sister.
>
> "You are, my son," replied Mr. Squeers, in a sentimental voice.
>
> "Oh my eye, won't I give it to the boys!" exclaimed the interesting child, grasping his father's cane. "Oh, father, won't I make 'em squeak again!"
>
> It was a proud moment in Mr Squeers's life to witness that burst of

enthusiasm in his young child's mind, and to see in it a foreshadowing of his future eminence. He pressed a penny into his hand, and gave vent to his feelings . . . in a shout of approving laughter. (108)

The penny pressed into little Wackford's fleshy hand echoes the irony of impression on which this passage depends: Squeers has impressed his values on his son, who is well prepared to take in hand both paternal economy and paternal cane. Squeers's pleasure derives from a sense of profit in his child, whose vicious avarice confirms that Squeers has raised him right—for the business of Dotheboys Hall, in any case.

The lesson of the Squeers patrimony suggests that children will learn all too well the lessons of their youth. Those lessons impinge not only on the future happiness of the family, but on the economic future of the nation. As *The Training of Young Children* suggests, "The habit of pilfering any thing, however slight, blunts the sense of honour, and leads to fraud and dishonesty. These are solemn reflections, and should lead you to see how important it is to sow the good seed early, and not to make excuse that you have not sufficient time for these things" (1863, 32). The necessity to invest in children, to see them as the nation's future harvest, suggests how maternal education was increasingly responsible for nipping bad economic traits in the bud. In 1844, Sarah Ellis wrote to the women of England: "You have deep responsibilities; you have urgent claims; a nation's moral worth is in your keeping" (1844, 18). In 1872, Mrs. Henry Wood's *Our Children* reiterated Ellis's message with renewed urgency, suggesting that England's future was in peril. Wood argues that the parent who will "wink at . . . the slight moving of a ball on the croquet lawn into a more advantageous position for its owner, or the sly peep at a companion's card, or the dexterous abstraction of a counter from the heap of a next neighbour" will reap an unhappy harvest for the country. "From whence," she asks, "come the clever forgers, the sharp practitioners, the unscrupulous speculators, the men and women who borrow without the intention of paying again? . . . Are they not . . . the fruit ripened from seed which has been for long years slowly but surely growing out of those small acts of dishonesty in the little child?" (135). Redefining the meaning of profit by encouraging parents to invest responsibly in a vision of responsible future traders, these works argue that both fraud and its prevention begin at home.

Thus for Wood, and for many of the manuals alongside which her book appeared, sound parental investment, in contrast to foolish speculation or benign neglect, offers a prophylactic approach to the perils of futures trading. Good education was a necessary preventative to the kinds of bad education that might produce little schoolboys like Wackford Jr.; or big business boys like Nick Leeson, whose duplicitous futures trading brought down Baring's Bank in 1995; or Jeffrey Skilling, whose inventive mark-to-market accounting allowed the Texas energy company Enron to count expected future profits as present assets throughout the 1990s. Obviously, a moral education was not adequate to counteract the lures of a capitalist society that increasingly measured value by the capacity to purchase consumer goods. The options market and the fraud that characterized it became the wave of the future, while the bad education of profiting by others' losses brought about the harvest we're still reaping today. In the shadow of Enron, in the company of bad children in supermarkets, the only truly safe investment in the future of nineteenth-century markets may have been latex after all.

Reading the Present

While writing this book, I have been living simultaneously in nineteenth-century Britain and twenty-first-century America. The recent scandals involving Enron and Martha Stewart suggest the enduring relevance of the paradigm I've been modeling in the preceding pages: it is significant that, as the biggest corporate swindle in recent years unfolded, both the government and the popular media turned their attention to the specter of a fallen domestic angel. Throughout the 1990s, Martha Stewart built an empire as a modern Mrs. Beeton. A successful television show, an international magazine, and product lines that included cookware, linens, and fresh flowers all helped to consolidate Stewart's reputation as America's reigning homemaking queen. However, when Stewart was indicted in 2003 on charges of obstruction of justice, conspiracy, making false statements and securities fraud, she toppled from her pedestal. By 2004, she had become the new poster child for corporate fraud.

The charges of economic malfeasance resulted from Stewart's sale of ImClone stock on December 27, 2001, one day before its value plummeted when its cancer drug, Erbitux, failed to obtain regulator approval. By selling on December 27, instead of the December 28, Stewart saved just over $50,000. ImClone CEO, Sam Waksal, also sold large quantities of ImClone stock on December 27. His broker, Peter Bacanovic, was Stewart's broker as well. Questioned by authorities, Stewart adamantly denied having received a tip, but when Bacanovic's assistant admitted to telling Stewart to sell, the indictments followed.

But, as Diane Brady reported in *Business Week,* "The trial of Martha Stewart was always about more than telling the truth" (2004). In the wake of the Enron scandal, Brady felt it necessary to remind her readers that Stewart's case "was no Enron, laying waste to billions of dollars of shareholder value. Martha Stewart didn't cook the books. She didn't loot her company. Nor did she set out to dupe her investors." Nonetheless, Stewart emerged as the most celebrated fraud of all—and this despite the fact that the securities-fraud charge against her was dropped.

The Enron debacle entered the public eye in late 2001, when the company's creative accounting practices finally failed to cover the fact that it was bankrupt. Although the Justice Department announced a criminal investigation in early 2002, it handed down no indictments of Enron's chief executives until early 2004. In the meantime, the Department indicted Martha Stewart. Martha's story was simpler, more homey, than the mess of Enron. As *The Guardian* reported, Stewart's own lawyers "asked if the justice department was attempting to deflect public attention from its failure to bring charges against senior executives of the firms involved in the most calamitous scandals of last year: Enron and WorldCom" (Teather 2003). Although Justice vehemently denied the allegation that they were attempting to distract the public, many media commentators opined otherwise.

I'm not a Martha defender, nor was I ever a member of Save Martha, but I watched with fascination as she took the hit for Enron, both publicly and legally. And I was hardly alone. The world responded with alternate horror, indignation, and delight as the domestic goddess, who seemed always to have a hot-glue gun at the ready, fell from grace. As Enron shareholders reeled from their losses, the public found Martha Stewart on the cover of every magazine and in the coverage of innumerable television programs. Enron was, it seems, too complicated, too terrible for popular engagement. Martha offered the opportunity to domesticate economic dishonesty, to take the frightening and confounding questions of fraud home for private consumption. Her sentence echoed that impulse, beginning with six months in a minimum-security prison, and concluding with a return to the domestic space on which she founded her empire. The specter of her house arrest was deliciously ironic.

I find an irony closer to my own work in the remarks U.S. Attorney James Comey offered at the press conference following her indictment. "This criminal case is about lying," he said, "lying to the FBI, lying to the SEC, and lying to investors. . . . It's a tragedy that could have been prevented if these two people [Stewart and her broker, Peter Bacanovic] had done—only done what parents have taught their children for eons. Even if you're in a tight spot, lying is not the way out" ("U.S. Attorney Makes Statement" [2003]).

Turning from the chaos of the stock market to the straightforward logic of childrearing, Comey implied that at least some responsibility for the corrupt state of modern economic practices lies with parents. In seeking answers to the densely complicated questions of commerce, it seems that, even now, there's no place like home.

The home is a space of cultivation and imagination in which one inevitably encounters the conflicts of the outer world. In my own home, in 2007, in the final stages of writing this book, I've been indulging myself by watching two recent television series about fraud: the BBC-produced *Hustle* and FX's *The Riches*.[7] Both the British and the American shows give swindling a domestic life. *The Riches* does so most obviously, in that it is about a literal family of cons who take illicit possession of a deceased wealthy couple's home and property. The British actors Eddie Izzard and Minnie Driver play the American Wayne and Dahlia Molloy, parents of Cael, Di Di and Sam. Together, they are a family of "travelers," or grifters, who at the season's start have been surviving on picking pockets and running short cons (in the pilot episode, the family crashes a high school reunion, stealing name tags and wallets in a dizzying spree of impersonation and theft). When first we meet the Molloys, they are part of a much larger band of "travelers," an extended family unit whose speech, style, and RV-living habits mark them out as stereotypical redneck trash. By the end of the pilot, however, the Molloys have stolen the "family" money and fled the "family" camp. When another pair of "travelers" pursues them in a high-speed chase, the result is the car accident that kills Doug and Cherien Rich, a wealthy couple on their way to a new million-dollar home in a new gated community. The Molloys take their keys, their papers, their laptops, and their identities, thereby grifting their way into the American dream. The show encourages its audience to side with the Molloys, not against them, cueing viewers to celebrate even as the family fleeces "buffers," or regular folk—folk like most of us. Illegitimately seizing the lifestyle to which many Americans aspire, the Molloys become con artists we learn to love.

It's easy to root for the Molloys, though, especially because the writers grant them far more ethical probity than their marks. Wayne and Dahlia are considerably more appealing than both the sleazy millionaires whose lives they assume, and the almost universally obnoxious wealthy characters that surround them. In one episode entitled "X Spots the Mark," for example, "Doug's" reprehensible boss insists that he bring in a wealthy investor or lose his job. "C'mon family, lots of easy marks around," Wayne cajoles, as he, Dahlia, and their children pore over recent newspapers in search of a likely dupe. Son Cael sums up the qualities of the ideal mark: "They can't know us, they can't be too smart, and they've got to be greedy as shit." The Molloys' eventual target compounds the moral reprobation of greed with statutory rape. A washed-out baseball player, Rudy Blue, has just finished doing time for seducing an underage girl when the Molloys seduce him, in turn, into an elaborate long con involving insider information, extortion, and the illegal development of environmentally protected land. Given that Rudy finds none of these ethical obstacles sufficient to offset the promise of exorbitant investor profits, it's hard to have much sympathy for him as the Molloy family (in concert with the residents of a local trailer park) stage a dramatic investors' meeting that ends in a fake murder. As Rudy flees the scene, leaving behind a supposedly dead supposed FBI agent (actually, the Riches' pool guy) and half a million dollars, the Molloys celebrate only briefly, as does the audience. Going directly into "Doug's" boss's coffers, the money *does* support a corrupt real-estate firm, which *does* build illegally on environmentally protected land, so that the swindle itself does little to advance the moral high ground. In effect, it allows the Molloys only to sustain their imposture, not to abandon it. At the close of the episode, Wayne and Dahlia discuss the scam as they make love. "Next time, we should keep the money," he says, musing. "I wouldn't have to pretend to be a lawyer." Dahlia's response sums up both the pleasures inherent in watching *The Riches* and various of the reasons it has less pleasure than it might. "Well," she says, "you got a job. I got a job. The kids are in school. We live here now." The Molloys have, in effect, become The Riches, and while the audience has learned to prefer the impostors to the originals, the Molloys have nonetheless acquired the domestic and professional headaches (household budgets and unpleasant dinner parties, job anxieties and unpleasant social obligations) that mark the daily lives of many modern Americans. In *The Riches*, after the fun of watching the cons infiltrate the gated community, the lines of impersonation begin to blur. "We're buffers now, baby," Dahlia says, and in that, the Riches are a little too close to home ("X Spots the Mark" [2007]).

The alternative family of *Hustle* has more style and fewer familiar threats than *The Riches*, in part because the writer, Tony Jordan, elected to leave domestic life off the screen. Inspired by old-school films like *The Sting* and newer heist movies like *Ocean's Eleven,* Jordan also did his homework, reading stacks of books on the art of the con. Fascinated by "the way that the knowledge of the long con had been passed through generations," Jordan elected to create a metaphorical grandfather, father, and son, so as to convey "this sense of someone passing it on to someone, passing it one to someone" (Jordan 2004). Early on, he says, he knew that he didn't want . . . to see any of their domestic lives. I didn't want to see where they li—it was all going to be hotels and all about, you know, cool. . . . So I didn't want to go and suddenly see 'em pull off this great long con, and then going home and cook an egg and chips. It just wasn't going to work. So then I thought, well, I'm going to have to replace that with something . . . [and] I realized that basically what I was doing was constructing a family. (ibid.)

Hustle's family isn't the couple with three kids who've moved in down the block. They are adults, and there's no blood between them. Beautiful and stylish, the show's characters, sets, and fashions are almost unrelentingly sleek. That shiny veneer not only works to cover over the games they play; it also belies the profound moral dedication they have to one another and to those for whom they care (one episode in the first season involves a major grift so as to help a fellow con artist who requires medical care). Behind the glamour and the dazzling sleights of hand, that is, *Hustle* offers some old-fashioned family values.

More broadly, *Hustle*'s agenda addresses directly the issues of personal and corporate greed that were so familiar to the Victorian public. There is a strict ethical code behind their choice of marks. "You see," the cast repeatedly reminds the audience, breaking the frame so as to create the connection and identification essential to the show's success, "The first rule of the con is, you can't cheat an honest man. It's never been done." One week, they scam a greedy government minister. In another episode, they take down a pair of corrupt investment bankers. As the executive producer, Simon Crawford Collins, remarks, "Our characters are not in the business of tricking defenceless old grannies out of their life-savings. Indeed when they learn they might have made an error of judgement—they are mortified and swift to take action to put the natural order back to rights. The 'marks' they target are given their just comeuppance" ("Producing *Hustle*" 2007). Expert acting, clever scripts, and slick cinematography together have made *Hustle*'s unusual "family" welcome in millions of British living rooms each week.[8]

These modern progeny of the Victorian domestic fraud plot transform the swindlers into families—families that many viewers might think they'd like to have to dinner. Yet, twenty-first-century consumers are generally a cagey bunch—and no wonder. We live in a world in which only the spam filter stands between us and the daily barrage of emails soliciting the unwary into more and less elaborate cons. Nor do recent events on the national stage do much to inspire confidence. Since I began my research, the Enron boys have been convicted, but Ken Lay died before going to prison and before handing over the Enron cash, which estate laws safely secured to his family.[9] Paul Wolfowitz has been forced out of the World Bank, Attorney General Alberto Gonzalez seems to have no memory of how "mistakes were made," and many of my compatriots share with me a distinct suspicion about the electoral process. As these names become history, I have little doubt that others will replace them, bringing fresh scandals to the international stage.

On the one hand, modern audiences can share with their nineteenth-century predecessors the pleasures of fraud safely packaged for entertainment, welcoming the opportunity to process virtually the events and circumstances that comprise the modern landscape. Yet, fraud is now so ubiquitous as to be de rigeur, and it is significant that the swindlers of *The Riches*, *Hustle*, and the latest *Ocean's* film encourage affiliation rather than rejection. Various Victorian authors (Wilkie Collins and Charles Dickens, in particular) had already begun to experiment with domesticating their con artists, making pets or, in rare cases, heroes of them.[10] The resulting serials, from Collins's *No Name* to *The Riches*, from *Our Mutual Friend* to *Hustle*, consistently remind their audiences that swindling permeates modern life, but they also complicate their basic premise that there's a sucker born every minute by underscoring the fierce loyalty among their family units. This new breed of popular swindlers promotes not only honor among thieves but also—ironically—a rare sense of secular faith.

And on that note I conclude. Throughout this book, I have been mulling the relationship between real events and popular representations. I have collected thousands of Victorian ballads, tales, melodramas, novels, illustrations, and legal records, all of which declare openly the enormous potential for fraud in the world. More recent forms address a world even more pandemically corrupt than its nineteenth-century counterpart. Yet, while suspicion offers at least a chance to avoid bad surprises, unrelenting vigilance seems not to be a particularly appealing psychological perspective. Thus, where earlier Victorian texts about swindling allowed their readers to practice accommodating themselves to risk, more modern domestic fraud plots offer something more. Rather than simply reiterating and reinforcing the values of wariness, they offer the rare, surprising, valuable capacity to practice trust.

Notes

———⌘———

Introduction

1. See the testimony of Josiah Wilkinson, of the firm Wilkinson, Gurney, and Stevens, at the inquest:

> The security he [Sadleir] lodged with me purported to be a deed given on the purchase of an estate in the Encumbered Estates Court. It was signed by two of the commissioners of the court and by two attesting witnesses in two different parts of the deed, and not a single signature was genuine. (Sensation.) It had a genuine seal of the Encumbered Estates Court attached to it, and the commissioners themselves admit the seal to be genuine. That seal might have been transferred from some other genuine deed to the spurious one, because the seal of the court is not impressed on the document or in wax, but on a large wafer, and attached to it. ("Adjourned Inquest" 1856)

2. In "Impressions of Theophrastus Such," George Eliot uses the benchmark of familial pity to evaluate a young lady's response to Sir Gavial Mantrap, a fraud who has been found out. When Melissa expresses her pity for Mantrap, Eliot's narrator responds,

> I should have thought you would rather be sorry for Mantrap's victims—the widows, spinsters, and hard-working fathers, whom his unscrupulous haste to make himself rich has cheated of all their savings, while he is eating well, lying softly, and after impudently justifying himself before the public, is perhaps joining in the General Confession with a sense that he is an acceptable object in the sight of God, though decent men refuse to meet him. (Eliot 1887, 386–87)

———⌘———

3. For a concise discussion of recent scholarship on separate spheres, see Levine 2006.

4. "In lived experience the norms and values of domesticity and privacy were found to be capable of obstructing one another" (McKeon 2005, xxi). As McKeon has recently, exhaustively, and brilliantly demonstrated, to argue that the separate spheres were not so separate is not to deny the historical division of knowledge, but rather to reinforce it: the very capacity to recognize the public in the private is to depend on definitions of public and private "as such." Leila Silvana May is presently at work on a project about the dangers of dismissing the power of separate-spheres ideology, even as we recognize its limited correlation with the actual functioning of Victorian households.

5. Until relatively recently, Ruskin's formulation was critical gospel. Fundamental to a wide swath of second-wave feminist criticism, the doctrine of separate spheres provided a foundation for critiquing various gendered inequities (wages, political rights, career opportunities, sexual freedoms and protections, and so on). However, as third-wave feminism substantially complicated too-easy generalizations of such categories as "woman" and "man," the rise of cultural criticism called attention to the too-easy distinction between spheres. Among the most influential of the many works that disassembled the commonplaces of separate spheres ideology are Mary Poovey's *Uneven Developments* (1998), Nancy Armstrong's *Desire and Domestic Fiction* (1987), Jeff Nunokawa's *The Afterlife of Property* (1994), and Catherine Gallagher's *The Industrial Reformation of English Fiction* (1980).

6. The Stowe papers at the Huntington Library include the accounts of the Duke of Buckingham and Chandos during and just prior to 1848, when the duke's estates were dissolved for debt. He accrued many of the massive bills he was ultimately unable to pay during a visit from Queen Victoria in 1846. His extravagances during that period were so great as to ruin him. The duke's interest in keeping up appearances was hardly an anomaly confined to the ruling classes, however; as Spencer's remarks indicate, the issue of domestic debt was pressing for the middle classes as well.

7. Robert Nichol, the surgeon who performed the postmortem on Sadleir's corpse, wrote to the *Times* declining to "occupy your valuable space by replying to the various other arguments by [those] … who believe that John Sadleir's very suicide was a swindle and that his last public act was a forgery of the hand of death itself. I believe in no instance has the identification of a body been more complete" (18 June 1856).

8. Catherine Gallagher's recent work (2006) on the relationship between "bioeconomic plots," which focus on circulation, and "somaeconomic plots," which focus on the ratio between pleasure and pain, brings narratives of political economy into conversation with popular Victorian fiction.

9. Page numbers refer to the two-volume New York edition; a three-volume London edition appeared in the same year.

10. Feminist sociologists use the category of "emotional capital" to address some of the gendered omissions in Bourdieu's schemata, wherein women appear more frequently as objects than agents of exchange. While, as Diane Reay observes, "Bourdieu himself never mentions emotional capital," it is basic to his contention that the family is the primary medium of cultural reproduction (2004, 57). Most of this scholarship concentrates on the emotional labor of mothers and has little to say about the affective investment of romantic love that so dominates the field of popular culture and therefore comprises a central concern of this book.

11. "The historical situations in which the artificially maintained structures of the

good-faith economy break up and make way for the clear, economical (as opposed to expensive) concepts of the economy of undisguised self-interest, reveal the cost of operating an economy which, by its refusal to recognize and declare itself as such, is forced to devote almost as much ingenuity and energy to disguising the truth of economic acts as it expends in performing them" (Bourdieu 1990, 114). For more on the relationship between credit and social forms of capital, see Finn 2003.

12. "Frankness, candour, sincerity, within the limits of good taste and justice, are fine and noble characteristics. Cunning, sly, suspicious, mysterious and equivocating people are not amiable; but the power to conceal one's own affairs, or the secrets of others, is a necessity—a very urgent need in our present state of individual and, consequently, social imperfection and discordance. 'Be ye therefore as wise as serpents and harmless as doves.' Every faculty is right when it has its right uses. None are evil but in excess, in lack, or in discordant or unbalanced action. The true character results from the healthy development and harmonious action of all the faculties, and the result of this harmony is true life." (S. Beeton 1875, 80)

13. In recent years, the Sadleir case has garnered considerable critical attention from economic historians, in part because it is frequently cited as the inspiration for Mr. Merdle and in part because of its intersections with recent scholarly interest in both literal and literary issues of value. Various critics have also linked Sadleir to Augustus Melmotte of Anthony Trollope's *The Way We Live Now*, although George Robb finds his specific context in the person of Albert Grant, who "would promote anything if he thought that it would bring him a profit and most of his floatations were trash foisted on a gullible public." According to Robb, "Augustus Melmotte, was almost certainly modeled after Albert Grant" (1992, 102). Russell finds more abstract forebears in the proliferating popularity and acceptance of credit companies that had little or no accountability to complete projects or to satisfy investors with either remuneration or explanation. As Russell notes, the Trollope who writes *The Way We Live Now* is "keenly aware that credit and credit financing, coupled with the feverish company promotion following the establishment of limited liability, have become acceptable to the higher ranks of society, and that the class from which Britain had for centuries derived its moral and social values was affected and corrupted by the new order of things" (1986, 152). Both texts, in short, have literal economic bases that make them as much historical adaptations as fictional narratives. These contexts are popular focal points for critical evaluations of these novels; because they have been so well documented by other authors, I give them little attention here.

14. The pamphlet offers a remedy as well: "Take enough of the Spirit of Fellowship to mix with an equal quantity of Truth and purity of feeling. Add to these two ounces at least of Goodwill for others and a little Respect for yourself. Drink often of this & mix with a few leaves of Proper respect and carefully skim therefrom all Personal feeling and wicked intent."

15. The financier's tendency to keep "his hands crossed under his uneasy coat-cuffs, clasping his wrists as if he were taking himself into custody" (*Dorrit*, 331) becomes one of the novel's dominant symptoms of Merdle's criminality. This mysterious "disease" illustrates the capacity of economic deceit to move freely among spaces and people and indeed to move right into that most intimate of domiciles, the body. The novel emphasizes that Merdle is no more at ease in the house he shares with his wife than he is in his own body. "Let Mrs. Merdle announce ... that she was At Home ever so many nights in a season," Dickens writes, "she could not announce more widely and unmistakably than Mr. Merdle

did that he was never at home" (335).

16. One might thus look back to that which the authorities sought to detain at Marseilles, when the Meagles party and Clennam meet in quarantine in the novel's second chapter. There, the Plague is the illness in question, but it resonates retrospectively with France's speculating mania under the reign of *Credit Mobilier* and other such companies.

17. I am indebted to the faculty workshop at the 2005 Dickens Universe, in which we discussed an earlier version of this argument. As Alex Woloch and Natalka Freeland noted then, Dickens has an odd and troubling tendency to implicate the working classes in the perpetuation of corporate fraud.

18. Martha Stewart's stint in jail provided a new, rich context for duplicitous homemaking behind bars. Some of the spoofs—for example, *Living … In Prison*—are powerfully and hilariously reminiscent of Dickens's novel. My conclusion deals briefly with Martha within the context of the Enron scandal.

19. The novel is vague about whether or not Arthur's father has committed bigamy. Mrs. Clennam refers to a "desecrated ceremony of marriage," but it is not at all clear when that ceremony takes place, nor whether it is "desecrated" because it is bigamous, unofficial, or simply in conflict with Mrs. Clennam's severe religious morality.

20. My thanks to Jim Buzard for his insight into the concordance between Mrs. Clennam's lies and Amy Dorrit's "gift" to her husband.

21. That Dickens wrote this novel in the final stages of his disintegrating marriage to his wife Catherine, whom he famously berated as a poor housekeeper, may help to account for his fixation on the virtues of peaceful domesticity, embodied most forcefully in Amy Dorrit. But the novel's plotlines depend on those figures—Blandois, Flintwinch, Mrs. Clennam, Mr. Merdle—who function to infect the domestic lives and spaces they encounter with economic and interpersonal deceit.

Chapter One

1. For more on the tensions between investment and speculation, see Itzkowitz 2002.

2. Fudging the Victorian distinction between terms, furthermore, allows me to avoid cosmetically the awkward substitution of "libidinal speculation" for the standard psychological term, "libidinal investment."

3. Even the most serious of scholars have been unable to resist the anecdotal allure of the Tichborne affair: work on this case inevitably begins with novelistic fanfare. David Richter (2002) writes, "Late in 1866 a man who had been a butcher in Wagga Wagga, Australia, calling himself Tomas Castro, arrived in England claiming to be Sir Roger Tichborne, the dissolute heir to a British baronetcy who had set sail from Rio de Janeiro in 1854 on a ship that had gone down with all hands." David Wayne Thomas commences with the assurance that he presents "a true story: in 1866, one Arthur Orton, wayfaring son of an East London butcher, quits his life of small adventure in Australia to return to England and assume the identity of Sir Roger Tichborne, who was presumed lost at sea over a decade prior" (2004, 83). And Janet Myers adds a holiday theme to the Claimant's return: "On Christmas day in 1866, an Australian immigrant arrived in London and claimed to be Roger Charles Doughty Tichborne, Baronet and heir to the Tichborne estates" (1999, 111). Less academic works simply succumb to temptation: for example, Robyn Annear's popular *The Man Who Lost Himself* begins with the lines, "Nobody knew what Tom Castro

knew. And up until August of the year 1865 nobody much cared" (2002, 3). As these and my own rendition demonstrate, this story is so ripe for colorful telling that it is almost impossible to relate its basic facts without recourse to the conventions of the novel.

4. In flatly calling the Claimant Arthur Orton, I divulge my perspective on the Claimant's claim: after years of research, the preponderance of evidence that linked the Claimant with Orton, and my sense that the real Sir Roger would most likely know how to spell his own name, I have come to concur with the courts that he was an impostor. Various popular sources, however, suggest that the case was never conclusively settled.

5. The civil case took 102 days, while the criminal case lasted 188 days; the latter was the longest trial to that date in British legal history. Orton served just ten years of his fourteen-year sentence.

6. See Thomas 2004 for a discussion of Tichborne as distraction from matters of greater political import.

7. George Cruikshank, "The Last Man on the Tichborne Jury." JJC Tichborne, Bodleian Library, Oxford. The passage is on the reverse of a card bearing an image of the same title.

8. Myers approaches the case from the perspective of emigration and the status of emigrants—particularly Australians—as citizens in England. My thanks to her for sharing her work with me.

9. This is true even of texts published early in the century. I attribute this discrepancy to two primary causes. First of all, as Tim Alborn notes, there was plenty of unlawful activity—so much that by midcentury "episodes of wrongdoing began to crowd out examples of smoothly-operating commercial principles in the bankers' own publications. What was 'pathological' ... started to appear normal and vice versa" (1995, 211). Furthermore, popular accounts were less concerned with ensuring the success of the new financial endeavors and hence served alternate purposes than the promotional tales of banking and investing on which Poovey and Freedgood focus.

10. See also *The Man of Business,* originally published in the U.S. in 1857 before being revised and reprinted for British audiences in 1864: "The community is startled when some great swindler absconds, leaving hundreds of widows and orphans beggared by his monstrous frauds" (1864, 40).

11. One exception to this rule was the futures market, which I discuss in my conclusion.

12. Janette Rutterford and Josephine Maltby note that, in discussing Joint Stock regulation and issues of limited liability, legislators tended "to bracket together women, the clergy, the reckless and the inexperienced in various combinations. . . . Women were portrayed as being short of funds (like clergy on small stipends), and both groups were lacking in judgment. They had little experience of the financial world and were likely to form unrealistic expectations of risk and return when they made investments" (2006, 17).

13. There was definite moral outrage about this condition. Morier Evans asserted, "In a commercial country such as England, no crime can be more heinous against society, as constituted, than a breach of mercantile trust" (1859, 123). The *Times* observed, more radically, "If the heinousness of crimes be measured by their consequences, the man who carries disaster, if not absolute ruin, into a hundred families is stained with deeper guilt than the mere ruffian who attacks life" (26 February 1856).

14. There were private wagers as well. Even Henry Hawkins, who later became famous as lead counsel for the Crown, had initially "laid several bets on the Claimant being the

man he said he was" (Gilbert 1957, 75). According to Michael Gilbert, Hawkins changed his mind early on:

> In 1867, he told one of his friends, a certain Mr Hodgman, that he had laid several bets on the Claimant being the man he said he was. Mr Hodgman was so impressed that he, and another sporting friend, took £400 to £200 to the same effect. Six months later the tide was on the change. Hawkins, meeting them, said "Bye the bye, did you back that man Tichborne?" "Indeed we did," said Mr Hodgman, "and got 2 to 1." "Then hedge it," said Hawkins. "I was wrong. He's an imposter, and I know just about enough to hang him." Hodgman hurried off and hedged. He had no difficulty. The plaintiff still had plenty of supporters. (75)

15. There are alternatives here as well: "Summiteering ... tends to highlight raw competition and struggle, while shadowing the conditions under which risk taking is carried out and individual effort supported. Mountaineering offers at least some preliminary clues as to how a deliberative public discourse about risk can be produced which empowers individuals and communities to respond to the risk that is often involuntarily imposed upon them" (Simon 2002, 182).

16. Cf. Christina Crosby's argument that literature "helps to render intelligible the abstractions of money ... [and] actively accommodates Victorians to the imaginary relations money effects" (1999, 226). See also Peter Brooks's contention in *Realist Vision* that realist fiction "claims to offer us a kind of reduction—*modèle reduit*—of the world, compacted into a volume that we know can provide, for the duration of our reading, the sense of a parallel reality that can almost supplant our own. More than most other fictions, the realist novel provides a sense of play very similar to that given by the scale model" (2005, 2–3). Brooks links that "sense of play" to the Freudian repetition compulsion so central to his *Reading for the Plot,* in which narrative rehearsal becomes a means of achieving at least the illusion of a mastery that might circumvent future trauma.

17. For more on the affective components of investment, see Jaffe 2002.

18. Lizzy remarks that "there was certainly some great mismanagement in the education of those two young men [Wickham and Darcy]. One has got all the goodness, and the other all the appearance of it" (*Pride,* 199).

19. Freedgood argues that ballooning texts invited readers to engage in what she terms "cultural masochism" (2000, 104)—that is, in forms of self-imposed suffering that would accustom them to the trials of late-Victorian global culture—and that "'literary' adventures generally give pain the last word, ensuring that risk-takers, in fiction and in the culture at large, are morally entitled to their rewards" (96).

20. The difference here is one of degree: Willoughby has *not* seduced Marianne, and as Elinor avers, "he has broken no positive engagement with my sister" (*Sense,* 170). Henry Crawford's affection for Fanny Price is true, despite the vanity that leads him to court a married woman with whom "he went off ... at last because he could not help it, regretting Fanny, even at the moment, but regretting her infinitely more, when all the bustle of the intrigue was over, and a very few months had taught him, by the force of contrast, to place a yet higher value on the sweetness of her temper, the purity of her mind, and the excellence of her principles" (*Mansfield,* 318). And Anne Elliot had never been taken in by her cousin; although she "could just acknowledge within herself such a possibility of having

been induced to marry him, as made her shudder at the idea of the misery which must have followed" (*Persuasion*, 198), she had suspected early on "something more than immediately appeared, in Mr. Elliot's wishing, after an interval of so many years, to be well received by them" (131). In none of these cases, that is to say, is there a loss of anything more than affectionate capital, which while hardly insignificant, is considerably more bearable when not compounded by the loss of significant personal property.

21. For more on *Nickleby*'s economic underpinnings, see Childers 1996. For an in-depth discussion of Victorian negotiations of capitalism within and around the nuclear family, see Cleere 2004.

22. He also testified that they had secretly been married by a Father Guidez. The priest later took the stand and denied all knowledge of the Claimant and of the events he claimed to recall.

23. See *The Tichborne trial: the evidence of handwriting: comprising autograph letters of Roger Tichborne, Arthur Orton and the defendant in fac-simile* (London: S. Tinsley, 1874).

24. One could argue as well that the prosecution wielded sentimentality as a double-edged sword. On the one hand, they used it in the sense that Laura Hanft Korobkin identifies in nineteenth-century adultery cases, as a "controlling mode for jury arguments that strive to convince jurors that their own deepest beliefs and emotions are at stake" (1998, 15). On the other hand, they drew upon the shift in attitudes toward emotional responsiveness that accompanied the decline of Romantic sympathy. As Barbara Benedict observes, "Sentimental literature, in rhetoric and structure, does not simply advocate feeling; it also warns the reader against some kinds of feeling or feelings associated with revolutionary or female culture. Sentimental fiction adheres to a dialectical structure that endorses yet edits the feelings in fiction" (1994, 1).

25. Anti-French sentiments in England run back to the seventeenth century, with nascent national and economic competition appearing in texts depicting the French as duplicitous and effeminate. Victorian popular texts reinforced the sense of duplicity in a tendency to characterize Catholicism as an irrational religion bound up with idol worship, materialistic interests, and a dubious sense of morality (the practice of absolution through confession, in particular, was regarded as a kind of free pass). See Charlotte Brontë's *Villette*: "*J'ai menti plusieurs fois*' formed an item of every girl's and woman's monthly confession: the priest heard unshocked, and absolved unreluctant" (82).

26. Janet Myers's analysis (1999, 139–48) of the case's relationship to sensation fiction also attends to the relationship between unveiling and undressing.

27. This element of the case actually bears a surprising resemblance to the triumphant exposure of Count Fosco at the end of *The Woman in White*, in which the corpse of Collins's "great fat man" lies in the window of the Paris Morgue. "There he lay, unowned, unknown; exposed to the flippant curiosity of a French mob! There was the dreadful end of that long life of degraded ability and heartless crime! Hushed in the sublime repose of death, the broad, firm, massive face and head fronted us so grandly, that the chattering Frenchwomen about me lifted their hands in admiration, and cried, in shrill chorus, 'Ah, what a handsome man!'" (*Woman*, 581). The displacement upward that this scene enacts (Hartright focuses his description on "the broad firm, massive face and head," noting only secondarily that Fosco's clothes hang above him: he is naked in the window), sterilizes the spectacle for popular novel readers, even as it effects the revenge on the villain that the novel's conclusion requires. The exposure of Fosco's body must stand in for the legal exposure that the novel so earnestly seeks. As Hartright remarks at the novel's start, "The Law

is still, in certain inevitable cases, the pre-engaged servant of the long purse; and the story is left to be told, for the first time, in this place. As the judge might once have heard it, so the Reader shall hear it now" (1).

28. While his cause maintained a certain popular utility among the working classes, who drew on it to demonstrate the legal system's inordinately harsh treatment of the poor, the Claimant's radically diminished credibility made him significantly less helpful as an illustration of inequity—and it didn't help matters that Thomas Keneally, Orton's counsel, was disbarred shortly following the conviction. David Wayne Thomas (2004) notes that the Claimant's conviction coincided with Gladstone's defeat, and thus with the defeat of a Liberal platform that marked a shift in national concerns and allegiances.

29. The film *The Tichborne Claimant* (1998) stars Robert Pugh as the Claimant and Stephen Fry as Henry Hawkins. Robyn Annear's biography, *The Man Who Lost Himself*, appeared in 2002. In 2006, the Hampshire City Council assembled a touring exhibit entitled "Who Does He Think He Is?" which included photographs, newly acquired legal documents, and popular ephemera. For recent essays on the case, see note 3 above.

30. In fact, the effort to generate an appealing illusion of creditability characterizes even agents of legitimate exchange, in both social and economic dealings. As Mary Poovey explains in *A History of the Modern Fact*, one of the earliest forms of business records, double-entry bookkeeping, originally included three books: the memorial, the journal, and the ledger. The memorial recorded each day's transactions in a mixture of prose and numbers; the other two books, the journal and the ledger, progressively converted language into numbers so as to achieve "the rhetorical function of the ledger—to display the merchant's honesty and thus his creditworthiness" (64). Ironically, the ledger recorded absent cash, in the forms both of debts owed and of credit extended, as if it were present, not only to make the balance sheet balance but also because "It was necessary ... for the merchant to represent himself as solvent even if he was not *in order* to establish the credit necessary to make himself so" (1998, 64; emphasis in original). Thus even the earliest forms of a practice designed to establish the honesty of an economic trader relied on significant deviations from the truth. Ledgers regularly and of necessity manufactured desirable fictions so as to solicit credit from their readers. That practice has significant relevance to the dynamics I have been discussing here.

31. See Althusser's famous argument about the relationship between the cognitive and the social in which he maintains, "It is not their real conditions of existence, their real world, that 'men' 'represent to themselves' in ideology, but above all it is their relation to those conditions of existence which is represented to them there" (1970, 164). His observation of the powerful influence of the "imaginary" on the "real," of representation upon lived experience, informs my argument in this chapter.

32. There are obvious concordances with the rise of fiction here. For more on the relationship between the novel and economic conditions, see Lynch 1992, Brantlinger 1996, and Poovey 2002.

33. The grammar is precisely akin: "the trial of David Anderson came on at last Yorkshire Assizes, when he was indicted for uttering, knowing them to be forged, two notes" (Yorkshire Assizes, Bodleian JJC Crime 1–Smaller Broadsides). In fact, counterfeit notes and counterfeit stories shared a great many features, most notably their aims. In both circumstances, the fictions worked to generate the effect of veracity in order to prompt their recipients to invest in them by granting some form of credit—perhaps the pound amount of a forged note, or the opportunity to accrue debt, or an invitation to join a particular social set.

Chapter Two

1. One such exception would be Nelly Dean of Emily Brontë's *Wuthering Heights*, but she is one of the few major characters who is a domestic servant, rather than a governess (Jane Eyre), wet nurse (Esther Waters), or farm laborer (Tess Durbeyfield). For more on the structural antagonisms between minor and major characters, see Woloch 2003.

2. "Rich merchant families had traditionally mingled comfortably and intermarried with aristocrats and landed gentry" (Morgan 1994, 49).

3. The London School of Economics has a wonderful online site that allows for detailed exploration of Booth's maps and classification systems. Available at http://booth.lse.ac.uk/static/a/4.html.

4. Thorstein Veblen notes that many servants served as no more than "evidence of ability to pay" (1899, 55).

5. See Burnett 1997. Robbins 1993 traces the caricature of the servant (and its corollary, the servant so clichéd as to be characterless) back to *The Odyssey*.

6. See especially Poovey 1988, Armstrong 1987, and Langland 1995 on the ideology of separate spheres as a fiction convenient in its day for obscuring the capitalist division of labor, and still convenient in our day for its neatness and simplicity.

7. Recognizing this problem, Frances Power Cobbe reminds her readers that "a servant is not now or henceforth a retainer, a dependant, a menial who, in receiving from his master food and wages, becomes his temporary property—somewhat between a child and a slave—to be ordered in all things concerning, or not concerning the master's service. He is simply a man who, instead of contracting to build a wall or make a pair of shoes, contracts to do certain indoor work, for whose performances it is generally desirable that he should eat and sleep under the employer's roof" (1868, 132).

8. Bell, otherwise known as Cousin Kate, was author of various works of morality literature, including *Horace and May; or, Unconscious Influence* and *Margaret Cecil; or, "I Can Because I Ought."*

9. Doors and windows often appear as portals through which the home may be sapped or contaminated. For example, of George Cruikshank's twelve illustrations for *The Greatest Plague of Life*, three include doorways. The most alarming of these depicts a constable standing in the darkened bedroom of the central family, the Sk–n–st–ns, who, attired in their nightclothes, peer at him with dismayed surprise: "Do you know as your street-door is open?" the caption reads. In the corresponding text, Mrs. Sk–n–st–n sends her husband down with the policeman to "see whether the spoons and forks were all right" (1847, 278). He returns "with the gratifying information that my treasure of a footman, who had stipulated to go to church, at least twice every Sunday, and lived for the last eighteen years with one of the bishops of the land, had gone off with the whole of our silver plate, and left nothing but that bilious-looking 'British' behind him" (278–79).

10. Matty's servant, Fanny, loses her post because "[s]he was forbidden, by the articles of her engagement to have 'followers.' ... But a vision of a man seemed to haunt the kitchen" (*Cranford*, 65).

11. As Anthea Trodd notes, "The section on female servants in Mayhew's *London Labour and the London Poor* voiced the general suspicion that the followers of maid-servants were often criminals seeking entry to the house" (1989, 53). Trodd goes on to discuss the alternate trajectory, in which the follower is not a criminal but a policeman. Both figures, she argues, jeopardize the ostensible privacy of the family.

12. Followers were frequently given the title of "cousin," so as to allow them visiting privileges (see *The Greatest Plague of Life* and Cruikshank's illustration "My cousin, m'am"). Variations on the discourse about servants' followers appear in Reynold's *Mary Price*, in which Mary's bad brother Robert robs his sister's employers.

13. Cf. "Wise Maxims" (1848): 60: "A good character is valuable to every one, but especially to servants, for it is their bread; and without it they cannot be admitted into a creditable family; and happy it is that the best of characters is in every one's power to deserve" (60). For more on the general notion of character in Victorian culture, see Joyce 1994.

14. A statute enacted under George III still in place in 1888 imposed fines or imprisonment on masters who gave false characters to their servants. "An action for deceit will lie against a person giving a false character to a servant." *Wilkin v. Reed* (1854) and *Foster v. Charles* (1830) were key cases in determining a master's liability. See Paterson (1885), 35–37 for more on character in legal cases:

> Any person giving a false character is liable to a penalty of £20, whether such character is written or verbal. Thus the defendant recommended an agent to the plaintiff, with the knowledge that his representation of the character of the agent was false. It was held in an action to recover damages arising from the misconduct of the agent, that it was not necessary by the plaintiff to prove a malicious or an interested motive by the defendant for the misrepresentation; if what the defendant said was false within his own knowledge and occasioned an injury to the plaintiff, it was a sufficient ground of action. (Hastings 1888, 39–40)

For a more humorous rendering of potential legal consequences, see *The Greatest Plague of Life*, in which Mrs. S. finds herself sued three times, once for giving a false character, then for libel when she gives an honest character, then again when she refuses to give a character at all (1847, 271–72).

15. Interestingly, Fielding and Defoe were at the forefront of the original hue and cry about false characters. Cf. Fielding: "one would imagine that half the Masters and Mistresses of this Kingdome, by the Characters they give of their Servants, live in fear of, and are dependent upon them" (quoted in Robbins 1993, 35–36). For more on the notion of character in fiction, see Lynch 1998.

16. For an actual case, see the ballads and broadsides concerning Mrs. Gurney, wife of an MP for Norfolk. Mrs. Gurney was independently wealthy and ran off to the Continent with her handsome footman. Popular materials include "The Blooming Lady Worth £500 and Her Footman," "Mrs. Gurney, the Divorced Lady!" and "The Two Elopements! Parson and Footman, Female Depravity." The Gurney case, while scandalous, did not involve fraud or theft, except from the perspective of some balladeers: "Oh the lucky lucky footman / He has done [a] trick so brown, / Got his masters lovely lady, / And five hundred thousand pound" ("The Blooming Lady").

17. A satire from *Punch* mocks servant sloth as well as infection theory, advising, "When visitors are expected, and you are honoured with instructions to clear out a bed room closet, . . . do so in as gentle a manner as you can, and spread clean paper on the shelves without disturbing the dust which there has peacefully accumulated." ("Hints to Make Houses Wholesome").

18. My thanks to John for sharing the manuscript copy of this work. Cf. "To under-

stand the concept of property it is decisive to recognize that the rigid demarcation between it and the self, between internal and external life, is quite superficial and that it should be made more fluid for the purpose of a deeper interpretation" (Simmel 2004, 322).

19. Cf. Mauss 1954, Hyde 1979, and Shell 1978.

20. Derrida argues that any gift *that is acknowledged as such* inevitably enters a temporal contract of exchange and deferral. He writes, "For there to be a gift, *it is necessary* [*il faut*] that the donee not give back, amortize, reimburse, acquit himself, enter into a contract, and that he never had contracted a debt. . . . It is thus necessary, at the limit, that he not *recognize* the gift as gift. If he recognizes it *as* gift, if the gift *appears to him as such,* if the present is present to him *as present,* this simple recognition suffices to annul the gift" (1992, 13; emphasis in original).

21. Ironically, Martineau's remarks on servants run directly counter to the calming effect she imparts in her writings about the marketplace proper. In *Illustrations of Political Economy*, Martineau conveys a "sense of a predictable and solid economic and social structure" meant to reassure her audience that the world is safe and benevolent. (quoted in Freedgood 2000, 29).

22. Following metonymic logic, those ladies who purposefully don the dresses of women beneath them inevitably wear those costumes to engage in behaviors that reveal their "real" nonaristocratic status, as in Charles Dickens's *Bleak House* when Lady Dedlock visits the grave of her lower-class lover in the dress of her French maid, Hortense. Much later in the novel, when Lady Dedlock flees Chesney Wold, she trades dresses with Jenny, an impoverished woman, to whom Esther refers as "the mother of the dead child." When Esther, Woodcourt, and Mr. Bucket finally find Lady Dedlock, lying dead at the cemetery gate in Jenny's dress, all Esther can see is the poor, suffering woman who was the bricklayer's wife. "She lay there," Esther writes, "a distressed, unsheltered, senseless creature" (915), which is precisely what Lady Dedlock has become.

23. Nineteen year-old Parr was indicted for stealing 80 pence, and 80 halfpence; the monies of Isaac Mitchell, his master. Found guilty, he was confined for four days.

24. Reynolds's novel stresses the dual culpability that many Victorian texts find in the perquisite system, arguing that the fraud inherent in it

is as much, if not more, the fault of masters and mistresses themselves than of their servants. This system is known to exist: it is tolerated—it may even be said to be winked at and encouraged: seldom is it that ever an attempt is made on the part of masters and mistresses to put a stop to it; and by their very indolence in looking after their own affairs, or else through the ridiculous pride which makes them consider any such interference to be beneath them, they wilfully shut their eyes to what is going on, and thus tacitly assent to the practice. Thus is it that the laziness and absurd vanity of aristocratic and wealthy families are both alike most demoralizing in their effects, and at least as culpable as the knavery of the systems which they generate or allow to exist. (1852, 65–66)

Chapter Three

1. See, for example, Michie 1992.

2. For food related readings, see Menke 1998, Cohen 1985, and D. Thompson 1991. For more market-based readings, see Helsinger 1991, Holt 1990, and Campbell 1990.

3. Dante Gabriel Rossetti is credited with the title "Goblin Market." Christina had originally entitled it "A Peep at the Goblins."

4. Helsinger writes, "'Come buy, come buy,' the iterated cry of the 'merchant men' that punctuates the poem, has few parallels in English poetry in the nineteenth century" (1991, 903). Helsinger's own reading of "Goblin Market" does focus on issues of buying and selling, but for her, the poem comments on how the market threatens to turn female consumers into products to be themselves consumed. "The story of survival offered in 'Goblin Market'—consumer power achieved by withholding female desire—culminates in the production of its heroines as 'public beings' who can publish female difference. . . . Rossetti herself is finally less interested in exposing the fictions of separate spheres through the transgressive figure of the female consumer (and her shadow sister, the prostitute), than in rescuing the possibility of utopian places for women outside the marketplace" (926–27).

5. Holt's focus on language and lack ultimately makes his reading more Lacanian than the cultural studies approach I offer here. For example, Holt observes that "The goblins' bargain is a cheat" (1990, 56)—a proposition that informs the current reading—but he does so to foreground the play between desire and lack that plagues the poem's female subjects.

6. On food adulteration, see Searle 1998, 91–97; Smith 1979, 203–15; and Wohl 1983, 52–55. Menke offers an interesting but different food-related observation, noting that the spring of 1859, during which Rossetti composed the poem, was a remarkably bad one for fruit. Early warmth and a late but severe frost made it unlikely that any but imported or engineered (that is, greenhouse-grown) fruit would have survived. "If the inventory of fruit in 'Goblin Market' seems dreamlike in its intense physicality," Menke writes, "the reasons for this paradox may in fact be legitimately historical: at the time the poem was written, fresh fruit would indeed have been largely the stuff of fantasy" (1998, 109). This reading, however, doesn't fully account for Laura's illness beyond the realm of metaphor.

7. See Gordon Bigelow's "Market Indicators" for a differently focused discussion of the relationship between the home and British market economics. Focusing on figurations of the Bank of England and the domestic woman, Bigelow argues, "We might conclude that the ideology of the domestic woman in the novel provides a space of essential value in a world of increasingly chaotic circulation" (2000, 600). However, as he demonstrates convincingly, the system of value under capitalism is representational; hence domestic value, like economic value, remains unsettlingly fluid.

8. My thanks to an anonymous reader for *Nineteenth-Century Literature* for noting the corollary with "Maud."

9. Over twenty texts on food adulteration were published in the 1850s. See, for example, *Adulteration of Food, Drink, and Drugs* (1855), Bronner 1856; Dalton 1857; Marcet 1856; *How to Detect Adulteration* (1855), and *Tricks of Trade* (1856).

10. Accum comments further on the deleterious effects of adulteration on the market itself. These remarks again turn to private concerns, concentrating on individual immorality and vulnerability. He notes that "the eager and insatiable thirst for gain, is proof against prohibitions and penalties; and the possible sacrifice of a fellow-creature's life, is a secondary consideration among unprincipled dealers" (1820, iv). In other words, "the eager and insatiable thirst for gain," indeed the very principle of capitalist economics, encourages an unprincipled climate that produces the poisonous fruits of merchant greed. According to Searle, Accum's work had been discredited by the 1850s (1998, 91 n. 85). However,

a range of popular texts from that period continue to cite him (see Hassall 1855, iii and passim, and Goderich 1852, 76, among others). Regardless of his scientific prowess (or lack thereof), Accum's comments on the private and moral implications of adulteration remained apropos to 1850s moral discourse on food adulteration.

11. See Hassall 1855, iii and passim; see also Searle 1998, 91–97.

12. See also *Political Blunders* (1872), which observes:

> Tea is sold in this country, made up of chopped straw and iron filings. Some importers unblushingly attempt to pass the Customs' officers with it, duty free; because, as they say, it is a manufactured article. This sort of stuff is sold in London at three to five farthings per pound. Butter is made out of Thames mud, swarming with worms and other loathsome things. It is also made at Dutch butter manufactories, out of measled port and flesh of still-born animals, and of rotten stuff that has been condemned by food inspectors as unfit for consumption, and which has been purchased for a halfpenny per pound. Other samples are mixed up with rags that have been reduced to a pulp; care has not even been taken to extract the colours out of the cloth. Such butter is sold to, and used by some confectioners in making up their morsels, which in the mouth are sweet, but in the stomach, a disease. Our flour and bread are mixed with alum and sulphate of copper. No wonder people are mumbling without teeth, and that the dentists and doctors drive a thriving trade. (13–14)

13. Laura ceases to sleep ("Goblin Market," 269–71); she "would not eat" (298); and, no longer able to hear or see the goblins, she wonders if she has "Gone deaf and blind" (259).

14. See also Searle (1998, 91) on representations of food adulteration. According to a VICTORIA List member, "Slomon" signifies a regular imbiber of sloe gin.

15. Hillel Schwartz observes that "the more adept the West has become at the making of copies, the more we have exalted uniqueness. It is within an exuberant world of copies that we arrive at our experience of originality" (1996, 212). But this formulation is too exuberant to accurately describe Victorian culture. Even if Laura's engagement with the goblins bespeaks fascination and desire, Lizzie's attitude maintains the mixed suspicion and regret that also strongly characterize Victorian perspectives on mimicry.

16. In Stern 1998, I examine the relationship between Judith Butler's work and the contradictory valences of repetition in Victorian culture.

17. Indeed, children who read such titles such as "She Who Would Help Others Must Be Self-Denying and Self-Watchful" were raised to be paranoid. The latter cautionary tale was collected in *Horace and May; or, Unconscious Influence* by "Cousin Kate" (Catherine D. Bell, the author of *Lily Gordon*).

18. The editor of the *English Churchman* wrote to Palmerston in 1854 about "the necessity of providing some machinery for preserving the poor from the evils of short weight, short measure, and the adulteration of their food. I venture to hope that your Lordship will consider that the duty undertaken by '*The Lancet*' is one which belongs especially to the Government." The editor included a recent clipping entitled "Detectives for the Poor," which dramatically illustrated the pandemic nature of the problem. This correspondence seems to have led to the formation of the Parliamentary Select Committee in 1855. It is available in the Public Record Office at Kew Gardens in Home Office file 45/5338.

19. For a thorough but quite different discussion of the Victorian interest in visual machinery, see Horton 1995. Of particular relevance here is the observation that the Victorian experience with new technologies of vision "was undoubtedly changing them" (13). Horton also links the growing realization that the eye could be tricked to narratives of the mystery novel.

20. Cf. my differences with Poovey and Freedgood in chapter 1, above.

21. My reading of this passage here reverses, to some extent, the reading I offer in the article-length version of this chapter, published in *Nineteenth-Century Literature* (Stern 2003). There I argued that Rossetti offered a logic of exception and singularity; the revision derives from the more complicated model of the relationship between reading and risk I developed while writing chapter 1.

22. Lizzie and Laura also share in this discourse; for all their likeness and for all ease of confusion between them, the two girls are quite different. Rossetti accentuates this after Laura's commerce with the goblin men, whence we find "Lizzie with an open heart, / Laura in an absent dream, / One content, one sick in part; / One warbling for the mere bright day's delight, / One longing for the night" (210–14). Helena Michie identifies this same characteristic of "Goblin Market" from a different perspective, arguing that "individuation threatens familial discourse" through a paradigm of sexual difference that includes a distinction between sexual purity and fall, and hence a distinction *between* women (1992, 34).

23. See Sedgwick 1997 for a more extended discussion of the psychology of avoiding the "bad surprise."

24. See, for example, Holt 1990 and Helsinger 1991. I am willing to follow Holt, who argues that Laura's "redemption offers a consoling fantasy of the subject's escape from power relations—an impossible exemption, in other words, from the very forces that give the subject existence. The consolation of what follows in 'Goblin Market' is plain, but the wishful, fantastic nature of this consolation—its historical discontinuousness and the impossibility of its realization in Rossetti's world—are equally apparent, as repressed threats return in the closing passages of the poem" (62). I find those "threats" more overt than repressed, which lends the poem an attitude more cautionary than fantastic.

25. Although Laura "Longed but had no money," the goblins assure her she can buy nonetheless: "'You have much gold upon your head,' / They answered all together / 'Buy from us with a golden curl'" (123–25). Like the system of credit on which the market operated, the wealth of Laura's looks allows her to trade without coin. The poem may be read as well, then, as a sermon on debt and the gambling that forms its subtext in much anti-capitalist literature. See Searle 1998, 230–33.

26. In a bizarre echo of "Goblin Market," many promoters used tropes of fertility and produce to denote the wary consumer's *duty* to participate in the market economy, to enrich national ground with individual wealth, so that England's bounty might increase. For example, *How to Obtain Wealth*, a sixpenny pamphlet, puffs "The Orchard Company," designed to "lease all the surplus lands on the banks of railways, which could be had at a very low rental, for the cultivation and improvement of all kinds of Fruit Trees and Vegetables. The sale of the fruit, etc., would produce a very handsome revenue, and the produce being close to the railway, the markets could be cheaply and quickly supplied" (n.d., 3). The impetus to speculate in such potentially fruitful ventures receives further reinforcement from the introduction to these schemes, which reminds the reader that: "If a Tree after it has been nurtured brings not forth good Fruit, it is cut down because it only

cumbereth the ground; so a man born with intellect, wealth, etc., if he does not apply these gifts of Providence which are lent to him to improve and benefit himself and neighbours, he likens himself to the unfruitful tree, and recedes further from God his Creator" (1). In other words, the Victorian public had a moral and religious responsibility to enter the market, populated by "goblins" though it might be.

27. George Eliot's short story "Brother Jacob" (1864; Eliot 1887) falls in this group. The aptly named David Faux steals from his mother, abandons his "idiot" brother, and reinvents himself as Edward Freely, a confectioner. While Eliot places him in close proximity to the sorts of confectionary that were notorious in her day, Faux is not an adulterator per se. Eliot writes, "A sharper can drive a brisk trade in this world: it is undeniable that there may be a fine career for him, if he will dare consequences; but David was too timid to be a sharper, or venture in any way among the man-traps of the law. He dared rob nobody but his mother. And so he had to fall back on the genuine value there was in him—to be content to pass as a good halfpenny, or, to speak more accurately, as a good confectioner" (506).

28. My thanks to Nancy Henry for bringing this novel to my attention. Page numbers refer to the double-columned American edition, published in the same year that the novel appeared in Britain.

29. Lawrence's moral fiber is not exactly tightly knit to start; he enters the adulteration business without much hesitation at all and he readily divorces the benefits of his actions from their consequences for others.

Chapter Four

1. See her novel *Martyrs to Circumstance*. See also J. R. O'Flanagan's *Gentle Blood* and Cyrus Redding's *A Wife and Not a Wife*.

2. Many historians trace the case's appeal to its engagement with the complications of marriage law in Great Britain. While the debates about Irish vs. Scotch vs. English marriage law certainly gave the case cachet within the legal community, popular materials about the case suggest a wider scope of public interest, concerned primarily with romantic betrayal.

3. A previous suit for Longworth's debts had been filed in England. The civil suit for money was settled in this court when Yelverton agreed to pay, which established the precedent that allowed the Dublin trial to take shape. See Erickson and McCarthy 1971, 278.

4. See Hastings and Davenport 1872:

> A husband married prior to the passing of "The Married Women's Property Act, 1870," still remains liable for his wife's debts incurred before marriage, of whatever amount, and whether he had any fortune with her or not. And he is also answerable for a breach of trust committed by her before marriage. A husband, however, married subsequent to the passing of "The Married Women's Property Act, 1870," is not responsible for his wife's debts contracted before marriage, her separate estate alone being liable for such debts. (41–42)

5. Henry Mansel famously critiqued the popular taste for sensation fiction, writing, "There is something unspeakably disgusting in this ravenous appetite for carrion, this vulture-like instinct which smells out the newest mass of social corruption, and hurries to

devour the loathsome dainty before the scent has evaporated" (*Quarterly Review*).

6. For nuanced discussions of the Matrimonial Causes Act and the complex economic debates surrounding it, see Shanley 1989, chap. 1, and Poovey 1988, chap. 3, and Poovey's remark that, "Even though the 1857 Married Women's Property bill did not become law, the controversy it aroused interjected the issues of women's rights, property, and work into parliamentary discussion, quarterly review articles, and popular novels as well" (Poovey 1995, 173).

7. See also Craig 2000. Although breach of promise suits fall neatly within the provenance of fraud, they are less immediately relevant to the debates about the Yelverton case.

8. Cf. "After the 1856 passage of new company law, financial fraud almost certainly became more common still, with mismanaging company directors and embezzling clerks joining fraudulent promoters in the pantheon of iniquity" (Poovey 2003, 18).

9. Armstrong's argument is more centered on issues of power than economy, largely due to her debt to Foucault. She notes of Richardson's ledger, "Although this novel claims to deal only with the sexual contract, doing so in this instance also revises the way in which political relationships are imagined" (1987, 112). For my purposes here, I want to highlight how that revision articulates equivalencies between the desirable body and money, goods, and land. The negotiations between B. and Pamela redistribute the properties men and women bring to the table in a sexual contract newly envisioned under capitalism.

10. The mood of this illustration is more gentle than the more scathing tone of the ballads I discuss below: despite those figures I cite, the majority of Cruikshank's lovers stand without monetary markers, and the overall effect is more comic than critical. There are sufficient smiles to moderate the sting of the illustrator's wit, as less obviously mercenary suitors nicely balance the swains who cluster around the "10,000 a Year" beauty.

11. Satires and other traces of personal ads emerge early in the century, suggesting that actual advertisements were appearing. See, for example, "The Matrimonial Hoax," a ballad that musically advises "Do not advertise for wives Sirs / For if you do as sure as fate / You lay yourselves to a pretty bait." John Dinely, whose public advertisement inviting women to compete for his hand, apparently inspired someone to exhibit his likeness in wax. See "A Capital Likeness" and "Wonderful Museum!" in JJC Human Freaks 4.

12. Another variation involves a young woman, made up to appear quite pregnant, who "offers her gold wedding-ring for sale, as she wants to get back to her suffering kids to give them something to eat." The ensuing conversation among the servant girls—"'oh, you'll want it, Mary, for John;' and another 'No, you'll want it first, Sally, for William.' But the woman has her eye on the one as says the least, as the likeliest of all to want it" (Mayhew 1861–2, 352), and so manages to elicit a healthy tip, if not half the ring's alleged value, from her flattered and hopeful target.

13. Further, because Mr. Taylor's interest in Mrs. Cooper emerges upon her mention of her "immense property," his desire for *her* reiterates precisely his desire for her avowed estate. Note how this revises Catherine Peters's evaluation of such desires: "Women in particular, both the downtrodden menials of the back-kitchens and their comparatively fortunate sisters in the back-drawing-rooms, could, except for a very few, hope to achieve status only through marriage, and the protective colouring of someone else's name" (1989, xviii). Here Cooper plays on the greedy *man's* interest in marrying up.

14. I am, with great restraint, leaving aside a potentially extended discussion of modern analogies to internet dating. I'll simply say that to use a picture that is more than five years old is, while not outright lying, to misrepresent oneself.

15. In the 1860s, Dickens would mock this form of dealing through the Lammles in *Our Mutual Friend*, whose marriage shares a chapter with the novel's famous passage on shares. "As is well known to the wise in their generation," Dickens writes, "traffic is the one thing to have to do with in this world. Have no antecedents, no established character, no cultivation, no ideas, no manners; have Shares" (159–60). Just after the Lammles' marriage, when the newlyweds discover that neither actually has any property, the "entrapped imposters" descend into a rattle of hostilities that ends in a pointed question: "'Do you pretend to believe,' Mrs. Lammle resumes, sternly, 'when you talk of my marrying you for worldly advantages, that it was within the bounds of reasonable probability that I would have married you for yourself?'" (170). They ultimately agree only that they are both adventurers: as Alfred Lammle says to his wife, "we have both been deceiving, and we have both been deceived. We have both been biting, and we have both been bitten" (172). See also Poovey: "the John Harmon plot works to rewrite 'value,' to exchange the false currency of literal money for the 'true,' metaphorical coin of love" (1995, 165). Tara McGann observes that "Sophronia and Alfred Lammle stand for what the novel takes to be a morally bankrupt speculative economy as well as representing and multiplying a disturbing transaction between mercenary marriage and speculation" (2002, 4).

16. Cf. "In circumstances he was not very well off; . . . He had an uncle on whose bounty he very much depended, who would be annoyed if he married" (*Yelverton Marriage Case* [1861], 10).

17. I cite the 1852 version of this text. A later edition revises as follows: "A clandestine marriage should be peremptorily declined. In too many cases it is a fraud committed by an elder and more experienced party upon one whose ignorance of the world's ways and confiding tenderness appeal to him for protection even against himself" (1865, 29–30).

18. J. L. Austin has compellingly discussed the performative nature of language with regard to the marriage ceremony: "I do" is a speech act that, when uttered under the proper circumstances, accomplishes what it describes (similar instances include "I promise" and "I bet"). However, he acknowledges that the "felicity," or success, of speech acts, depends on a number of conditions, which include the following:

> (A. 2) The particular persons and circumstances in a given case must be appropriate for the invocation of the particular procedure invoked. . . .
> (Γ. 1) Where, as often, the procedure is designed for use by persons having certain thoughts or feelings, or for the inauguration of certain consequential conduct on the part of any participant, then a person participating in and so invoking the procedure must in fact have those thoughts or feelings, and the participants must intend so to conduct themselves, and further
> (Γ. 2) must actually so conduct themselves subsequently. (1975, 15)

Austin's formulation echoes nearly precisely that of the Scottish and English courts that subsequently heard the Yelverton case: As the Lord Ordinary, Lord Ardmillian, insisted,

> Marriage is a consensual contract. Consent alone, if freely, seriously, and deliberately given, constitutes marriage. No ceremony, civil or religious, is necessary. The interchange of mutual consent is sufficient. The celebration of the ordinance of marriage in facie ecclesiæ is only the regular, and the most becoming, and the best mode of proving the mutual consent which constitutes marriage.

But other modes of proof are recognized as sufficient,—the general and permanent rule being, that the serious and deliberate consent—the mutual intention of the parties to enter into the contract of marriage—shall clearly appear. Nothing less will suffice. Light words—words of doubtful import—words used merely to give a colour to cohabitation, to escape scandal, or to obtain access to lodgings or hotels,—these are not sufficient proof of that mutual consent to marry which the law requires, and which must be seriously entertained and deliberately expressed. (*Cases Decided* [1863], 112)

19. The statute in question was 19 Geo. II. c. 13, s. 1. Furthermore, under 23 Geo. II, c. 10, s. 3, any priest who performed such a marriage was guilty of a felony. See Erickson and McCarthy 1971, 287–88. A subsequent law under Victoria (5 & 6 Vic., c. 28) determined that any priest who performed such a ceremony was punishable by seven years transportation.

20. See note 18, above.

21. See *Cases Decided* (1863) for specific records of the appeals and verdicts.

22. See note 1, above.

23. The most notable of these accounts, Erickson and McCarthy 1971, continues to be the definitive historical account. Crow 1966 offers a more creative, but less historically reputable, interpretation.

24. See Erickson and McCarthy 1971, Maceachen 1950, and Page 1995.

25. See also Page's introduction to Wilkie Collins's *Man and Wife,* in which he argues that "The Yelverton case brought the questions of bigamy and of irregularly contracted marriages dramatically to public notice. . . . It has been estimated," he continues, "that in the four years following the Yelverton trial, between twelve and sixteen 'bigamy novels' appeared each year" (1983, x).

26. The seduction plots of many nineteenth-century novels offer ready paradigms through which to interpret Yelverton's behavior: Gaskell's *Ruth*, Wood's *East Lynne*, and Eliot's *Adam Bede*, among others, feature a male protagonist who plays upon a woman's romantic ideals, gets her pregnant, and disappears.

27. In the Scottish trial, the Lord Ordinary writes,

> The tone and tenor of these letters is very far from indicating those feelings and hopes by which the statements which she has put on record are true. . . . [T]he only passage of a more cheerful kind is that relating to "bon bons"—"not real ones," which she hopes to get—words to which the defender attaches meaning of a kind which it is not necessary to mention, and which the Lord Ordinary, who does not adopt the defender's meaning, does not at present understand, but of which the pursuer has offered no intelligible explanation. (*Cases Decided* [1863], 107)

28. It may do so inadvertently, for the Vickers report is explicitly sympathetic to Longworth. However, the illustrations, contributed by various artists, offer considerably more complicated renditions of Longworth than does the text. See also my discussion of the illustration "Visions of Gentle-Blooded Life," below.

29. The *Full Report* quotes Brewster saying, "If he were forty times his client he would not stand up in that court to justify him" (1861, 53). See Rosenman 2003, 156–57 for

further discussion of Yelverton's lawyers' posture with regard to their client.

30. This interpretation may gain credence from the small prone figure that grips two sheets of paper at the bottom of the illustration, stabbed at the heart with a quill. The small letters identifying this figure as John Swain mark what seems to be a rivalry between engravers (Swain worked for and eventually became the head of engraving at *Punch*, while Julian Portch, whose signature sprawls beside the figure, was a less powerful, albeit still popular, illustrator).

31. See, for example, the Vickers report, which explicitly uses Yelverton's term to describe Longworth's family background:

> The defendant was a man of noble family, the heir apparent to the peerage of Avonmore. Teresa [*sic*] Yelverton, his wife, whose maiden name was Longworth, was also of gentle blood. She belonged to an ancient and honourable family in England, and having lost her mother in early life, she was taken to France to be educated. . . . She had a sister married in France to the son of the Chief Justice of that empire. (*Yelverton Marriage Case* [1861], 9–10)

However respectable her family may have been, they did not come close to matching the Yelvertons in hereditary oomph.

32. Sergeant Armstrong took rather a different line: "To be told that [the Scotch marriage] was an honest marriage, or a marriage at all, would be a blow to virtue, to the security of families, to the peace, and honour, and tranquillity of married life greater than ever had been inflicted upon that sacred connexion. God forbid that such a transaction, even if it occurred, would receive the stamp of approbation from an honest jury" (*Yelverton Marriage Case* [1861], 140).

33. The full passage runs as follows:

> The defender having thus informed the pursuer that he was a confirmed bachelor, and intended to remain so, proceeds in a subsequent letter to tell the pursuer what she may expect from him [from which he cites a long passage. . . . There is no deception or disguise in this. When a gentleman in the course of such a correspondence as this, resolutely refrains from responding to dexterous suggestions, and even direct invitations, to make proposals of marriage,—when he tells the lady that he is a confirmed bachelor, and yet has no Rubicon beyond which he does not mean to pass, if he can, then he has certainly given her no encouragement to expect marriage, but on the contrary has said enough to put her to some extent on her guard. (*Cases Decided* [1863], 96)

34. Arguments that the Longworth–Yelverton hearings foregrounded discrepancies among marriage laws within Great Britain are most pertinent to this phase of the case.

35. See the Lord Ordinary in the Scotch hearing:

> Nor can this Irish ceremony receive effect as a renewal of a previous marriage, regular or irregular, in Scotland. Of such previous marriage there is no proof; and no acknowledgment of any such previous marriage was made by the defender to the priest; nor was any statement of such previous marriage so

made by the pursuer as to imply the acquiescence of the defender. If no such previous marriage existed, it could not be renewed; and whatever effect, as a renewal of a previous marriage, the ceremony might have had in Ireland if previous marriage had been proved, the Irish ceremony can have no effect in Scotland in the constitution of marriage, in regard to which there is no proof of previous interchange of matrimonial consent. (*Cases Decided* [1863], 108)

36. See Rosenman 2003, 129 on the transcript of Longworth's appeal.

Conclusion

1. The Zazoo ad is easy to find by searching "Zazoo" at www.youtube.com.

2. Other forms included refuses and puts. A "refuse" was an option to buy a stock, a "put" was an option to sell stock, and a time bargain was a promise (and in this sense not an option) to buy stock at a fixed price; all on some set future date.

3. As David Itzkowitz has remarked, those "legitimate transactions" were also technically time-bargains. "Stocks bought or sold on the Exchange did not … have to be delivered or paid for at the time of purchase," he writes (2002, 131). Because they would be held until the settling day, "Virtually all transactions on the Exchange were what we would now refer to as 'futures,' though the time between sale and delivery was relatively short" (ibid.). Furthermore, Teresa Michals notes that basically *all* credit transactions deal in unknown futures, because a "marketplace of credit is essentially a 'futures' market," whereby the extension of credit is a gamble on the likelihood of future reimbursement (usually with interest) (1994, 8).

4. For Edelman, the reproductive characteristics of "futurism" so profoundly privilege heteronormativity as to render impossible a truly political homosexual identity. Edelman's *No Future* (2004) works through the oppositional logic of homophobic rhetoric to extrapolate a broader homophobic logic behind the (Lacanian) Symbolic order. Edelman refuses the recuperative bent of liberalism, espousing instead a politics that is itself premised on refusal, particularly of the future:

> Politics (as the social elaboration of reality) and the self (as mere prosthesis maintaining the future for the figural Child), are what queerness, again as figure, necessarily destroys—necessarily insofar as this "self" is the agent of reproductive futurism and this "politics" the means of its promulgation as the order of social reality. But perhaps, as Lacan's engagement with Antigone in Seminar 7 suggests, political self-destruction inheres in the only act that counts as one: the act of resisting enslavement to the future in the name of having a life. (30)

5. My thanks to Susan for sharing her work with me.

6. The *Guides* unfortunately lack pagination.

7. I suspect that, in my addiction to serial forms, I am participating in a weakness to which Victorianists are especially prone.

8. The show is less popular in America (reruns air on AMC far too early in the morning for most viewers, and iTunes does not yet offer it). I was, however, happy to find the first three seasons readily available through Netflix.

9. Lay's death continues to be shrouded in a mystery reminiscent of John Sadleir; various sources report spotting him in Vail, in Paris, in Greece.

10. Particular examples of the fraud-made-familiar include Collins's Captain Wragge and Dickens's John Harmon in *Our Mutual Friend*. Thackeray's Becky Sharp (*Vanity Fair*) would be another likely candidate, did not the author's punishment of his character (to say nothing of his illustration of her in ch. XLIV) suggest strongly his decided ambivalence about trusting the likes of Rebecca anywhere near his family hearth.

Works Cited

Accum, Frederick. 1820. *A Treatise on Adulterations of Food, and Culinary Poisons, Exhibiting the Fraudulent Sophistications of Bread, Beer, Wine, Spiritous Liquors, Tea, Coffee, Cream, Confectionery, Vinegar, Mustard, Pepper, Cheese, Olive Oil, Pickles, and Other Articles Employed in Domestic Economy. And Methods of Detecting Them.* London: Longman, Hurst, Rees, Orme, and Brown.

"Adjourned Inquest on Mr. Sadleir, M.P." 1856. *The Times*, 26 February.

Adulteration of Food, Drink, and Drugs. Being the Evidence Taken before the Parliamentary Committee. 1855. London: David Bryce.

"Advice to Servants." 1848. *The Servants' Magazine; or Female Domestics Instructor.* London: Ward & Co. Vol. 11: 238–89.

"The Adulteration of Food and Drugs." 1869. *Westminster Review* 91 (January): 185–206.

Ahmed, Sara. 2004. "Affective Economies." *Social Text* 79: 117–39.

Alborn, Tim. 1995. "The Moral of the Failed Bank: Professional Plots in the Victorian Money Market." *Victorian Studies* 38: 199–225.

Althusser, Louis. 1970. "Ideology and Ideological State Apparatuses." Reprinted in *Lenin and Philosophy and Other Essays.* Translated by Ben Brewster. New York: Monthy Review Books, 1971. French original, 1968.

Annear, Robyn. 2002. *The Man Who Lost Himself: The Unbelievable Story of the Tichborne Claimant.* London: Robinson.

Armstrong, Nancy. 1987. *Desire and Domestic Fiction: A Political History of the Novel.* New York: Oxford University Press.

———. 2005. *How Novels Think: The Limits of Individualism from 1719–1900.* New York: Columbia University Press.

Atlay, J. B. 1899. *Famous Trials of the Century.* Chicago and New York: Herbert S. Stone and Co.; London: Grant Richards.

Austen, Jane. 1811. *Sense and Sensibility.* Edited by James Kinsley. Oxford World's Classics. New York: Oxford University Press, 1998.

————. 1813. *Pride and Prejudice*. Edited by James Kinsley. Oxford World's Classics. New York: Oxford University Press, 1998.

————. 1814. *Mansfield Park*. Edited by Claudia L. Johnson. New York: W.W. Norton, 1998.

————. 1817. *Persuasion*. Edited by Gillian Beer. New York: Penguin, 2003.

Austin, J. L. 1962. *How to Do Things with Words*. Edited by J. O. Urmson. 2nd ed., edited by Marina Sbisà. Cambridge: Harvard University Press, 1975.

Bagehot, Walter. 1876. "The Transferability of Capital." Reprint. *The Postulations of English Political Economy*. London: Longmans, Green and Co., 1885.

Bailey, Peter. 1979. "'Will the Real Bill Banks Please Stand Up?' Towards a Role Analysis of Mid-Victorian Working-Class Respectability." *Journal of Social History* 12: 336–53.

Banner, Stuart. 1998. *Anglo-American Securites Regulation*. Cambridge: Cambridge University Press.

Barrington, G. 1832. *The London Spy; or, The Frauds of London Detected*. Boston: n. pub.

Beeton, Isabella. 1861. *Mrs Beeton's Book of Household Management*. Reprint. Edited by Nicola Humble. New York: Oxford University Press, 2000.

Beeton, Samuel Orchart. 1875. *Beeton's Manners of Polite Society; or, Etiquette for Ladies, Gentlemen, and Families*. London: Ward, Lock, and Tyler.

Bell, Catherine D. [Cousin Kate, pseud.] n.d. *Horace and May; or, Unconscious Influence*. London: Frederick Warne.

————. 1857. *Kind Words to Domestic Servants*. London: T. Nelson.

————. 1868. *Lily Gordon; or, the Young Housekeeper*. London: Frederick Warne.

————. N.d. *Margaret Cecil; or, "I Can Because I Ought."* Edinburgh: n. pub.

Benedict, Barbara M. 1994. *Framing Feeling: Sentiment and Style in English Prose Fiction 1745–1800*. New York: AMS Press.

Bigelow, Gordon. 2000. "Market Indicators: Banking and Domesticity in Dickens's *Bleak House*." *ELH* 67: 589–615.

"The Blooming Lady Worth £500 and Her Footman." N.d.. Ballad. Harding 13 (142). Bodleian Library.

Bourdieu, Pierre. 1977. *An Outline of a Theory of Practice*. Translated by Richard Nice. Cambridge: Cambridge University Press.

————. 1984. *Distinction: A Social Critique of the Judgement of Taste*. Translated by Richard Nice. Cambridge: Harvard University Press.

————. 1986. "The Forms of Capital." Translated by Richard Nice. In *Handbook of Theory and Research for the Sociology of Education*, edited by John G. Richardson, 241–58. New York: Greenwood.

————. 1990. *The Logic of Practice*. Translated by Richard Nice. Stanford, CA: Stanford University Press.

Bowen, John. 1996. "Performing Business, Training Ghosts: Transcoding *Nickleby*." *English Literary History* 63: 153–75.

Braddon, Mary Elizabeth. 1862. *Lady Audley's Secret*. Reprint. Edited by David Skilton. Oxford and New York: Oxford University Press, 1987.

Brady, Diane. 2004. 'The System Served Martha an Injustice." *Business Week* 8 March. Available at http://www.businessweek.com/bwdaily/dnflash/mar2004/nf2004039_0886_dbo45.htm

Brantlinger, Patrick. 1996. *Fictions of State: Culture and Credit in Britain, 1694–1994*. Ithaca: Cornell University Press.

Bronner, Edward, M.D. 1856. *The Chemistry of Food and Diet: with a Chapter on Food Adulterations.* London: Houlston and Stonement.

Brontë, Charlotte. 1847. *Jane Eyre.* Edited by Margaret Smith. 2nd ed. Oxford World's Classics. Oxford and New York: Oxford University Press, 2000.

———. 1853. *Villette.* Edited by Helen M. Cooper. New York: Penguin, 2004.

Brontë, Emily. 1847. *Wuthering Heights.* Edited by Pauline Nestor. New York: Penguin, 2003.

Brooks, Peter. 2005. *Realist Vision.* New Haven: Yale University Press.

Brown, J. B. 1871. *First Principles of Ecclesiastical Truth.* London: Hodder & Staughton.

Burnett, Mark Thornton. 1997. *Masters and Servants in English Renaissance Drama and Culture: Authority and Obedience.* New York: St. Martin's.

Campbell, Elizabeth. 1990. "Of Mothers and Merchants: Female Economics in Christina Rossetti's 'Goblin Market.'" *Victorian Studies* 33: 393–410.

"A Capital Likeness of John Dineley, Bart." 1801. Windsor: C. Knight.

Carlisle, Janice M. 1975. "*Little Dorrit:* Necessary Fictions." *Studies in the Novel* 7: 195–214.

"The Case of Major Yelverton." 1858. London *Times.* 25 November.

Cases Decided in the Court of Session, &c. 1863. *Longworth or Yelverton v. Yelverton, and Yelverton v. Longworth, December 19, 1862.* Reported by Norman Macpherson, Robert Lee, Andrew B. Bell, Middleton Rettie, and Alex. S. Kiinnear, Esquires, Advocates. Edinburgh: T and T Clark; London: V. & R. Stevens, Sons, & Haynes.

Central Criminal Court. *Minutes of Evidence.* 1847. Trial of Cornelius Parr. Vol. XXVI. London: George Herbert.

———. 1847. Trial of Janet Rose and Mary McIntosh. Vol. XXVI. London: George Herbert.

———. 1859–60. Trial of Jane and Eliza Robinson. Vol. LI. London: Butterworths.

"The Chapter of Cheats, or Every Man Is a Rogue." N. pub. n.d. Bodleian Library, Firth collection. Shelfmark Firth c. 17 (276).

Childers, Joseph W. 1996. "*Nicholas Nickleby*'s Problem of *Doux Commerce.*" *Dickens Studies Annual: Essays on Victorian Fiction* 25: 49–65.

"The Claimant's Woes" or "Roger the Dodger." N.d.. Written by Frank W. Green, arranged by Alfred Lee. London: C. Sheard.

Cleere, Eileen. 2004. *Avuncularism: Capitalism, Patriarchy, and Nineteenth-Century English Culture.* Stanford, Calif.: Stanford University Press.

Cobbe, Frances Power. 1862. "Celibacy v. Marriage." *Fraser's Magazine* 65 (February): 228–335. Reprint in *'Criminals, Idiots, Women, and Minors': Victorian Writing by Women on Women,* edited by Susan Hamilton, 74–83. Orchard Park, NY: Broadview Press, 1995.

———. 1862. "What Shall We Do With Our Old Maids?" *Fraser's Magazine* 66 (November): 594–610.

———. 1868. "Household Service." *Fraser's Magazine* 77 (January): 121–34.

Cohen, Monica. 1998. *Professional Domesticity in the Victorian Novel: Women, Work, and Home.* Cambridge: Cambridge University Press.

Cohen, Paula Marantz. 1985. "Christina Rossetti's 'Goblin Market': A Paradigm for Nineteenth-Century Anorexia Nervosa." *University of Hartford Studies in Literature* 17: 1–18.

Collins, Wilkie. 1860. *The Woman in White.* Edited by John Sutherland. New York: Oxford University Press, 1996.

———. 1862. *No Name.* Edited by Virginia Blain. New York and Oxford: Oxford University Press, 1986.

———. 1870. *Man and Wife.* Reprint. New York: Dover, 1983.

A Complete History of the Yelverton Family since the Reign of Edward II. To which is added some account of the Longworth family. N.d. Manchester: Abel Hayword; London: George Vickers.

"The Conviction of the Claimant." Harding Ballad. Bodleian Library, The University of Oxford.

The Cookmaid's Complete Guide and Adviser: on the Best, Quickest, and Most Easy Methods of Correctly Performing all the Business of the Cookmaid, in Respectable Families. [1846]. London: Thos. Dean.

"The Cooks Rout, or High Life below Stairs." 1794. Engraving. Bodleian Library, JJC Trades and Professions 4, April 28. London: J. Evans.

Coyne, J. Stirling, Esq. 1857. *Fraud and Its Victims: A Drama in Four Acts, Preceded by a Prologue.* London: Thomas Hailes Lacy. Lacy's Acting Edition of Plays. Vol. 29.

Craig, Randall. 2000. *Promising Language.* Albany: SUNY Press.

Crosby, Christina. 1999. "Financial." In *A Companion to Victorian Literature & Culture,* edited by Herbert F. Tucker, 225–43. Malden, MA: Blackwell.

Crow, Duncan. 1996. *Theresa: The Story of the Yelverton Case.* London: Rupert Hart-Davis.

Cruikshank, George. "The Last Man on the Tichborne Jury." JJC Tichborne, Bodleian Library, Oxford.

"A Cure for Deceit." N.d. JJC Street Ballads 30. Bodleian Library, Oxford.

"A Curious Speculation." 1856. *The Times,* 2 April.

Dalton, William. 1857. *"Is Killing Murder?" A Key to the Adulteration of Our Daily Food, Compiled from the Evidence Given before the Committee of the House of Commons in the Years 1855–6.* London: Marlborough.

Darwin, Ellen. 1890. "Domestic Service." *The Nineteenth Century* 39, no. 162 (August): 286–96.

David, James Edward, Esq. 1868. *The Master and Servant Act, 1867.* London: Butterworths.

"Death of Mr. John Sadleir, M.P. for Sligo." 1856. *The Times,* 18 February.

Derrida, Jacques. 1992. *Given Time,* Part 1: *Counterfeit Money.* Translated by Peggy Kamuf. Chicago: University of Chicago Press. French original, 1991.

Dickens, Charles. 1839. *Nicholas Nickleby.* Edited by Mark Ford. New York: Penguin, 2003.

———. 1850. *David Copperfield.* Edited by Jeffrey Tambling. New York: Penguin, 1996.

———. 1853. *Bleak House.* Edited by Nicola Bradbury. New York: Penguin, 1997.

———. 1857. *Little Dorrit.* Edited by Harvey Peter Sucksmith. Oxford University Press, 1982.

———. 1859. *A Tale of Two Cities.* Edited by Richard Maxwell. New York: Penguin, 2003.

———. 1861. *Great Expectations.* Edited by Charlotte Mitchell. New York: Penguin, 1996.

———. 1865. *Our Mutual Friend.* Edited by Stephen Gill. New York: Penguin, 1985.

Dickens, Charles, Jr. 1888. *Dickens's Dictionary of London: An Unconventional Handbook.* No. 8. Reprint as *Dickens's Dictionary of London 1888.* Moretonhampstead, Devon: Old House Books, 2001.

Eccles' Household Almanack. 1875. Woodstock: Eccles & Son.

———. 1877. Woodstock: Eccles & Son.

Edelman, Lee. 2004. *No Future: Queer Theory and the Death Drive.* Durham: Duke University Press.

Eliot, George. 1871–72. *Middlemarch.* Edited by David Carroll. Oxford World's Classics. New York: Oxford University Press, 1998.

———. 1887. *Miscellaneous Essays, Impressions of Theophrastus Such, The Veil Lifted, Brother Jacob. George Eliot's Complete Works.* Boston: Estes and Lauriat.

———. *Adam Bede.* 1859. Edited by Valentine Cunningham. Oxford and New York: Oxford University Press, 1996.

Ellis, Sarah Stickney. 1844. *The Daughters of England.* London: Fisher, Son.

Ellis, William Fitz-Norman. 1873. *The Heir of Tichborne.* 11th ed. Southampton: Paul and Sons.

Erickson, Arvel B., and Fr. John R. McCarthy. 1971. "The Yelverton Marriage Case: Civil Legislation and Marriage." *Victorian Studies* 14: 275–91.

Etiquette of Courtship and Matrimony: With a Complete Guide to the Forms of a Wedding. 1852. London: David Bogue.

———. 1865. London: Routledge, Warne, and Routledge.

Evans, D. Morier. 1859. *Facts, Failures, and Frauds: Revelations, Financial, Mercantile, Criminal.* London: Groombridge.

"Eye Service." 1846. *The Servants' Magazine; or Female Domestics' Instructor.* London: Ward & Co. Vol. 9: 17.

Fahnestock, Jeanne. 1981. "Bigamy: The Rise and Fall of a Convention." *Nineteenth-Century Fiction* 36, no. 1: 47–71.

Feltes, N. N. 1978. "'The Greatest Plague of Life': Dickens, Masters and Servants." *Literature and History* 8: 197–213.

Finn, Margot. 2003. *The Character of Credit: Personal Debt in English Culture, 1740–1914.* Cambridge: Cambridge University Press.

Forster, John. 1874. *The Life of Charles Dickens.* 3 vols. Philadelphia: Lippincott.

Foucault, Michel. 1979. *Discipline and Punish: The Birth of the Prison.* Translated by Alan Sheridan. New York: Vintage. French original, 1975.

Francis, John. 1850. *Chronicles and Characters of the Stock Exchange.* London: Willoughby and Co.

"Frauds and Pickpockets, or *Rogues All!*" N.d. 7 Dials, London: Pitts Printer.

The Frauds of London, Displaying the Numerous and Daring Cheats and Robberies Practised upon the Stranger and the Unwary: The Whole Consisting of the Facts Derived from the Most Authentic Sources; And Being the Most Complete Account of Metropolitan Villany Ever Presented to the Public Eye. [1826–27]. By An Old Bow Street Officer. London: William Cole.

Freedgood, Elaine. 2000. *Victorian Writing about Risk: Imagining a Safe England in a Dangerous World.* New York: Cambridge University Press.

Frith, W. P. R.A. 1888. *My Autobiography and Reminiscences.* 4th ed. 3 vols. London: Richard Bentley.

Frost, Ginger. 1995. *Promises Broken: Courtship, Class, and Gender in Victorian England.* Charlottesville: University of Virginia Press.

Full Report of the Important Trial Thelwall versus Yelverton. 1861. Glasgow: William Syme & Co.

Gallagher, Catherine. 1980. *The Industrial Reformation of English Fiction*. Chicago: University of Chicago Press.

———. 2006. *The Body Economic: Life, Death, and Sensation in Political Economy and the Victorian Novel*. Princeton, NJ: Princeton University Press.

Gallagher, Catherine, and Stephen Greenblatt. 2000. *Practicing New Historicism*. Chicago: University of Chicago Press.

Garnier, Rev. Thos. B.C.L. [The Rector and Chaplain to the House of Commons]. 1851. "The Duty of Servants." In *Domestic Duties. A Series of Sermons Preached in Trinity Church, Saint Marylebone*. London: J. Laver.

Gaskell, Elizabeth Cleghorn. 1853. *Cranford*. Edited by Peter Keating. New York: Penguin, 1976.

———. 1853. *Ruth*. Edited by Angus Easson. New York: Penguin Classics, 1997.

Gilbert, Michael. 1957. *The Claimant*. London: Constable.

Goderich, Viscount. 1852. "On the Adulteration of Food and Its Remedies." In *Meliora*. 2nd. ed. Ed. Viscount Ingestre. London, 76–87.

Great Tichborne Case, A Literary & Pictorial Record. N.d. London: British Library.

"The Great Yelverton Case." 1861. *Harpers Weekly: Journal of Civilization* 5, no. 223 (6 April): 221–22.

"Greatest Wonder of the Age! The Singing Mouse." John Johnson Collection of Printed Ephemera. Animals on Show 2. Bodleian Library, Oxford.

Greenland, Maureen, and Russell E. Day. 1991. *Compound-plate Printing*, Part 1: *Historical Survey*. Oxford: The Foundation for Ephemera Studies.

Hardy, Thomas. 1891. *Tess of the D'Urbervilles*. Edited by Tim Dolin. New York: Penguin Classics, 1998.

Harris, Richard. 1884. *Illustrations in Advocacy, Including Two Breaches of Promise of Marriage; Analysis of Sir Henry Hawkins's Speech in the Tichborne Prosecution for Perjury. His Cross-Examination of "Old Bogle" as to the Tattoo Marks. Analysis of Cicero's Defense of Roscius for Murder. County Court Entertainments, A Humble Address to Our Future Judges, &c., &c.* London: Waterlow Bros. & Layton.

Hassall, Arthur Hill, M.D. 1855. *Food and its Adulterations; Comprising the Reports of the Analytical Sanitary Commission of "The Lancet" for the Years 1851 to 1854 Inclusive, Revised and Extended: Being Records of the Results of Some Thousands of Original Microscopial and Chemical Analyses of the Solids and Fluids Consumed by All Classes of the Public; and Containing The Names and Addresses of the Various Merchants, Manufacturers, and Tradesmen of Whom the Analysed Articles Were Purchased*. London: Longman, Brown, Green, and Longmans.

———. 1857. *Adulterations Detected; or, Plain Instructions for the Discovery of Frauds in Food and Medicine*. London: Longman, Brown, Green, Longmans, and Roberts.

Hastings, Sydney, B.A. 1888. *A Short Treatise on the Law Relating to Fraud and Misrepresentation*. London: William Clowes.

Hastings, Sidney, and John Davies Davenport. 1872. *The Rights and Liabilities of Husband and Wife,* by John Fraser MacQueen, Esq. Q.C. 2nd ed. London: H. Sweet.

Hawkins, William and John Curwood. 1824. *A Treatise of the Pleas of the Crown*. 8th ed. Vol. I. London: C. Howorth.

"The He She Lady's Maid." N.d. 7 Dials, London: J. Catnach.

Helsinger, Elizabeth K. 1991. "Consumer Power and the Utopia of Desire: Christina Rossetti's 'Goblin Market.'" *English Literary History* 58: 903–33.

Works Cited

"Hints to Make Houses Wholesome." 1873. *Punch* (15 February).

Holt, Terrence. 1990. "'Men sell not such in any town': Exchange in *Goblin Market*." *Victorian Poetry* 28: 51–67.

Horton, Susan R. 1995. "Were They Having Fun Yet? Victorian Optical Gadgetry, Modernist Selves." In *Victorian Literature and the Victorian Visual Imagination,* edited by Carol T. Christ and John O. Jordan, 1–26. Berkeley and Los Angeles: University of California Press.

Household Work; or, The Duties of Female Servants, Practically and Economically Illustrated, Through the Respective Grades of Maid-of-all-work, House and Parlour-maid, and Laundry-maid: With Many Valuable Recipes for Facilitating Labour in Every Department. N.d. Prepared for the Use of the National and Industrial Schools of the Holy Trinity, at Finchley. 11th ed. London: Joseph Masters.

How to Detect Adulteration in Our Daily Food and Drink: A Complete Analysis of the Frauds and Deceptions Practised upon Articles of Domestic Consumption, by Tradesmen and Manufacturers; With Full Directions to Detect Genuine from Spurious, by Simple and Inexpensive Means. [1855]. London: Groombridge.

How to Obtain Wealth, Honour and Position! A Programme of New Plans, Projects, etc., For the Formation and Establishment of Various Commercial Undertakings, Associations, Benefit Societies & Companies. N.d. Dedicated to All Who Are Desirous of Employing their Energy, Intellect, Influence, Wealth, etc., in Creating for Themselves a Name, Position, and of Benefitting Their Country. London: Steel & Jones and W. H. Guest.

Hyde, Lewis. 1979. *The Gift: Imagination and the Erotic Life of Property.* New York: Vintage Books.

Itzkowitz, David C. 2002. "Fair Enterprise or Extravagant Speculation: Investment, Speculation, and Gambling in Victorian England." *Victorian Studies* 45: 121–47.

Jackson, Thomas. 1810. *Marriage and Adultery Considered: A Sermon, Preached at the New Chapel, Stockwell, June 3, 1810.* Chelsea: J. Tilling.

Jaffe, Audrey. 2002. "Trollope in the Stock Market: Irrational Exuberance and *The Prime Minister*." *Victorian Studies* 45: 43–64.

James, G. P. R. 1845. *The Smuggler: A Tale.* 3 vols. London: Smith Elder..

Jane Wright; or, The Young Servant. [1865]. London: Society for Promoting Christian Knowledge.

Jerrold, Douglass [the late Captain Barabbas Whitefeather, pseud.]. 1839. *The Hand-Book of Swindling.* Edited by John Jackdaw (pseud.). London: Chapman and Hall.

"Jolly Old Sir Roger." 1872. Ballad. London: Disly, Printer (April).

Jordan, John O. 1998. "Domestic Servants and the Victorian Home." In *Homes and Homelessness in the Victorian Imagination,* edited by Murray Baumgarten and H. M. Dealeski, 79–90. New York: AMS Press.

Jordan, Tony. 2004. "Assembling the Team." *Hustle.* DVD. Directed by Bharat Nalluri. London: BBC Video.

Joyce, Patrick. 1994. *Democratic Subjects: The Self and the Social in Nineteenth-Century England.* Cambridge: Cambridge University Press.

"Kate's Young Man." N.d. Ballad. Firth c. 17(141). Bodleian Library.

Korobkin, Laura Hanft. 1998. *Criminal Conversations: Sentimentality and Nineteenth-Century Legal Stories of Adultery.* New York: Columbia University Press.

"The Lady Beat the Soldier." N.d. Ballad. Harding B13 (133). Bodleian Library.

Lalor, John. *Money and Morals: A Book for the Times.* 1852. London: John Chapman.

Langland, Elizabeth. 1995. *Nobody's Angels: Middle-Class Women and Domestic Ideology in Victorian Culture*. Ithaca: Cornell University Press.

"The Latest Tichborne Alphabet." N.d. London: Alfred Ritchie.

Levine, Caroline. 2006. "Strategic Formalism: Toward a New Method in Cultural Studies." *Victorian Studies* 48: 625–57.

[Lewes, George Henry (Slingsby Lawrence, Esq., pseud.)]. 1861. *The Game of Speculation: A Comedy in Three Acts*. London: Samuel French.

Litvak, Joseph. 1992. *Caught in the Act: Theatricality in the Nineteenth-Century English Novel*. Berkeley and Los Angeles: University of California Press.

———. 1997. *Strange Gourmets: Sophistication, Theory, and the Novel*. Durham, NC: Duke University Press.

Loftus, Donna. 2002. "Capital and Community: Limited Liability and Attempts to Democratize the Market in Mid-Nineteenth-Century England." *Victorian Studies* 45: 93–120.

"London Adulterations." N.d. John Johnson Collection of Printed Ephemera. Street Ballads 6. Bodleian Library B24 (1130).

Longworth, Maria Theresa. 1861. *Martyrs to Circumstance*. 2 vols. London: Richard Bentley.

Lynch, Deidre Shauna. 1998. *The Economy of Character: Novels, Market Culture, and the Business of Inner Meaning*. Chicago: University of Chicago Press.

Lyndall, Joseph. 1854. *Business: As It Is, and As It Might Be*. Prize Essay, Young Men's Christian Association. London: Walton and Maberly.

M. M. 1869. *Susan Dering; or, A Cook's Perquisites*. London: Society for Promoting Christian Knowledge.

Maceachen, Dougald B. 1950. "Wilkie Collins and British Law." *Nineteenth-Century Fiction* 5: 121–39.

The Man of Business Considered in Six Aspects: A Book for Young Men. 1864. Rev. ed. Edinburgh: William P. Nimmo. U.S. original, 1857.

[Mansel, Henry.] 1863. "Sensation Novels." *Quarterly Review* 113 (April): 481–514.

Marcet, W., M.D., F.C.S. 1856. *On the Composition of Food and How It Is Adulterated, with Practical Directions for its Analysis*. London: John Churchill.

Martineau. Harriet. 1832–4. *Illustrations of Political Economy*. London: Charles Fox.

———. 1862. "Modern Domestic Service." *Edinburgh Review* 115 (April): 409–39.

"The Matrimonial Hoax." N.d. Harding B11 (2883). Bodleian Library.

"Matrimony by Advertisement." 1846. *Our Own Times* (July): 104–7.

Mauss, Marcel. 1954. *The Gift*. Trans. W. D. Halls. New York: W.W. Norton and Co., 1990. Originally published in French 1950.

Mayhew, Henry. 1861–2. *London Labour and the London Poor*. 4 vols. New York: Dover, 1968.

———, and Augustus Septimus Mayhew. 1847. *"The Greatest Plague of Life"; or, The Adventures of a Lady in Search of A Good Servant*. By one who has been "almost Worried to Death." 6 parts. London: David Bogue.

McCuskey, Brian W. 2000. "The Kitchen Police: Servant Surveillance and Middle-Class Transgression." *Victorian Literature and Culture* 28: 359–75.

McGann, Tara. 2002. "Domesticating Finance in *Our Mutual Friend*." Paper presented at the Narrative conference, East Lansing, Michigan, March.

McKeon, Michael. 2005. *The Secret History of Domesticity: Public, Private, and the Division of Knowledge.* Baltimore: Johns Hopkins University Press.

McWilliam, Rohan. 2007. *The Tichborne Claimant: A Victorian Sensation.* London: Hambledon Continuum.

———. 1991. "Radicalism and Popular Culture: The Tichborne Case and the Politics of 'Fair Play,' 1867–1886." In *Currents of Radicalism: Popular Radicalism, Organised Labour and Party Politics in Britain, 1850–1914,* edited by Eugenio F. Biagini and Alastair J. Reid, 44–64. Cambridge: Cambridge University Press.

Menke, Richard. 1998. "The Political Economy of Fruit: *Goblin Market.*" In *The Culture of Christina Rossetti: Female Poetics and Victorian Contexts.* Edited by Mary Arseneau, Anthony H. Harrison, and Lorraine Janzen Kooistra, 105–36. Athens: Ohio University Press.

Michals, Teresa. 1994. "Commerce and Character in Maria Edgeworth." *Nineteenth-Century Literature* 49: 1–20.

Michie, Helena. 1992. *Sororophobia: Differences among Women in Literature and Culture.* New York: Oxford University Press.

Miller, Andrew H. 1997. *Novels behind Glass: Commodity Culture and Victorian Narrative.* Cambridge and New York: Cambridge University Press.

Miller, D. A. 1988. *The Novel and the Police.* Berkeley and Los Angeles: University of California Press.

Moore, George. 1894. *Esther Waters.* Edited by Lionel Stevenson. Boston: Houghton Mifflin, 1963.

Morgan, Marjorie. 1994. *Manners, Morals and Class in England, 1774-1858.* New York: St. Martin's Press.

Morrison, Paul. 1991. "Enclosed in Openness: *Northanger Abbey* and the Domestic Carceral." *Texas Studies in Literature and Language* 33: 1–23.

Morse, John T., Jr. 1874. *Famous Trials: The Tichborne Claimant, Troppmann, Prince Pierre Bonaparte, Mrs. Wharton, The Meteor,—Mrs. Fair.* Boston: Little, Brown.

Mr. Timothy Wiggins. 1860. s.n. JJC The Social Day 2. Bodleian Library.

"Mrs. Gurney, the Divorced Lady!" N.d. Ballad. London: H. Such.

Myers, Janet C. 1999. "The Voyage Out: Portable Domesticity and Emigration to Australia in the Victorian period." PhD diss., Rice University.

The "Newsman"'s Full and Revised Report of the Extraordinary Marriage Case, Thelwall v. Yelverton. [1861]. London: Penny Newsman's Office.

Nunokawa, Jeff. 1994. *The Afterlife of Property: Domestic Security and the Victorian Novel.* Princeton, NJ: Princeton University Press.

O'Flanagan, J. R. 1861. *Gentle Blood; or, The Secret Marriage: A Tale of High Life.* Dublin: M'Glashan & Gill; Edinburgh: J. Menzies; Manchester: J. Heywood.

"Oh, Crikey! Oh, Good Gracious!" [1850]. Ballad. Manchester: G. Jacques.

Oliphant, Margaret. 1866. *Miss Marjoribanks.* Edited by Elizabeth Jay. New York: Penguin, 1998.

Osteen, Mark. 2002. "Introduction: questions of the Gift." *The Question of the Gift.* New York and Oxford: Oxford University Press.

Page, Norman. 1995. "Introduction: *Man and Wife,* by Wilkie Collins, edited by Norman Page. New York and Oxford: Oxford University Press.

Palmerston, Lord. 1865. Speech at the South London Industrial Exhibition. 25 March. In James Ewing Ritchie. *The Life and Times of Viscount Palmerston.* London: Printing and Publishing Company, Ltd., 1866.

Pardoe, Julia. 1834. *Speculation*. 3 vols. London: Saunders and Otley. 2 vols. New York: Harper.

"A Particular Account of the Life, &c. of the Notorious George Miller." Broadside. JJC Crime 1. Bodleian Library, University of Oxford.

Paterson, James. 1885. *Notes on the Law of Master and Servant*. London: Shaw and Sons.

"Perquisites." 1844. *The Servants Magazine, or Female Domestics' Instructor*. Vol. VII: 8–10. London: Ward & Co.

Peters, Catherine. 1989. "Introduction." *Armadale*, by Wilkie Collins. Edited by Catherine Peters. New York and Oxford: Oxford University Press.

Plotz, John. 2008. *Portable Property: Victorian Culture on the Move*. Princeton: Princeton University Press.

Political Blunders and Public Frauds; or, A Consideration of a Few Questions Which Are Evidently Tending to Britain's Decline. [1872]. By a Politician. London: F. Pitman.

Poole, Miss. [1870]. *Without a Character: A Tale of Servant Life*. London: Society for Promoting Christian Knowledge.

Poovey, Mary. 1988. *Uneven Developments: The Ideological Work of Gender in Mid-Victorian England*. Chicago: University of Chicago Press.

———. 1995. *Making a Social Body: British Cultural Formation, 1830–1864*. Chicago: University of Chicago Press.

———. 1998. *A History of the Modern Fact: Problems of Knowledge in the Sciences of Wealth and Society*. Chicago: University of Chicago Press.

———. 2002. "Writing about Finance in Victorian England: Disclosure and Secrecy in the Culture of Investment." *Victorian Studies* 45: 17–41.

———. 2003. Introduction to *The Financial System in Nineteenth-Century Britain*, edited by Mary Poovey, 1–33. New York: Oxford University Press.

Practical Jobber. 1816. *The Art of Stock-Jobbing Explained*. London.

Practical Mistress of a Household. 1859. *Domestic Servants, As They Are & As They Ought to Be*. Brighton: Curtis.

"Producing *Hustle*." BBC. Accessed 30 May 2007, http://www.bbc.co.uk/drama/hustle/ backstage2.shtml.

Reay, Diane. 2004. "Gendering Bourdieu's Concept of Capitals? Emotional Capital, Women and Social Class." *Sociological Review* 52, no. 2: 57–74.

Records of Whitecross Street Prison: Comprising Biographical Sketches of Celebrated Characters; As well as Many Curious and Graphic Delineations of Swindles and Swindlers—Laughable Episodes—Melancholy and Romantic Incidents of Prisoners—and Other Extraordinary Reminiscences of Prison Life. [1866]. By an Eye-Witness. London: Henry Vickers.

Redding, Cyrus. 1867. *A Wife and Not a Wife*. London: Saunders, Otley.

Reynolds, G. W. M. [1852]. *Mary Price; or, the Memoirs of a Servant-Maid*. 2 vols. London: John Dicks.

Richter, David. 2002. "Cases of Identity: La femme sans nom, *The Woman in White*, and the Tichborne Claimant." Paper presented at Narrative Conferrence, East Lansing, Mich., April. Text available at http://qcpages.qc.cuny.edu/ENGLISH/Staff/richter/ femme2001.htm.

Riddell, Mrs. J. H. 1866. *The Race for Wealth*. New York: Harper.

Robb, George. 1992. *White-Collar Crime in Modern England: Financial Fraud and Business Morality, 1845–1929*. New York: Cambridge University Press.

Robbins, Bruce. 1993. *The Servant's Hand: English Fiction from Below*. Raleigh, NC: Duke University Press.

Rose, T. H. 1847. *The People's Important Guide for Remedy and Easy Recovery in Cases of Fraud and other Misconduct of Debtors under Twenty Pounds, in the Local and Other Courts Throughout England*. London: Sherwood.

Rosenman, Ellen Bayuk. 2003. *Unauthorized Pleasures: Accounts of Victorian Erotic Experience*. Ithaca: Cornell University Press.

Rossetti, Christina. "Goblin Market." 1862. In *The Complete Poems of Christina Rossetti: A Valorium Edition*, edited by R. W. Crump, 1: 11–26. Baton Rouge: Louisiana State University Press, 1979.

Ruskin, John. 1865. *Sesame and Lilies*. Edited by Harold Bloom. New York: Chelsea House, 1983.

Russell, Norman. 1986. *The Novelist and Mammon: Literary Responses to the World of Commerce in the Nineteenth Century*. Oxford: Clarendon.

Rutterford, Janette, and Josephine Maltby. 2006. "'The Widow, the Clergyman and the Reckless': Women Investors in England, 1830–1914." *Feminist Economics* 12: 111–38.

Sandeman, [Robert]. 1800. *The Honour of Marriage Opposed to All Impurities: An Essay*. Edinburgh: G. Caw.

Schwartz, Hillel. 1996. *The Culture of the Copy: Striking Likenesses, Unreasonable Facsimiles*. New York: Zone Books.

Searle, G. R. 1998. *Morality and the Market in Victorian Britain*. Oxford: Clarendon.

Sedgwick, Eve Kosofsky. 1990. *Epistemology of the Closet*. Berkeley and Los Angeles: University of California Press.

———. 1997. "Paranoid Reading and Reparative Reading; or, You're So Paranoid, You Probably Think This Introduction is About You." In *Novel Gazing: Queer Readings in Fiction*, edited by Eve Kosofsky Sedgwick, 1–37. Duke University Press.

The Servants' Magazine; or Female Domestics' Instructor. 1846–48. Vols. 9–11. London: Published for the London Female Mission, by Ward & Co.

Shakespeare, William. 2004. *Henry IV, Part One*. Edited by Barbara A. Mowat and Paul Werstine. New York: Washington Square Press.

Shanley, Mary Lyndon. 1989. *Feminism, Marriage, and the Law in Victorian England*. Princeton: Princeton University Press.

Shell, Marc. 1978. *The Economy of Literature*. Baltimore: The Johns Hopkins University Press.

Shepherd, Charles Pitman. 1858. "Sins of the Tongue, Lying, and Other Fraud, A Sermon, Preached in South Lambeth Chapel." London: A. M. Pigott.

Simmel, Georg. 2004. *The Philosophy of Money*. 3rd ed. Edited by David Frisby. Translated by Tom Bottomore and David Frisby. London: Routledge.

Simon, Jonathan. 2002. "Taking Risks: Extreme Sports and the Embrace of Risk in Advanced Liberal Societies." In *Embracing Risk: The Changing Culture of Insurance and Responsibility*, edited by Tom Baker and Jonathan Simon, 177–208. Chicago: University of Chicago Press.

Smith, F. B. 1979. *The People's Health 1830–1910*. New York: Holmes & Meier.

Spencer, Herbert. 1859. "The Morals of Trade." *Westminster Review* (April). Reprinted in *Essays: Scientific, Political, and Speculative*, 3: 113–51. New York: Appleton, 1891.

Stern, Rebecca. 2003. "Adulterations Detected: Food and Fraud in Christine Rossetti's

'Goblin Market.'" *Nineteenth-Century Literature* 57: 477–511.

————. 1998. "Moving Parts and Speaking Parts: Situating Victorian Antitheatricality." *English Literary History* 65: 423–49.

Stoker, Bram. 1910. *Famous Imposters.* New York: Sturgis & Walton.

"Suicide of Mr. John Sadleir, M.P." 1856. *The Times,* 19 February.

Sutherland, John. 1989. *The Stanford Companion to Victorian Fiction.* Stanford, CA: Stanford University Press.

Taylor, Tom. 1880. *The Race for Wealth. A Series of Five Pictures by W. P. Frith, R.A. Now exhibiting at the King Street Galleries, 10, King Street, St. James's.* London: William Clowes.

Teather, David. 2003. "Bad taste day as Martha Stewart arrives in court." *The Guardian,* 5 June.

Tennyson, Alfred, Lord. 1855. "Maud." In *Maud and Other Poems.* London: Edward Moxon.

Thackeray, William Makepeace. 1847–48. *Vanity Fair.* Edited by Peter L. Shillingsburg. New York: W. W. Norton, 1995.

Thomas, David Wayne. 2004. *Cultivating Victorians.* Philadelphia: University of Pennsylvania Press.

Thompson, Deborah Ann. 1991. "Anorexia as a Lived Trope: Christina Rossetti's 'Goblin Market.'" *Mosaic* 24, nos. 3–4: 89–106.

Thompson, F. M. L. 1988. *The Rise of Respectable Society: A Society History of Victorian Britain, 1830–1900.* Cambridge: Harvard University Press.

Thompson, James. 1996. *Models of Value: Eighteenth Century Political Economy and the Novel.* Durham, NC: Duke University Press.

The Tichborne Trial: The Evidence of Handwriting: Comprising Autograph Letters of Roger Tichborne, Arthur Orton and the Defendant in Fac-simile. 1874. London: S. Tinsley.

The Tichborne Malformation. Intended for the Perusal of Men Only. [1878?]. London: British Library.

"The Tichbourne [*sic*] A.B.C." N.d. Handbill. Bodleian 2803 d. 3(14).

The Training of Young Children. 1863. London: Society for Promoting Christian Knowledge.

"The Treatment of Fraud." 1856. *The Saturday Review of Politics, Literature, Science and Art* (1 March): 340–41.

Tricks and Traps of London. An Exposure of the Frauds, Vices, &c., of Metropolitan Life. London: T. Owen, [1868].

The Tricks of Trade in the Adulterations of Food and Physic; With Directions for the Detection and Counteraction. 1856. London: David Bogue.

Trodd, Anthea. 1989. *Domestic Crime in the Victorian Novel.* New York: St. Martin's Press..

Trollope, Anthony. 1861–62. *The Struggles of Brown, Jones, and Robinson.* Edited by N. John Hall. Oxford Worlds Classics. Oxford and New York: Oxford University Press, 1992.

————. 1875. *The Way We Live Now.* Edited by Sir Frank Kermode. New York: Penguin, 1994.

"The Two Elopements! Parson and Footman, Female Depravity." [1859–60]. Norwich: Wm. Stewardson.

"U.S. Attorney Makes Statement about Stewart Case." 2003. CNN Breaking News, 4 June.

Accessed 28 September 2006, http://transcripts.cnn.com/TRANSCRIPTS/0306/04/bn.05.html.

Veblen, Thorstein. 1899. *The Theory of the Leisure Class: An Economic Study of Institutions.* Edited by C. Wright Mills. Somerset, NJ: Transaction, 1991.

Victoria, Queen of England. 1858. Letter to the Princess Royal. 3 May. Reprinted in *Dearest Child: Letters between Queen Victoria and the Princess Royal, Previously Unpublished.* Edited by Roger Fulford. New York: Holt Rinehart, 1964.

"The Virgin Only 19 Years Old." N.d. Johnson Ballads 2957. Bodleian Library.

"We'll Not Forget Poor Roger Now." [1874]. London: Disley.

Willcox, William B., and Walter Arnstein. 2001. *The Age of Aristocracy 1688–1830.* 8th ed. Boston: Houghton Mifflin.

"Wise Maxims for Servants." 1848. *The Servants' Magazine; or Female Domestics' Instructor.* Vol. XI: 60–62. London: Ward & Co.

Wohl, Anthony S. 1983. *Endangered Lives: Public Health in Victorian Britain.* Cambridge: Harvard University Press.

Woloch, Alex. 2003. *The One vs. the Many: Minor Characters and the Space of the Protagonist in the Novel.* Princeton: Princeton University Press.

"Wonderful Museum!" N.d. Handbill. JJC Human Freaks 4. Bodleian Library.

Wood, Mrs. Henry. 1861. *East Lynne.* Edited by Sally Mitchell. New Brunswick, NJ: Rutgers University Press, 1984.

———. 1876. *Our Children.* London: Daldy, Isbister & Co.

Woodruff, Douglas. 1957. *The Tichborne Claimant: A Victorian Mystery.* New York: Farrar, Straus, and Cudahy.

"X Spots the Mark." 2007. *The Riches.* FX Networks. Cablecast 30 April.

"The Yelventon [*sic*] Case; or, The Major in a Minor Key." [1860–5]. *The Yelverton Songster.* London: Bishop.

The Yelverton Marriage Case, Thelwall v. Yelverton, Comprising an Authentic and Unabridged Account of the Most Extraordinary Trial of Modern Times, with All Its Revelations, Incidents, and Details Specially Reported. [1861]. London: George Vickers.

Zieger, Susan, 2006. "Children, Class, and Sexuality in Dickens' and McGrath's *Nicholas Nickleby.*" Paper presented at Dickens Universe, Santa Cruz, CA, 2 August. Conference.

Index

Index